Stillwater

CREATED BY

CHIP ZDARSKY

AND

RAMÓN K PEREZ

CHIP ZDARSKY
CREATOR / WRITER

RAMÓN K PEREZ
CREATOR / ARTIST

MIKE SPICER
COLORIST

RUS WOOTON
LETTERER

JON MOISAN
EDITOR

ANDRES JUAREZ
LOGO / DESIGN

FOR SKYBOUND ENTERTAINMENT

ROBERT KIRKMAN *Chairman*
DAVID ALPERT *CEO*
SEAN MACKIEWICZ *SVP, Editor-in-Chief*
SHAWN KIRKHAM *SVP, Business Development*
BRIAN HUNTINGTON *VP, Online Content*
SHAUNA WYNNE *Sr. Director, Corporate Communications*
ANDRES JUAREZ *Art Director*
ARUNE SINGH *Director of Brand, Editorial*
ALEX ANTONE *Senior Editor*
JON MOISAN *Editor*
ARIELLE BASICH *Associate Editor*
CARINA TAYLOR *Graphic Designer*
JOHNNY O'DELL *Social Media Manager*
DAN PETERSEN *Sr. Director of Operations & Events*

Foreign Rights & Licensing Inquiries:
contact@skybound.com

SKYBOUND.COM

FOR IMAGE COMICS, INC.

TODD MCFARLANE *President*
JIM VALENTINO *Vice President*
MARC SILVESTRI *Chief Executive Officer*
ERIK LARSEN *Chief Financial Officer*
ROBERT KIRKMAN *Chief Operating Officer*
ERIC STEPHENSON *Publisher / Chief Creative Officer*
NICOLE LAPALME *Controller*
LEANNA CAUNTER *Accounting Analyst*
SUE KORPELA *Accounting & HR Manager*
MARLA EIZIK *Talent Liaison*
JEFF BOISON *Director of Sales & Publishing Planning*
DIRK WOOD *Director of International Sales & Licensing*
ALEX COX *Director of Direct Market Sales*
CHLOE RAMOS *Book Market & Library Sales Manager*
EMILIO BAUTISTA *Digital Sales Coordinator*
JON SCHLAFFMAN *Specialty Sales Coordinator*
KAT SALAZAR *Director of PR & Marketing*
DREW FITZGERALD *Marketing Content Associate*
HEATHER DOORNINK *Production Director*
DREW GILL *Art Director*
HILARY DILORETO *Print Manager*
TRICIA RAMOS *Traffic Manager*
MELISSA GIFFORD *Content Manager*
ERIKA SCHNATZ *Senior Production Artist*
RYAN BREWER *Production Artist*
DEANNA PHELPS *Production Artist*

IMAGECOMICS.COM

STILLWATER VOLUME 1. FIRST PRINTING. ISBN: 978-1-5343-1837-3.
Published by Image Comics, Inc. Office of publication: PO BOX 14457, Portland, OR 97293.

PRINTED IN USA.

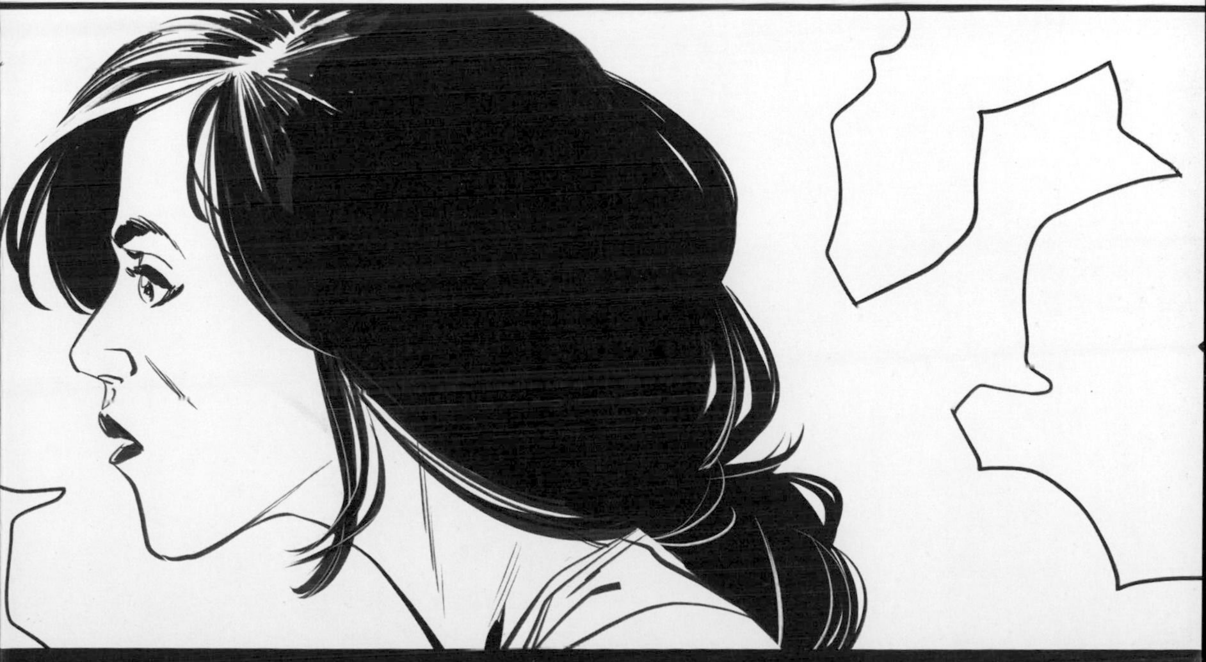

VOLUME ONE
"RAGE, RAGE."

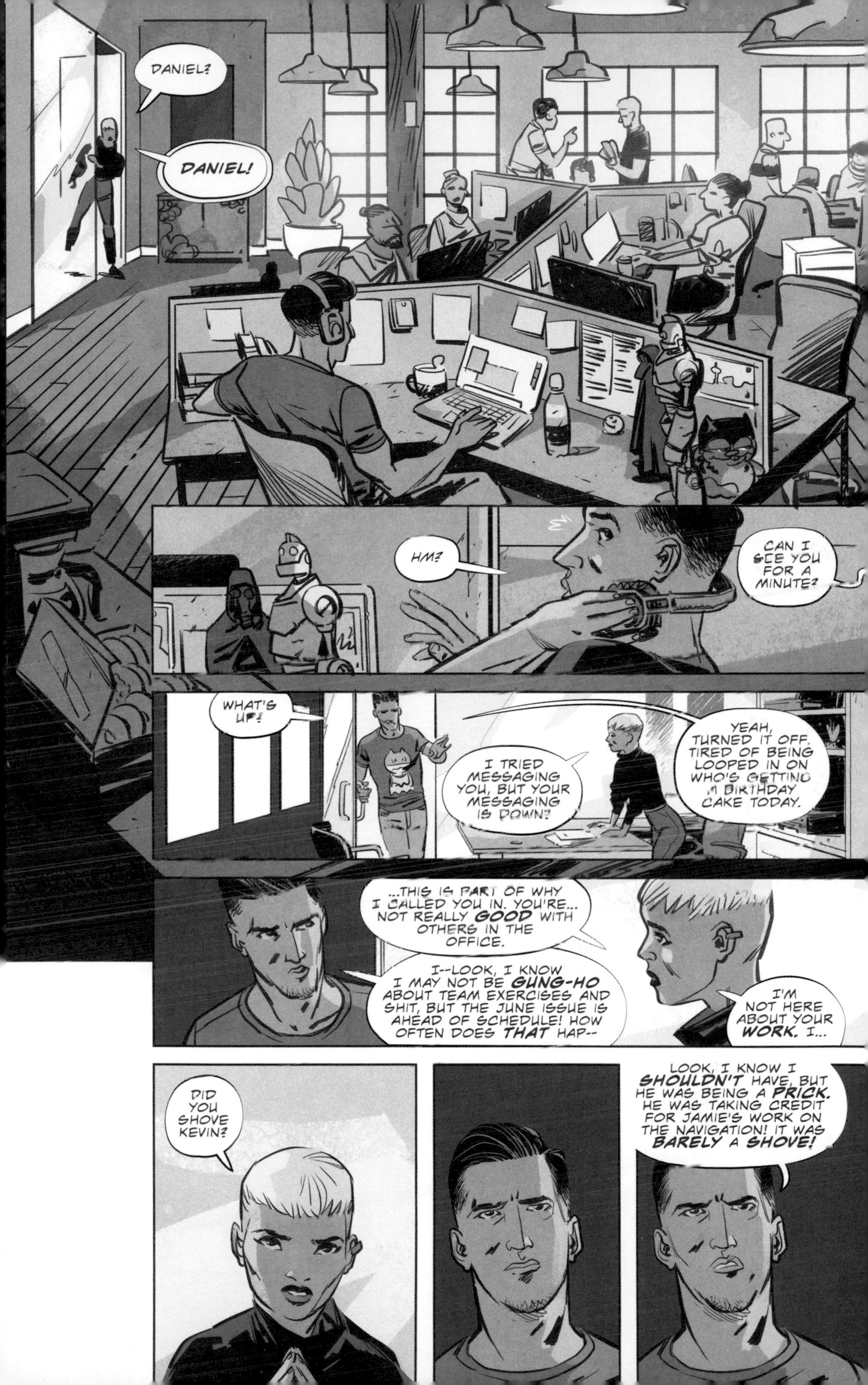
DANIEL?
DANIEL!
HM?
CAN I SEE YOU FOR A MINUTE?
WHAT'S UP!
I TRIED MESSAGING YOU, BUT YOUR MESSAGING IS DOWN?
YEAH, TURNED IT OFF. TIRED OF BEING LOOPED IN ON WHO'S GETTING A BIRTHDAY CAKE TODAY.
...THIS IS PART OF WHY I CALLED YOU IN. YOU'RE... NOT REALLY GOOD WITH OTHERS IN THE OFFICE.
I--LOOK, I KNOW I MAY NOT BE GUNG-HO ABOUT TEAM EXERCISES AND SHIT, BUT THE JUNE ISSUE IS AHEAD OF SCHEDULE! HOW OFTEN DOES THAT HAP--
I'M NOT HERE ABOUT YOUR WORK. I...
DID YOU SHOVE KEVIN?
LOOK, I KNOW I SHOULDN'T HAVE, BUT HE WAS BEING A PRICK. HE WAS TAKING CREDIT FOR JAMIE'S WORK ON THE NAVIGATION! IT WAS BARELY A SHOVE!

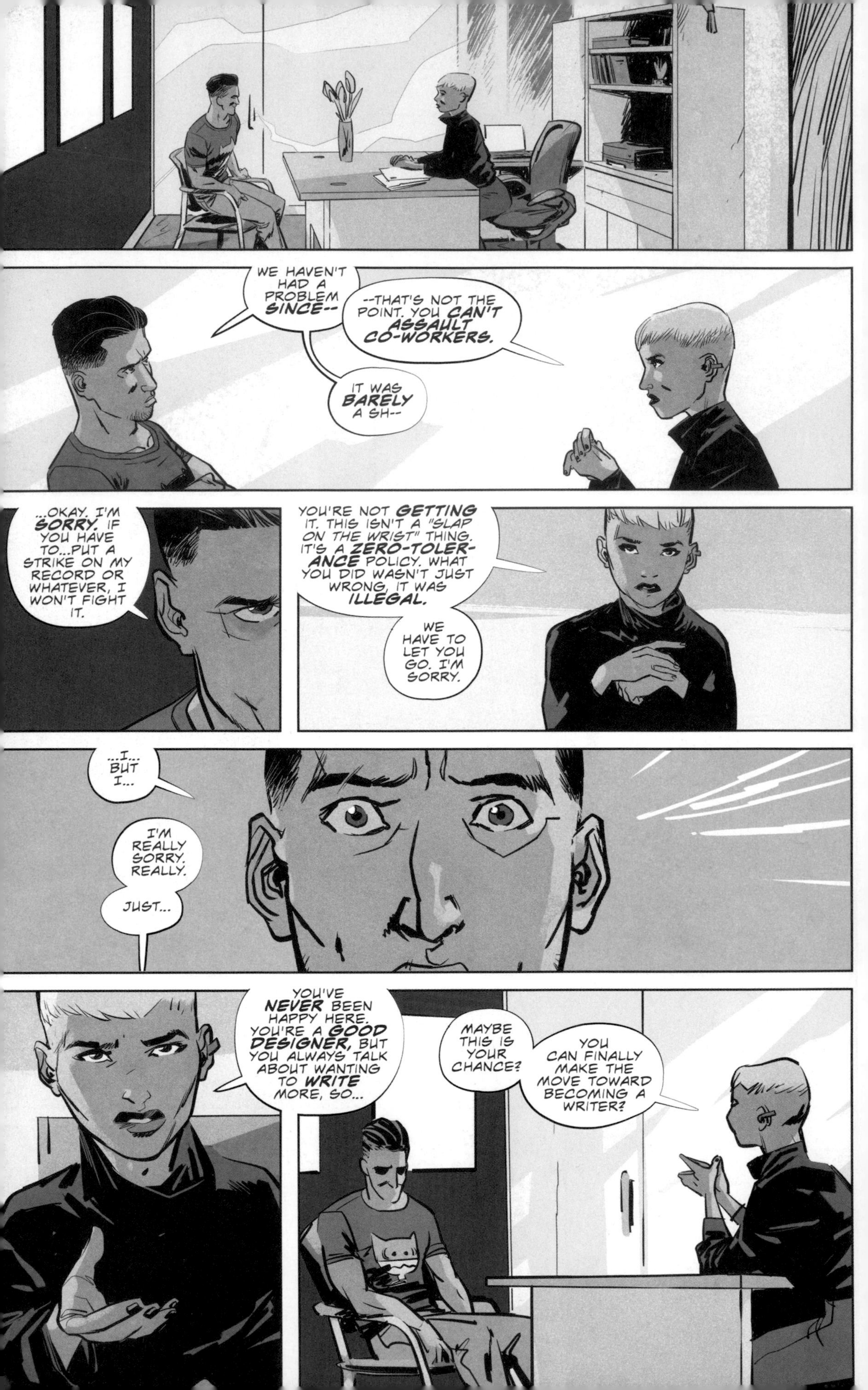
WE HAVEN'T HAD A PROBLEM SINCE--
--THAT'S NOT THE POINT. YOU CAN'T ASSAULT CO-WORKERS.
IT WAS BARELY A SH--
...OKAY. I'M SORRY. IF YOU HAVE TO...PUT A STRIKE ON MY RECORD OR WHATEVER, I WON'T FIGHT IT.
YOU'RE NOT GETTING IT. THIS ISN'T A "SLAP ON THE WRIST" THING. IT'S A ZERO-TOLERANCE POLICY. WHAT YOU DID WASN'T JUST WRONG, IT WAS ILLEGAL.
WE HAVE TO LET YOU GO. I'M SORRY.
...I... BUT I...
I'M REALLY SORRY. REALLY.
JUST...
YOU'VE NEVER BEEN HAPPY HERE. YOU'RE A GOOD DESIGNER, BUT YOU ALWAYS TALK ABOUT WANTING TO WRITE MORE, SO...
MAYBE THIS IS YOUR CHANCE?
YOU CAN FINALLY MAKE THE MOVE TOWARD BECOMING A WRITER?

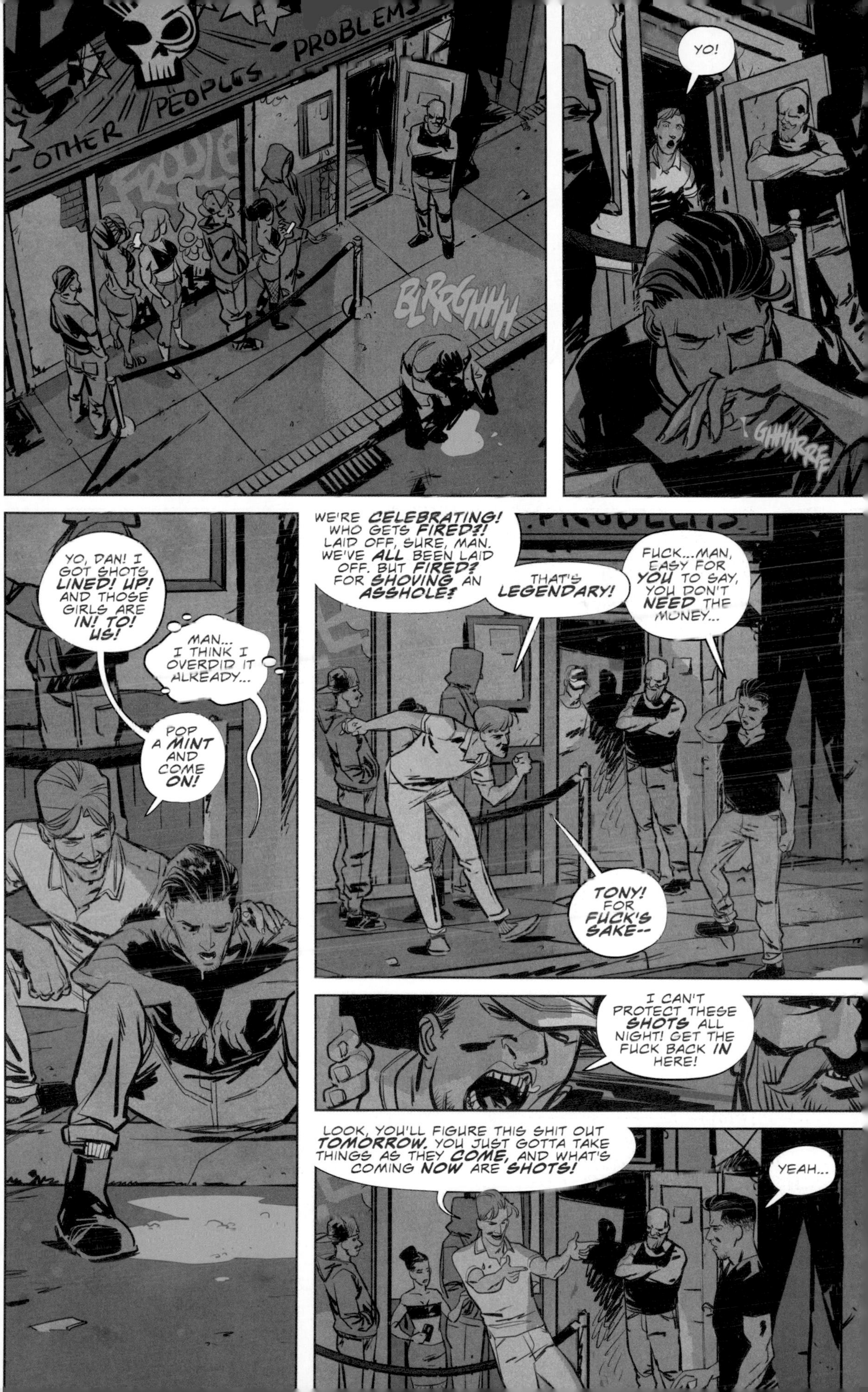
OTHER PEOPLES PROBLEMS
BLRRGHHH
YO!
GHHHRRFF
YO, DAN! I GOT SHOTS LINED! UP! AND THOSE GIRLS ARE IN! TO! US!
MAN... I THINK I OVERDID IT ALREADY...
POP A MINT AND COME ON!
WE'RE CELEBRATING! WHO GETS FIRED?! LAID OFF, SURE, MAN. WE'VE ALL BEEN LAID OFF. BUT FIRED? FOR SHOVING AN ASSHOLE?
THAT'S LEGENDARY!
FUCK...MAN, EASY FOR YOU TO SAY, YOU DON'T NEED THE MONEY...
TONY! FOR FUCK'S SAKE--
I CAN'T PROTECT THESE SHOTS ALL NIGHT! GET THE FUCK BACK IN HERE!
LOOK, YOU'LL FIGURE THIS SHIT OUT TOMORROW. YOU JUST GOTTA TAKE THINGS AS THEY COME, AND WHAT'S COMING NOW ARE SHOTS!
YEAH...

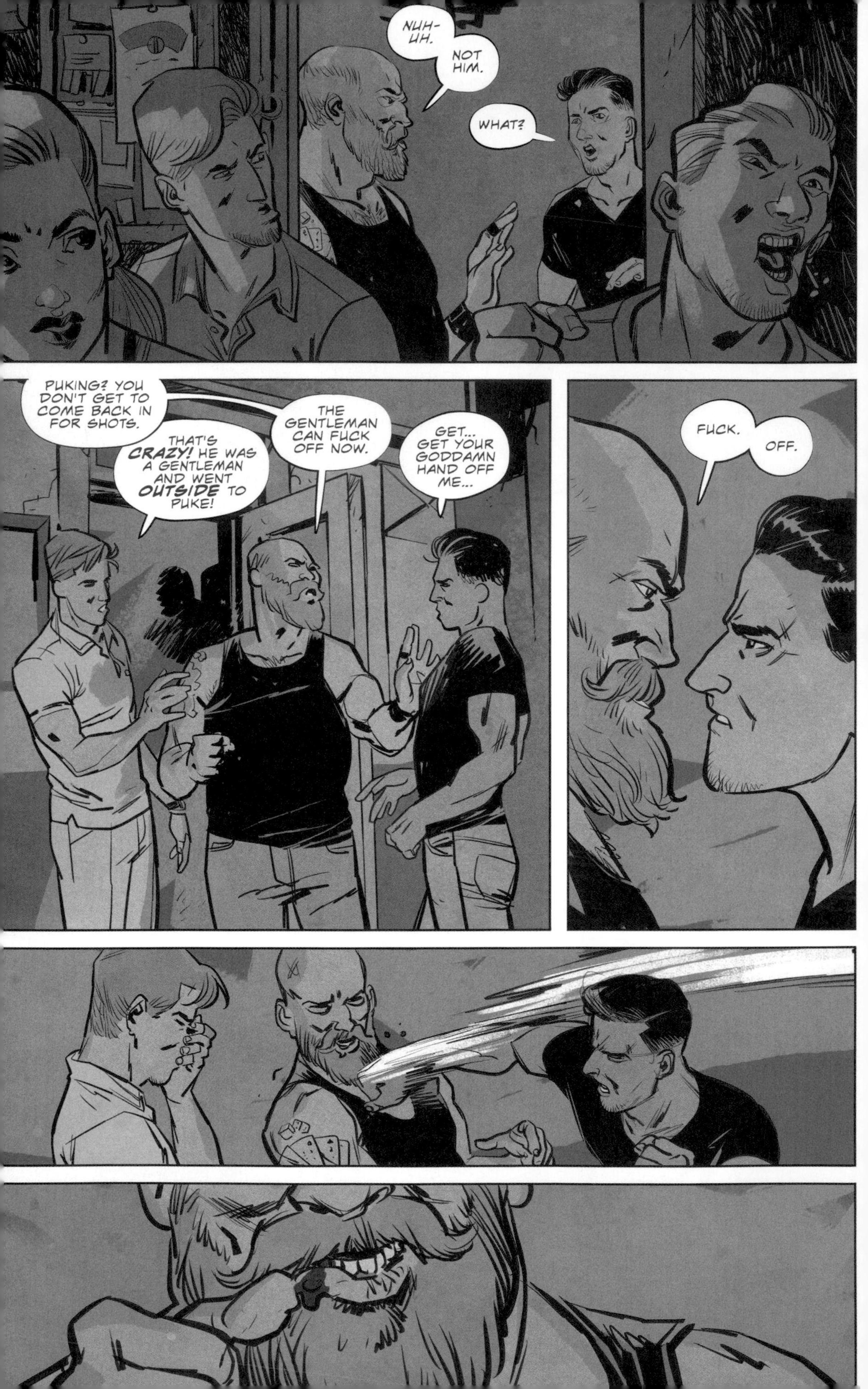
NUH-UH.
NOT HIM.
WHAT?
PUKING? YOU DON'T GET TO COME BACK IN FOR SHOTS.
THAT'S CRAZY! HE WAS A GENTLEMAN AND WENT OUTSIDE TO PUKE!
THE GENTLEMAN CAN FUCK OFF NOW.
GET... GET YOUR GODDAMN HAND OFF ME...
FUCK.
OFF.

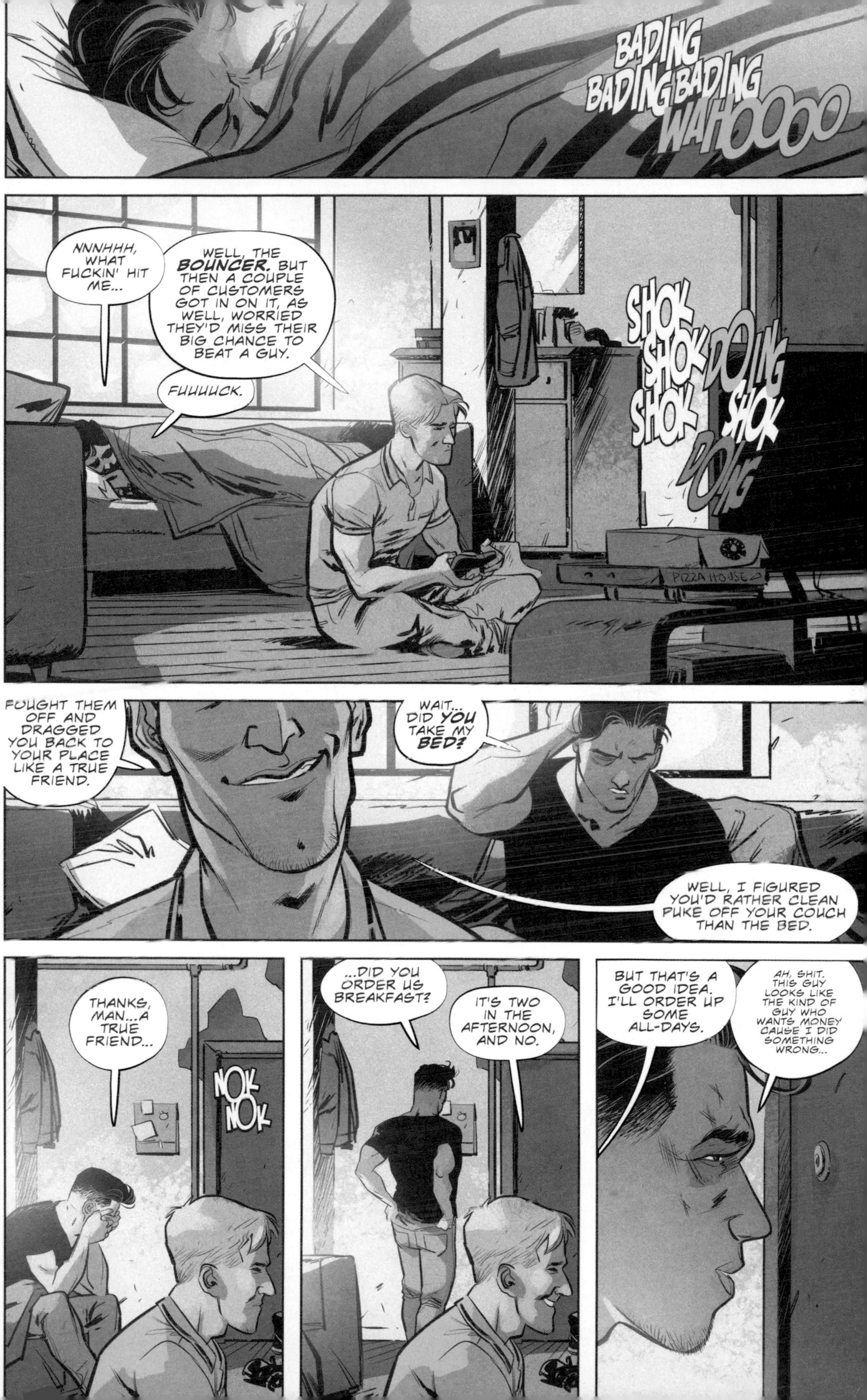
BADING BADING BADING WAHOOOO
NNNHHH, WHAT FUCKIN' HIT ME...
WELL, THE BOUNCER. BUT THEN A COUPLE OF CUSTOMERS GOT IN ON IT, AS WELL, WORRIED THEY'D MISS THEIR BIG CHANCE TO BEAT A GUY.
FUUUUCK.
SHOK SHOK SHOK DOING SHOK DOING
PIZZA HOUSE
FOUGHT THEM OFF AND DRAGGED YOU BACK TO YOUR PLACE LIKE A TRUE FRIEND.
WAIT... DID YOU TAKE MY BED?
WELL, I FIGURED YOU'D RATHER CLEAN PUKE OFF YOUR COUCH THAN THE BED.
THANKS, MAN...A TRUE FRIEND...
NOK NOK
...DID YOU ORDER US BREAKFAST?
IT'S TWO IN THE AFTERNOON, AND NO.
BUT THAT'S A GOOD IDEA. I'LL ORDER UP SOME ALL-DAYS.
AH, SHIT. THIS GUY LOOKS LIKE THE KIND OF GUY WHO WANTS MONEY CAUSE I DID SOMETHING WRONG...

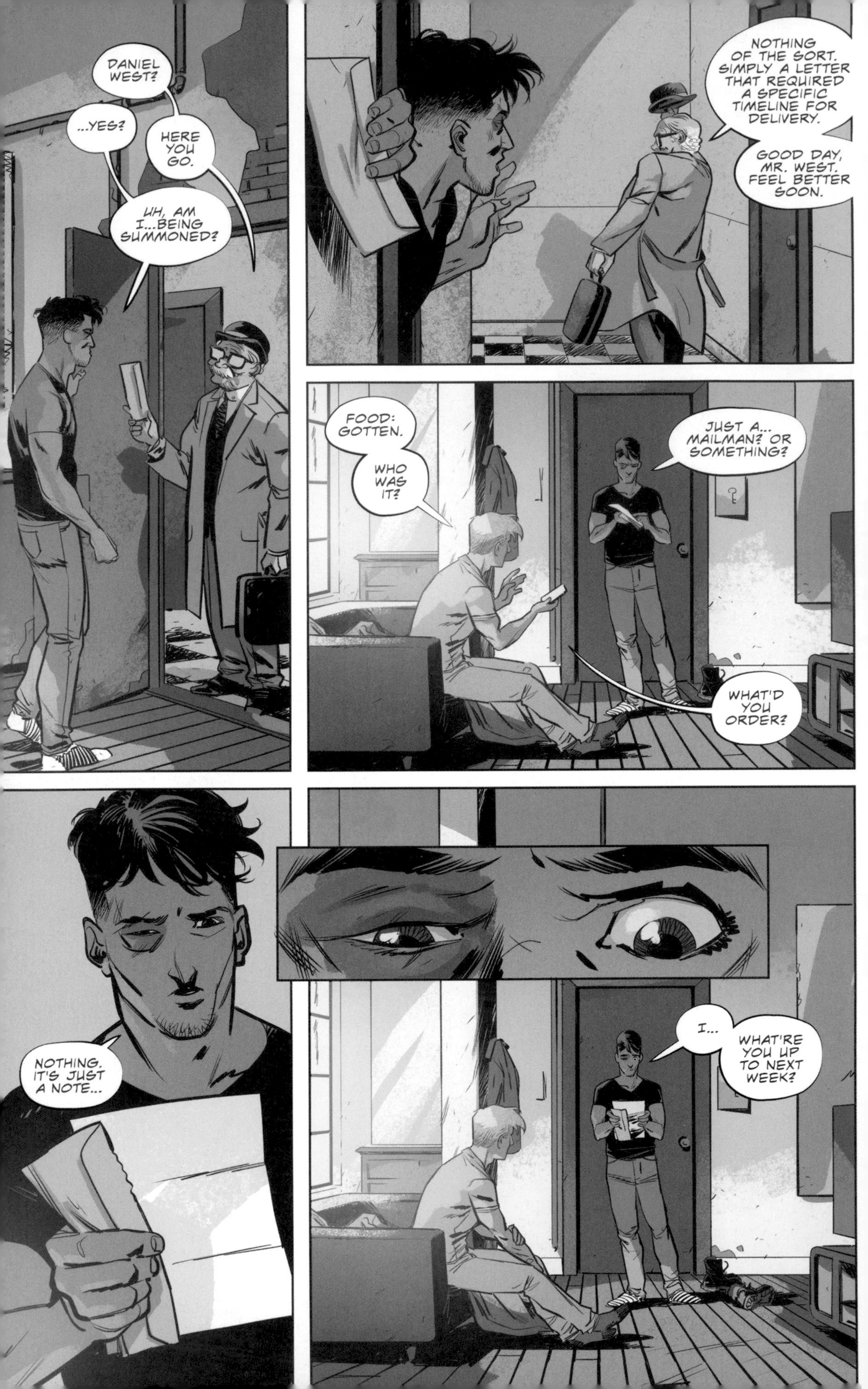
DANIEL WEST?
...YES?
HERE YOU GO.
UH, AM I...BEING SUMMONED?
NOTHING OF THE SORT. SIMPLY A LETTER THAT REQUIRED A SPECIFIC TIMELINE FOR DELIVERY.
GOOD DAY, MR. WEST. FEEL BETTER SOON.
FOOD: GOTTEN.
WHO WAS IT?
JUST A... MAILMAN? OR SOMETHING?
WHAT'D YOU ORDER?
NOTHING. IT'S JUST A NOTE...
I...
WHAT'RE YOU UP TO NEXT WEEK?

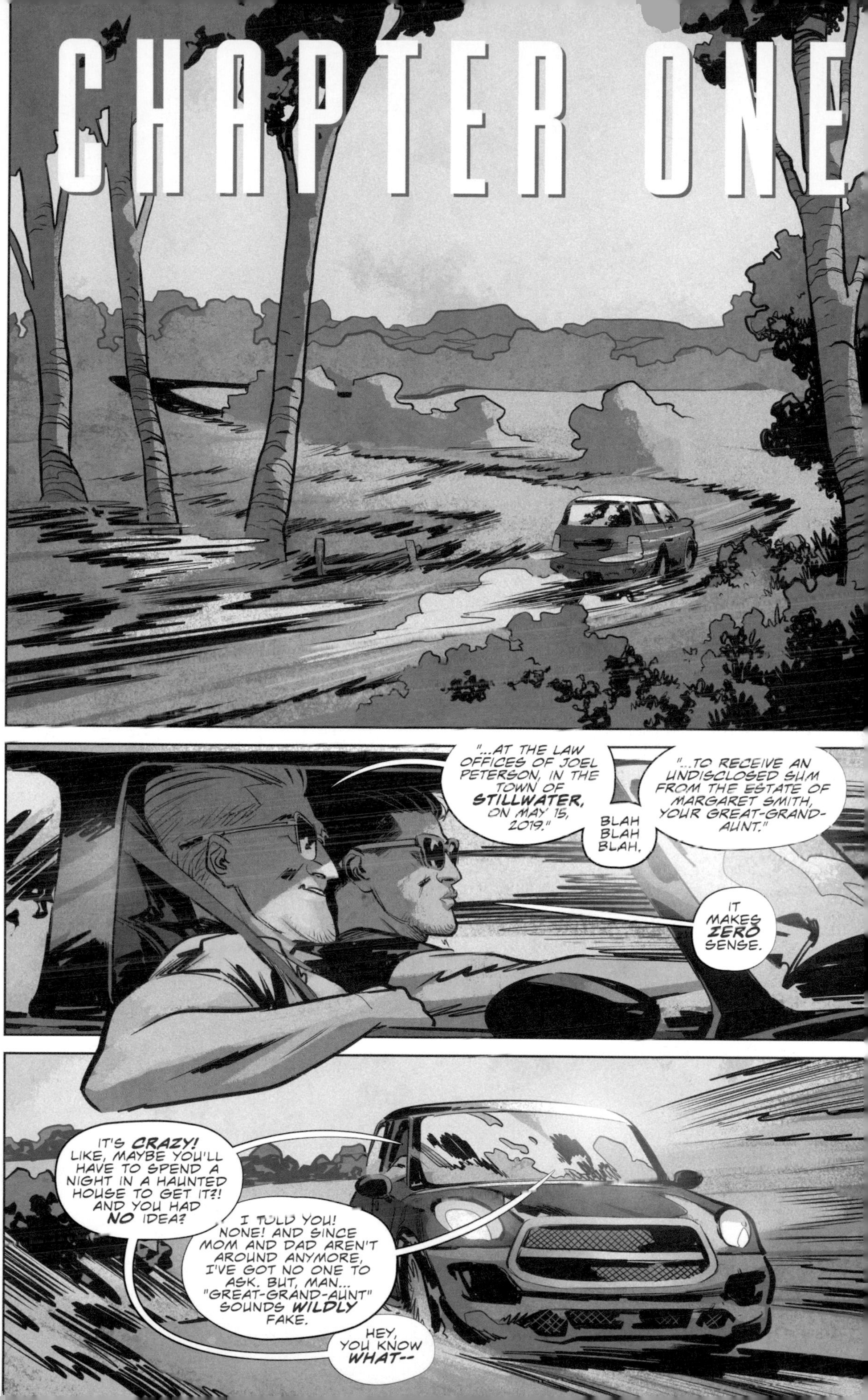
CHAPTER ONE
"...AT THE LAW OFFICES OF JOEL PETERSON, IN THE TOWN OF STILLWATER, ON MAY 15, 2019."
BLAH BLAH BLAH.
"...TO RECEIVE AN UNDISCLOSED SUM FROM THE ESTATE OF MARGARET SMITH, YOUR GREAT-GRAND-AUNT."
IT MAKES ZERO SENSE.
IT'S CRAZY! LIKE, MAYBE YOU'LL HAVE TO SPEND A NIGHT IN A HAUNTED HOUSE TO GET IT?! AND YOU HAD NO IDEA?
I TOLD YOU! NONE! AND SINCE MOM AND DAD AREN'T AROUND ANYMORE, I'VE GOT NO ONE TO ASK. BUT, MAN... "GREAT-GRAND-AUNT" SOUNDS WILDLY FAKE.
HEY, YOU KNOW WHAT--

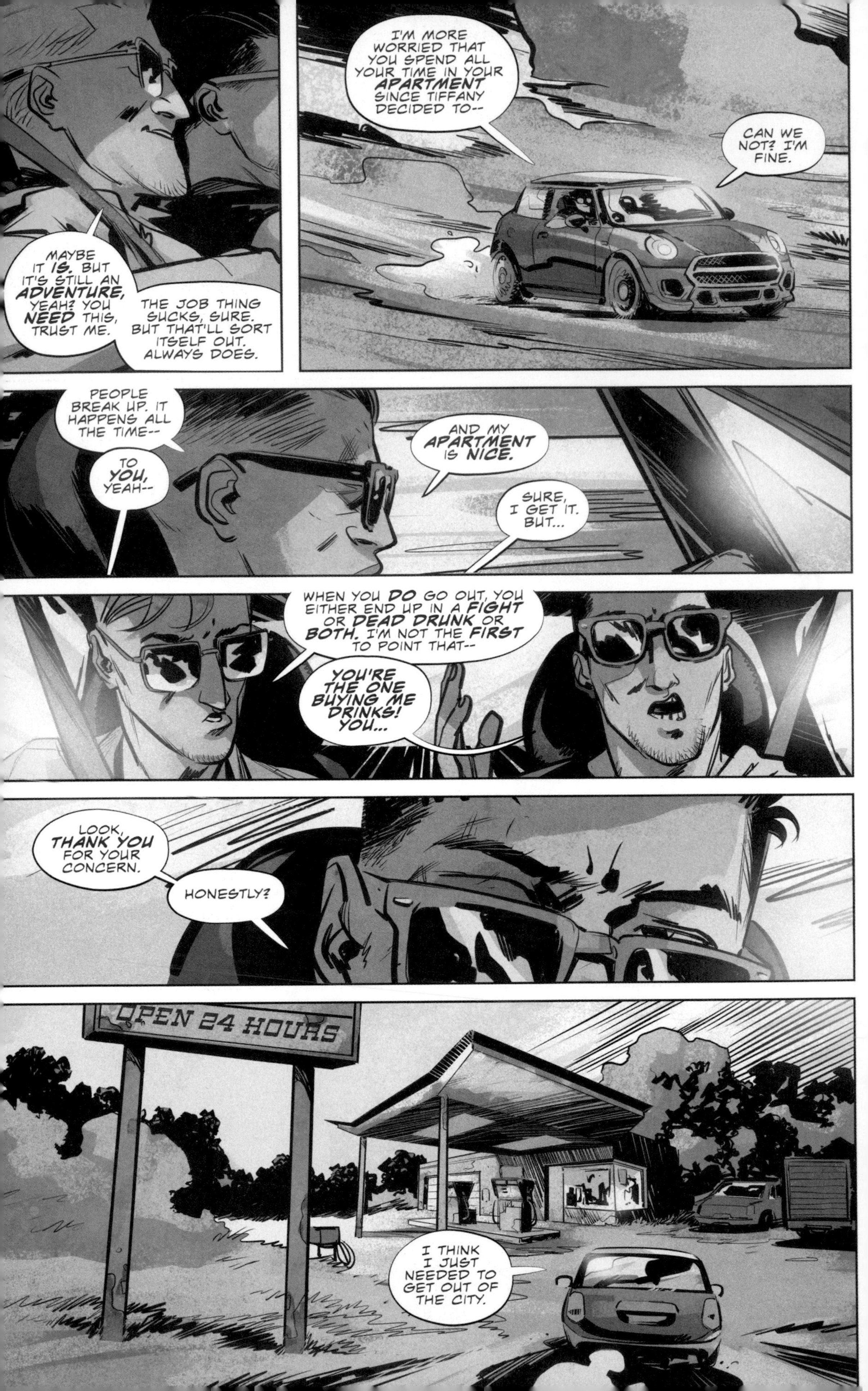
MAYBE IT IS. BUT IT'S STILL AN ADVENTURE, YEAH? YOU NEED THIS, TRUST ME.
THE JOB THING SUCKS, SURE. BUT THAT'LL SORT ITSELF OUT. ALWAYS DOES.
I'M MORE WORRIED THAT YOU SPEND ALL YOUR TIME IN YOUR APARTMENT SINCE TIFFANY DECIDED TO--
CAN WE NOT? I'M FINE.
PEOPLE BREAK UP. IT HAPPENS ALL THE TIME--
TO YOU, YEAH--
AND MY APARTMENT IS NICE.
SURE, I GET IT. BUT...
WHEN YOU DO GO OUT, YOU EITHER END UP IN A FIGHT OR DEAD DRUNK OR BOTH. I'M NOT THE FIRST TO POINT THAT--
YOU'RE THE ONE BUYING ME DRINKS! YOU...
LOOK, THANK YOU FOR YOUR CONCERN.
HONESTLY?
OPEN 24 HOURS
I THINK I JUST NEEDED TO GET OUT OF THE CITY.

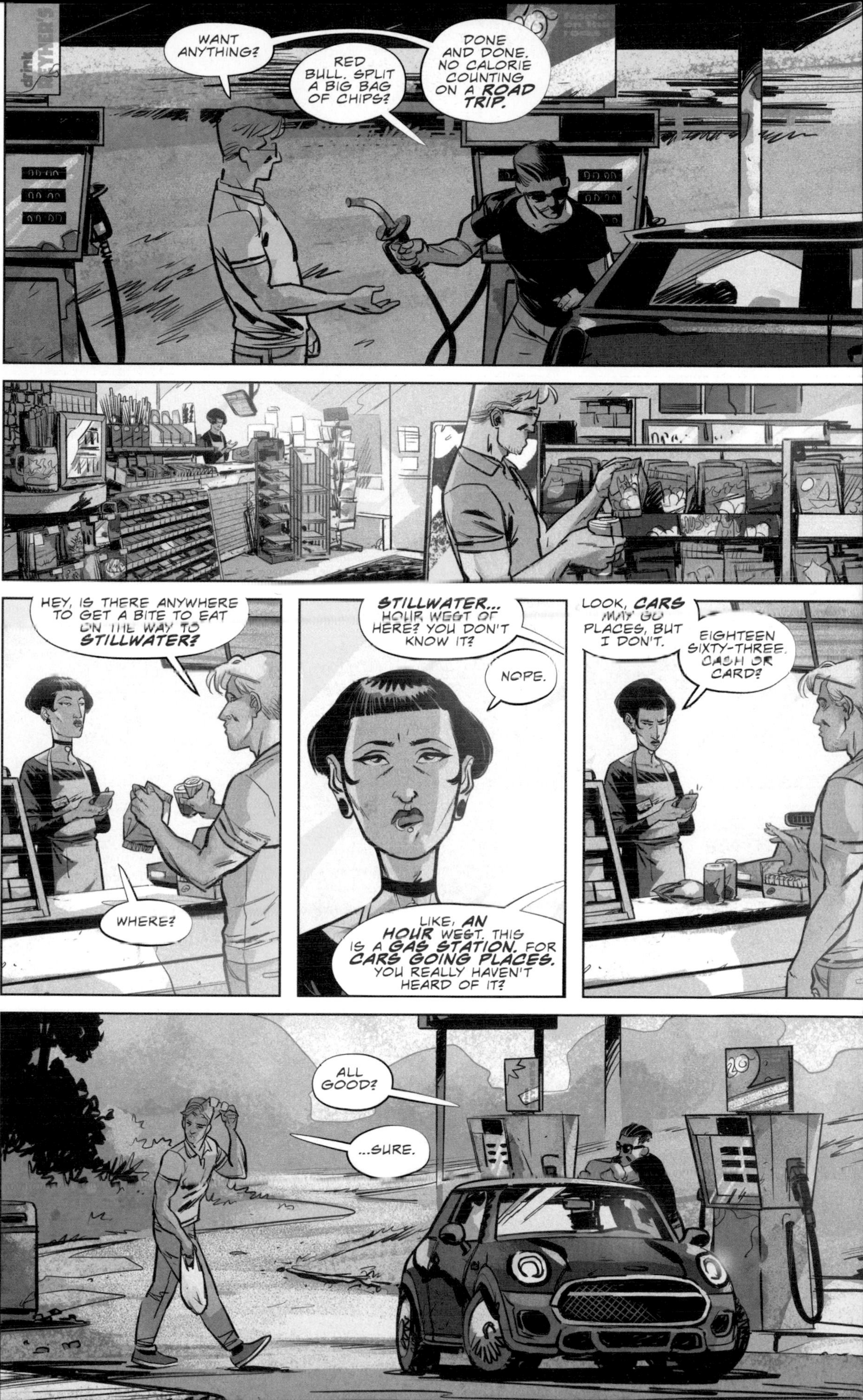
WANT ANYTHING?
RED BULL. SPLIT A BIG BAG OF CHIPS?
DONE AND DONE. NO CALORIE COUNTING ON A ROAD TRIP.
HEY, IS THERE ANYWHERE TO GET A BITE TO EAT ON THE WAY TO STILLWATER?
WHERE?
STILLWATER... HOUR WEST OF HERE? YOU DON'T KNOW IT?
NOPE.
LIKE, AN HOUR WEST. THIS IS A GAS STATION. FOR CARS GOING PLACES. YOU REALLY HAVEN'T HEARD OF IT?
LOOK, CARS MAY GO PLACES, BUT I DON'T.
EIGHTEEN SIXTY-THREE. CASH OR CARD?
ALL GOOD?
...SURE.

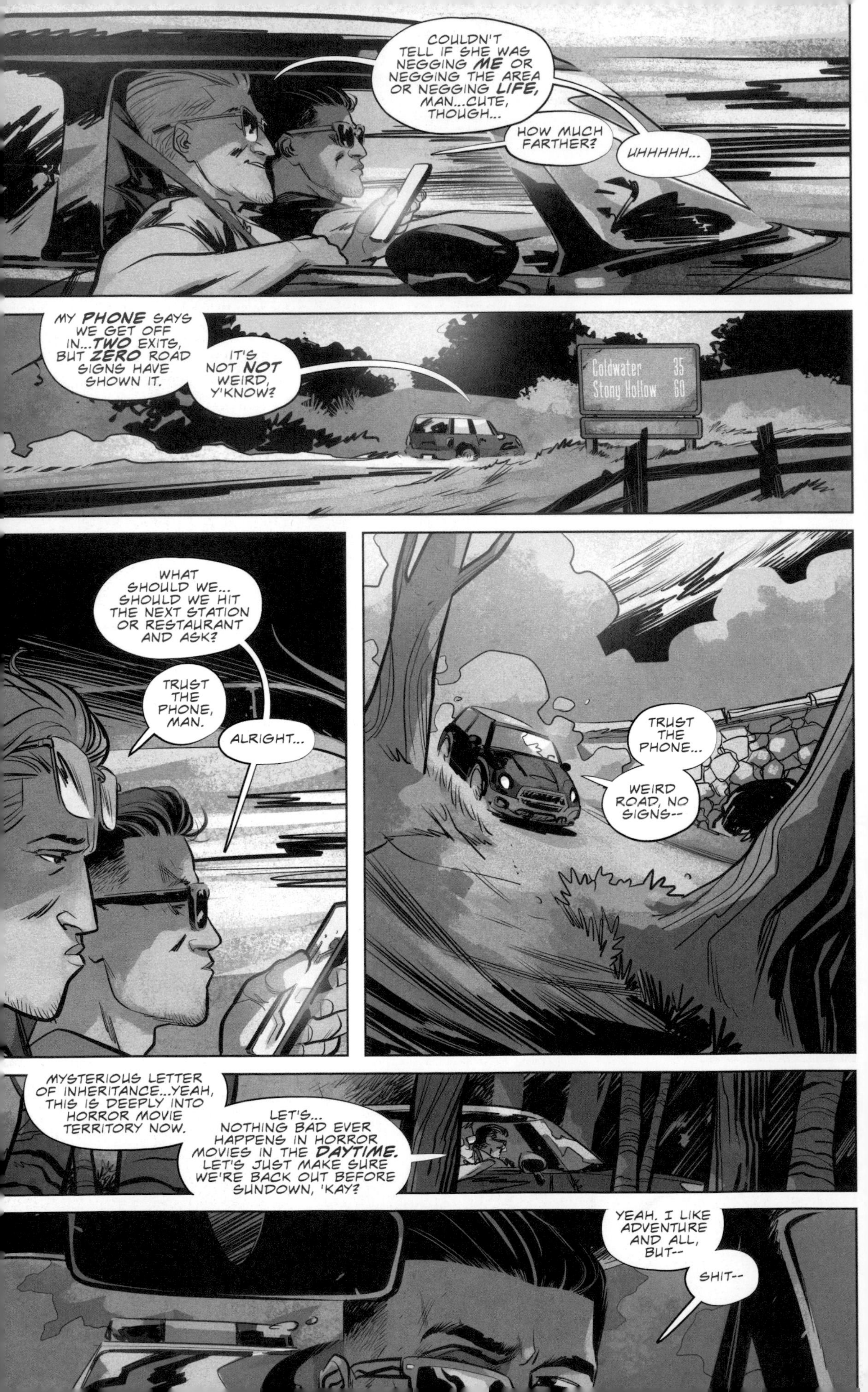
COULDN'T TELL IF SHE WAS NEGGING ME OR NEGGING THE AREA OR NEGGING LIFE, MAN...CUTE, THOUGH...
HOW MUCH FARTHER?
UHHHHH...
MY PHONE SAYS WE GET OFF IN...TWO EXITS, BUT ZERO ROAD SIGNS HAVE SHOWN IT.
IT'S NOT NOT WEIRD, Y'KNOW?
Coldwater 35
Stony Hollow 60
WHAT SHOULD WE... SHOULD WE HIT THE NEXT STATION OR RESTAURANT AND ASK?
TRUST THE PHONE, MAN.
ALRIGHT...
TRUST THE PHONE...
WEIRD ROAD, NO SIGNS--
MYSTERIOUS LETTER OF INHERITANCE...YEAH, THIS IS DEEPLY INTO HORROR MOVIE TERRITORY NOW.
LET'S... NOTHING BAD EVER HAPPENS IN HORROR MOVIES IN THE DAYTIME. LET'S JUST MAKE SURE WE'RE BACK OUT BEFORE SUNDOWN, 'KAY?
YEAH. I LIKE ADVENTURE AND ALL, BUT--
SHIT--

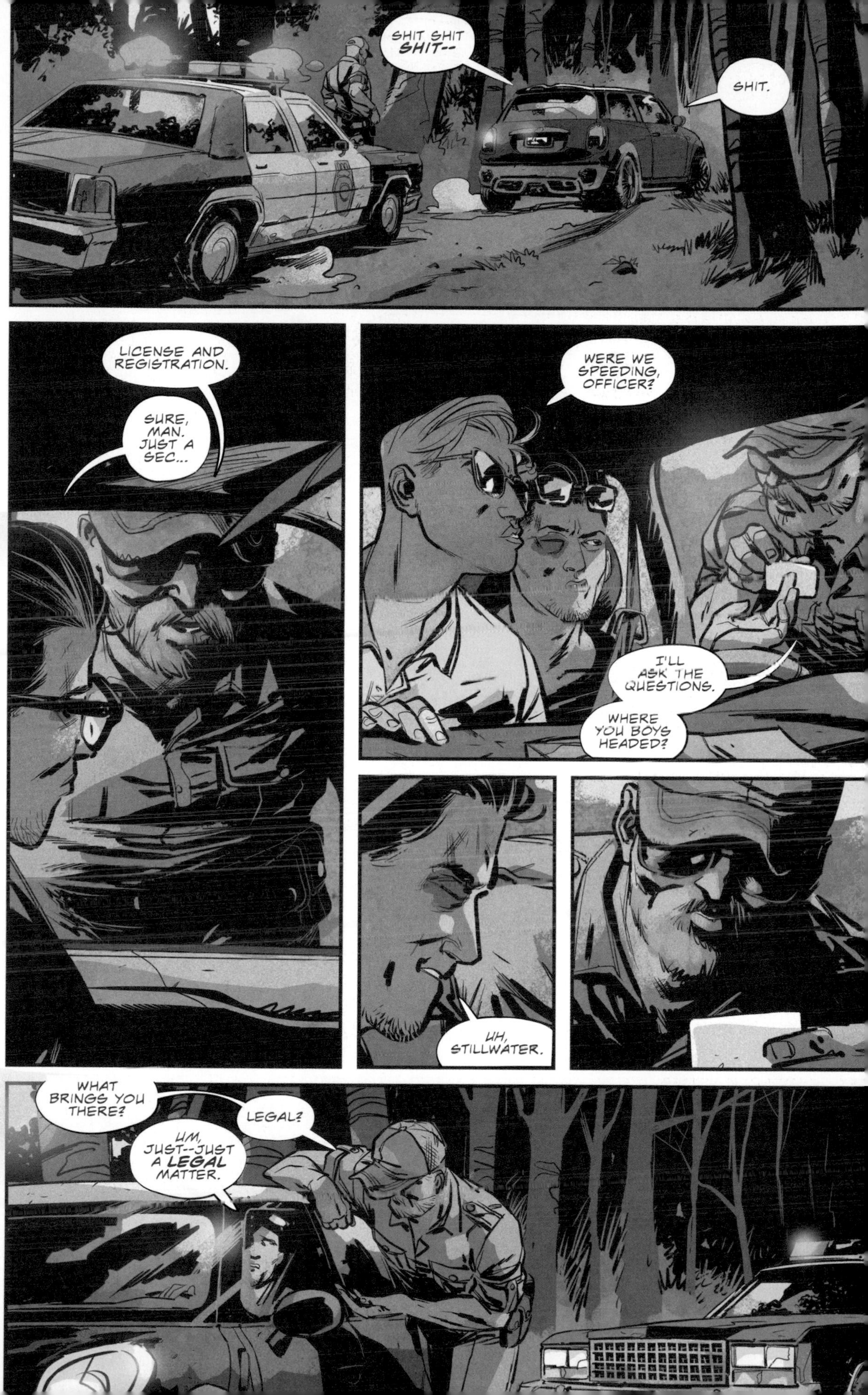
SHIT SHIT SHIT--
SHIT.
LICENSE AND REGISTRATION.
SURE, MAN. JUST A SEC...
WERE WE SPEEDING, OFFICER?
I'LL ASK THE QUESTIONS.
WHERE YOU BOYS HEADED?
UH, STILLWATER.
WHAT BRINGS YOU THERE?
UM, JUST--JUST A LEGAL MATTER.
LEGAL?

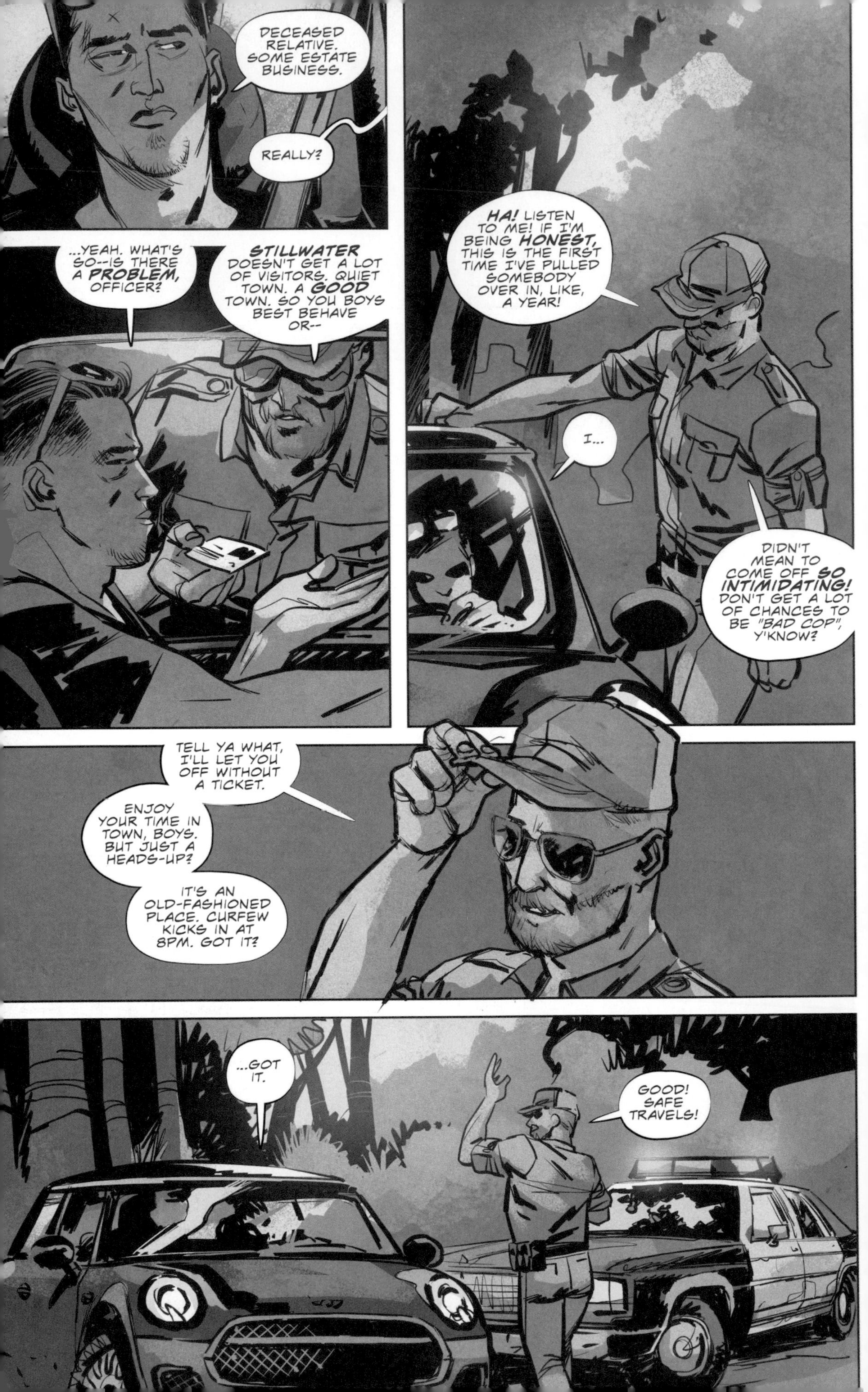
DECEASED RELATIVE. SOME ESTATE BUSINESS.
REALLY?
...YEAH. WHAT'S SO--IS THERE A PROBLEM, OFFICER?
STILLWATER DOESN'T GET A LOT OF VISITORS. QUIET TOWN. A GOOD TOWN. SO YOU BOYS BEST BEHAVE OR--
HA! LISTEN TO ME! IF I'M BEING HONEST, THIS IS THE FIRST TIME I'VE PULLED SOMEBODY OVER IN, LIKE, A YEAR!
I...
DIDN'T MEAN TO COME OFF SO INTIMIDATING! DON'T GET A LOT OF CHANCES TO BE "BAD COP", Y'KNOW?
TELL YA WHAT, I'LL LET YOU OFF WITHOUT A TICKET.
ENJOY YOUR TIME IN TOWN, BOYS. BUT JUST A HEADS-UP?
IT'S AN OLD-FASHIONED PLACE. CURFEW KICKS IN AT 8PM. GOT IT?
...GOT IT.
GOOD! SAFE TRAVELS!

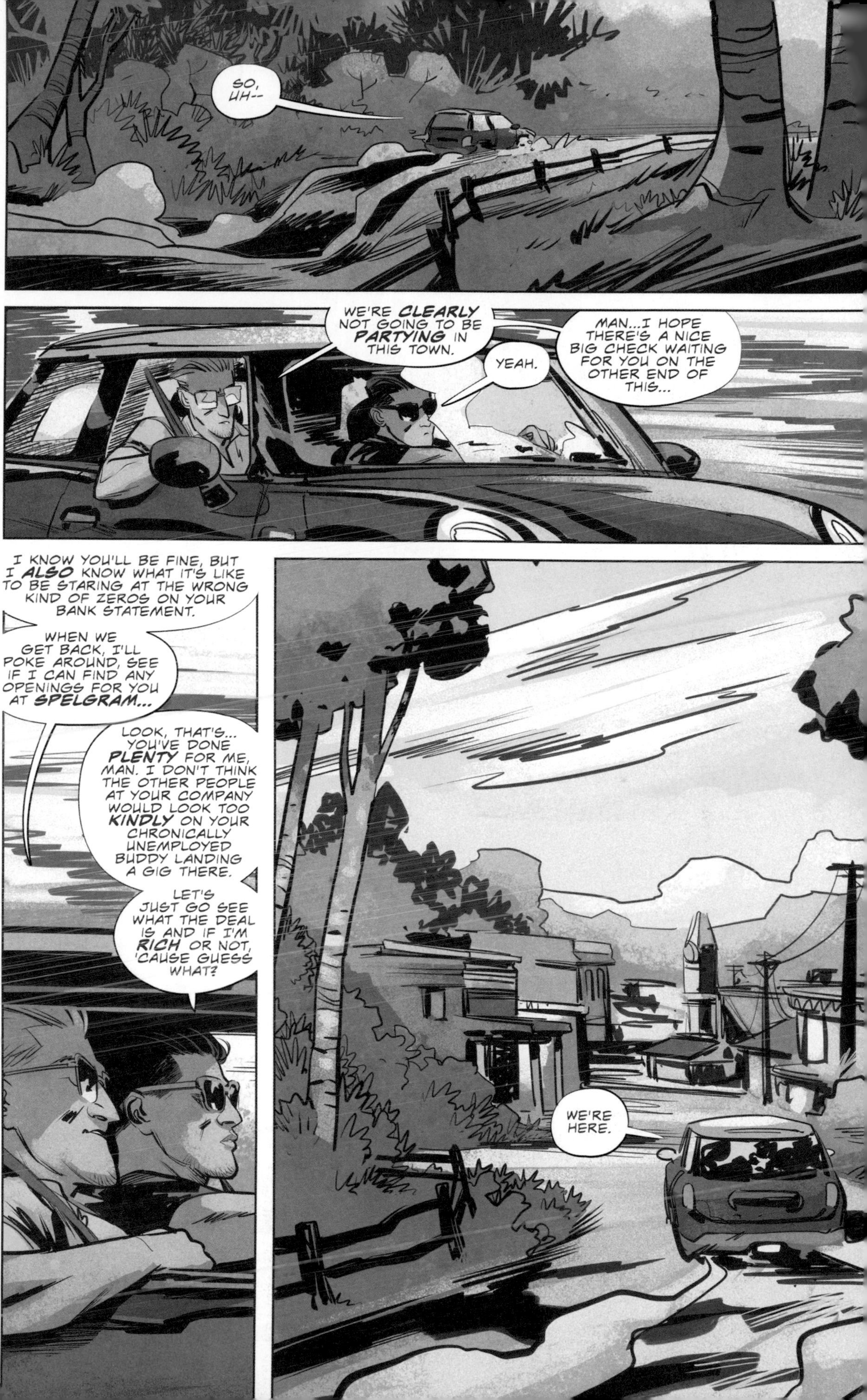
SO, UH--
WE'RE CLEARLY NOT GOING TO BE PARTYING IN THIS TOWN.
YEAH.
MAN...I HOPE THERE'S A NICE BIG CHECK WAITING FOR YOU ON THE OTHER END OF THIS...
I KNOW YOU'LL BE FINE, BUT I ALSO KNOW WHAT IT'S LIKE TO BE STARING AT THE WRONG KIND OF ZEROS ON YOUR BANK STATEMENT.
WHEN WE GET BACK, I'LL POKE AROUND, SEE IF I CAN FIND ANY OPENINGS FOR YOU AT SPELGRAM...
LOOK, THAT'S... YOU'VE DONE PLENTY FOR ME, MAN. I DON'T THINK THE OTHER PEOPLE AT YOUR COMPANY WOULD LOOK TOO KINDLY ON YOUR CHRONICALLY UNEMPLOYED BUDDY LANDING A GIG THERE.
LET'S JUST GO SEE WHAT THE DEAL IS AND IF I'M RICH OR NOT, 'CAUSE GUESS WHAT?
WE'RE HERE.

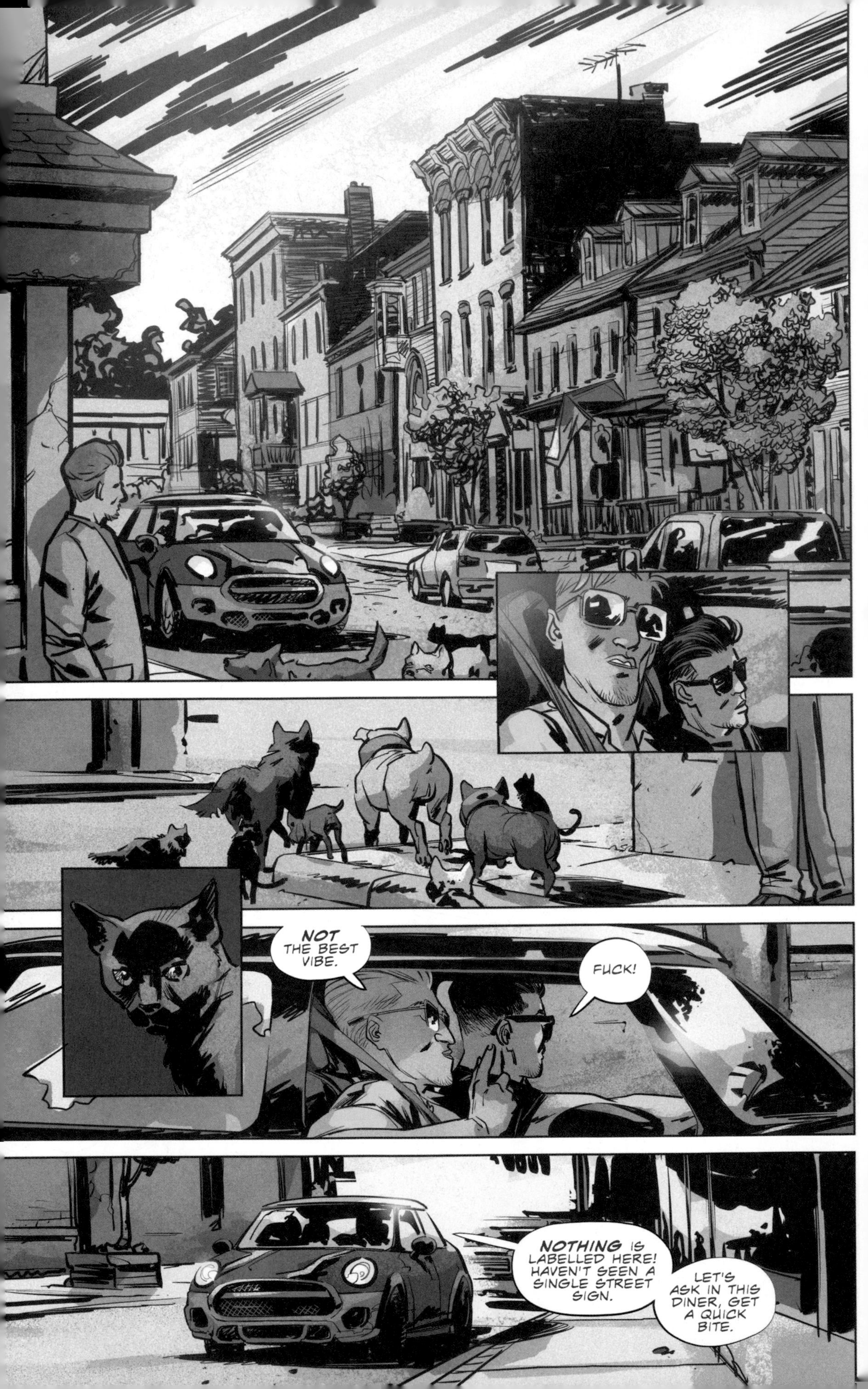
NOT THE BEST VIBE.
FUCK!
NOTHING IS LABELLED HERE! HAVEN'T SEEN A SINGLE STREET SIGN.
LET'S ASK IN THIS DINER, GET A QUICK BITE.

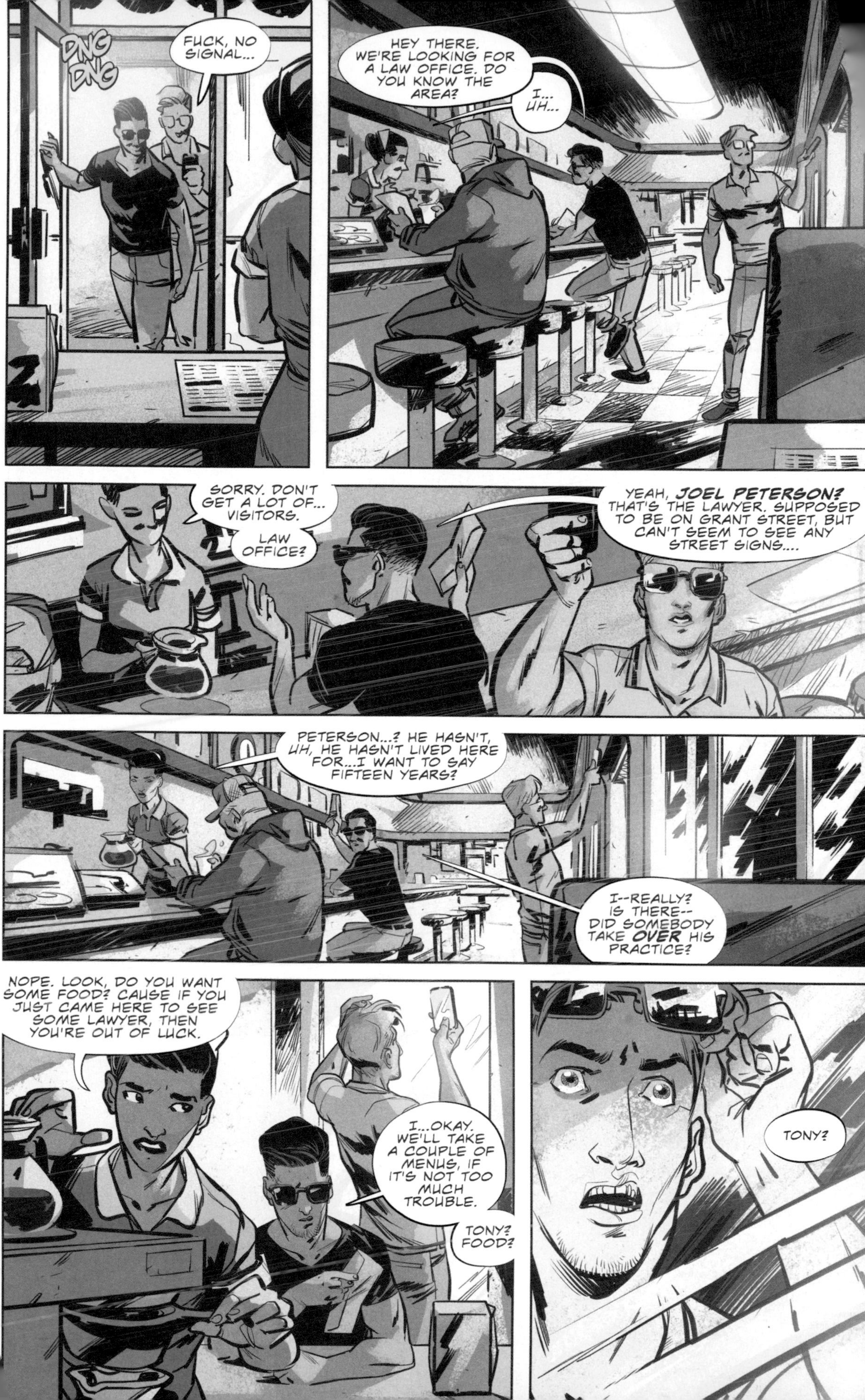
DNG DNG
FUCK, NO SIGNAL...
HEY THERE. WE'RE LOOKING FOR A LAW OFFICE. DO YOU KNOW THE AREA?
I... UH...
SORRY. DON'T GET A LOT OF... VISITORS.
LAW OFFICE?
YEAH, JOEL PETERSON? THAT'S THE LAWYER. SUPPOSED TO BE ON GRANT STREET, BUT CAN'T SEEM TO SEE ANY STREET SIGNS....
PETERSON...? HE HASN'T, UH, HE HASN'T LIVED HERE FOR...I WANT TO SAY FIFTEEN YEARS?
I--REALLY? IS THERE-- DID SOMEBODY TAKE OVER HIS PRACTICE?
NOPE. LOOK, DO YOU WANT SOME FOOD? CAUSE IF YOU JUST CAME HERE TO SEE SOME LAWYER, THEN YOU'RE OUT OF LUCK.
I...OKAY. WE'LL TAKE A COUPLE OF MENUS, IF IT'S NOT TOO MUCH TROUBLE.
TONY? FOOD?
TONY?

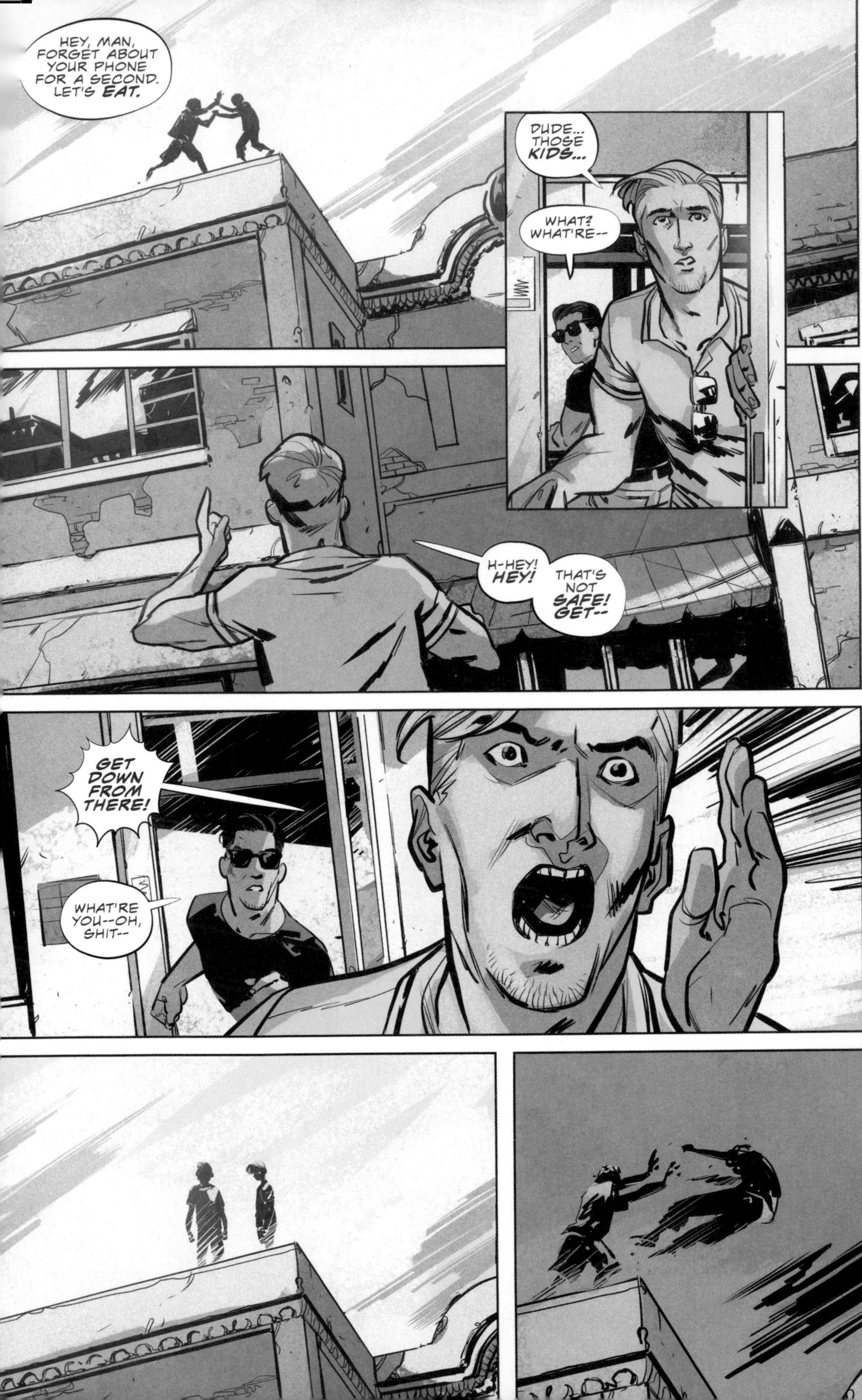
HEY, MAN, FORGET ABOUT YOUR PHONE FOR A SECOND. LET'S EAT.
DUDE... THOSE KIDS...
WHAT? WHAT'RE--
H-HEY! HEY!
THAT'S NOT SAFE! GET--
GET DOWN FROM THERE!
WHAT'RE YOU--OH, SHIT--

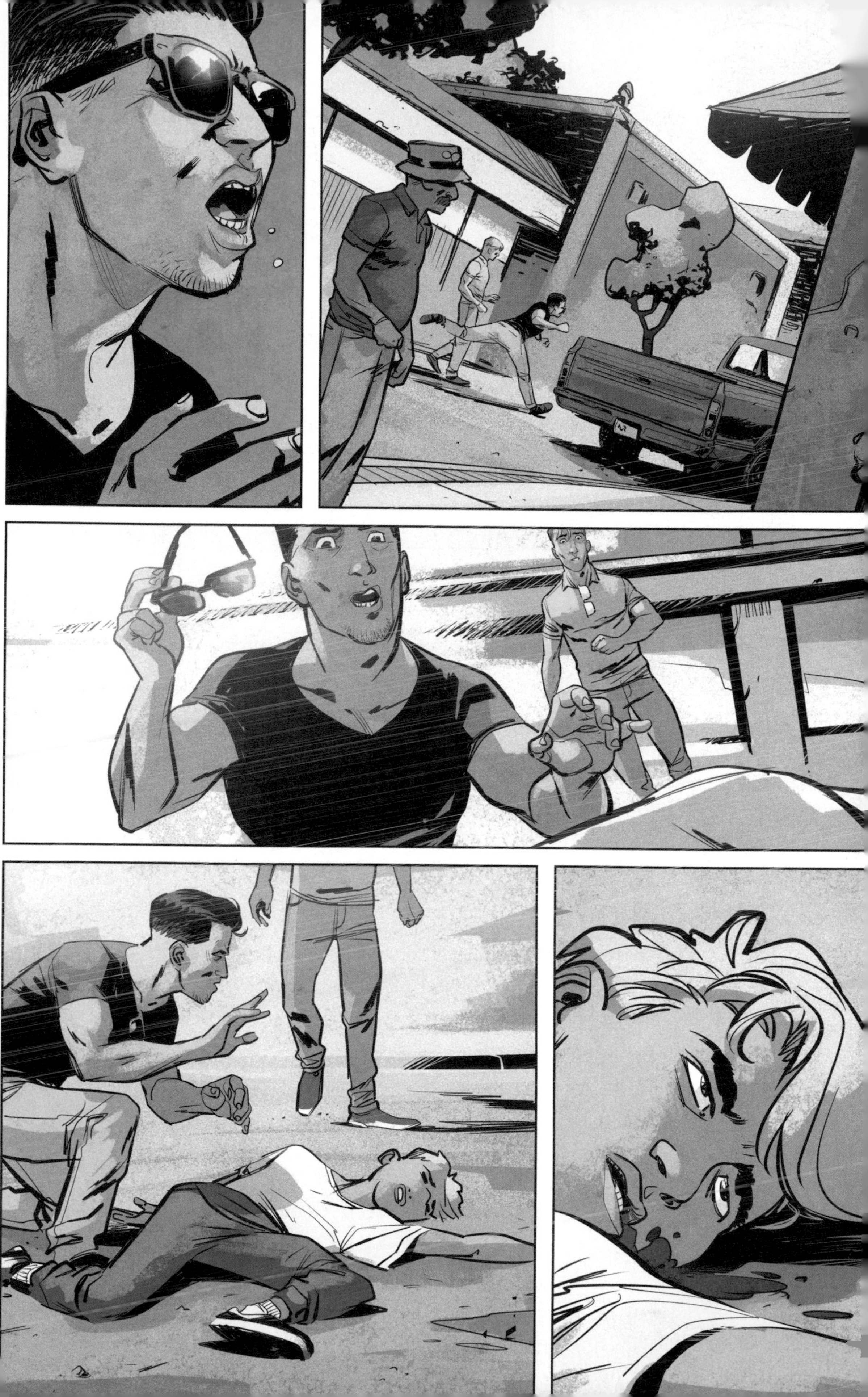

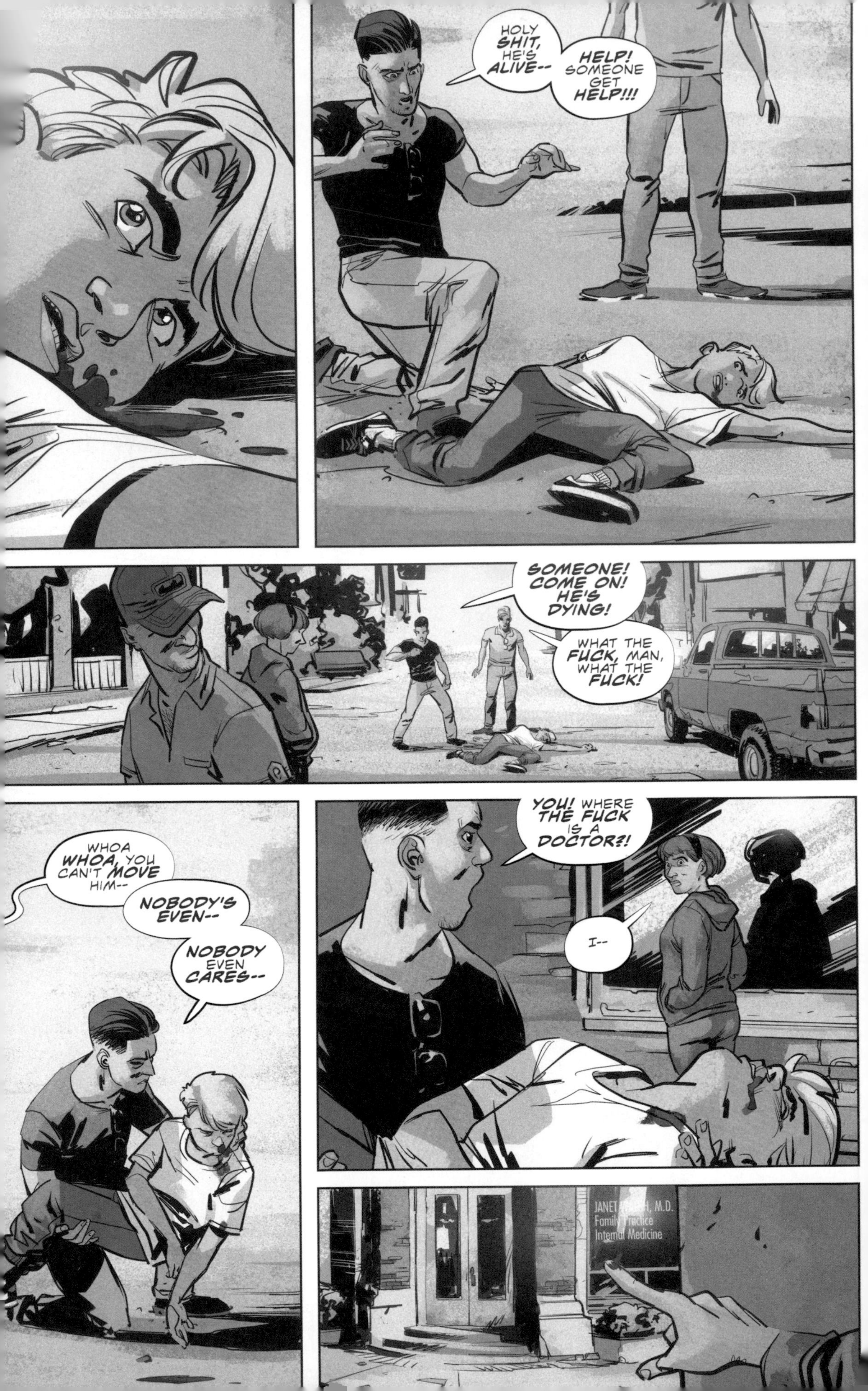
HOLY SHIT, HE'S ALIVE--
HELP! SOMEONE GET HELP!!!
SOMEONE! COME ON! HE'S DYING!
WHAT THE FUCK, MAN, WHAT THE FUCK!
WHOA WHOA, YOU CAN'T MOVE HIM--
NOBODY'S EVEN--
NOBODY EVEN CARES--
YOU! WHERE THE FUCK IS A DOCTOR?!
I--
Family Practice
Internal Medicine

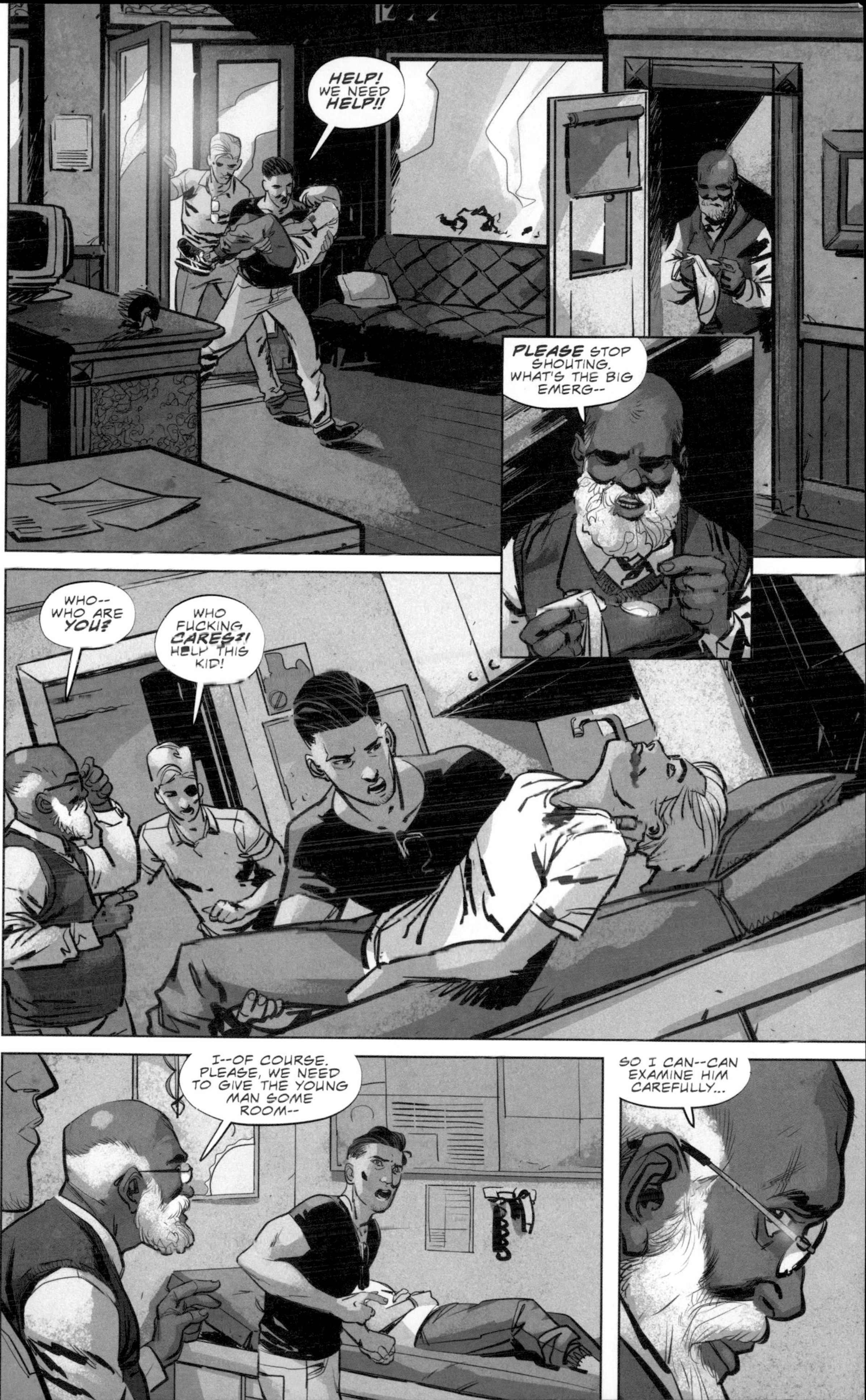
HELP! WE NEED HELP!!
PLEASE STOP SHOUTING. WHAT'S THE BIG EMERG--
WHO-- WHO ARE YOU?
WHO FUCKING CARES?! HELP THIS KID!
I--OF COURSE. PLEASE, WE NEED TO GIVE THE YOUNG MAN SOME ROOM--
SO I CAN--CAN EXAMINE HIM CAREFULLY...

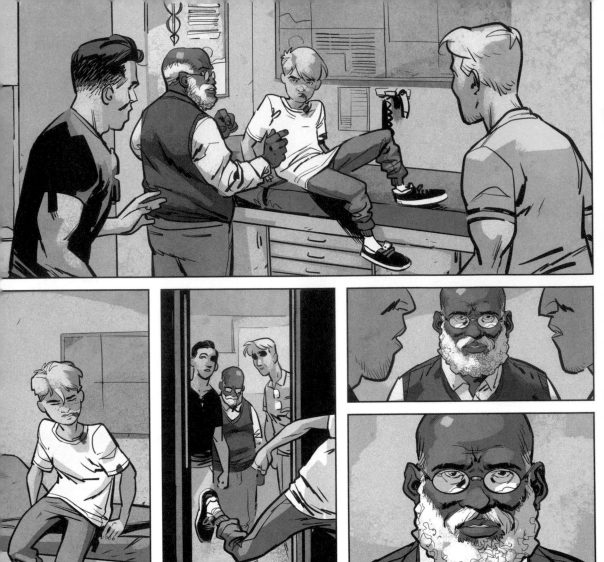

GET IN YOUR CAR AND *GO*. PLEASE, YOU *HAVE* TO TRUST ME. THIS WILL NOT END WELL, OTHERWISE.

I CAN'T PROTECT YOU. NO ONE CAN.

D-DANIEL?

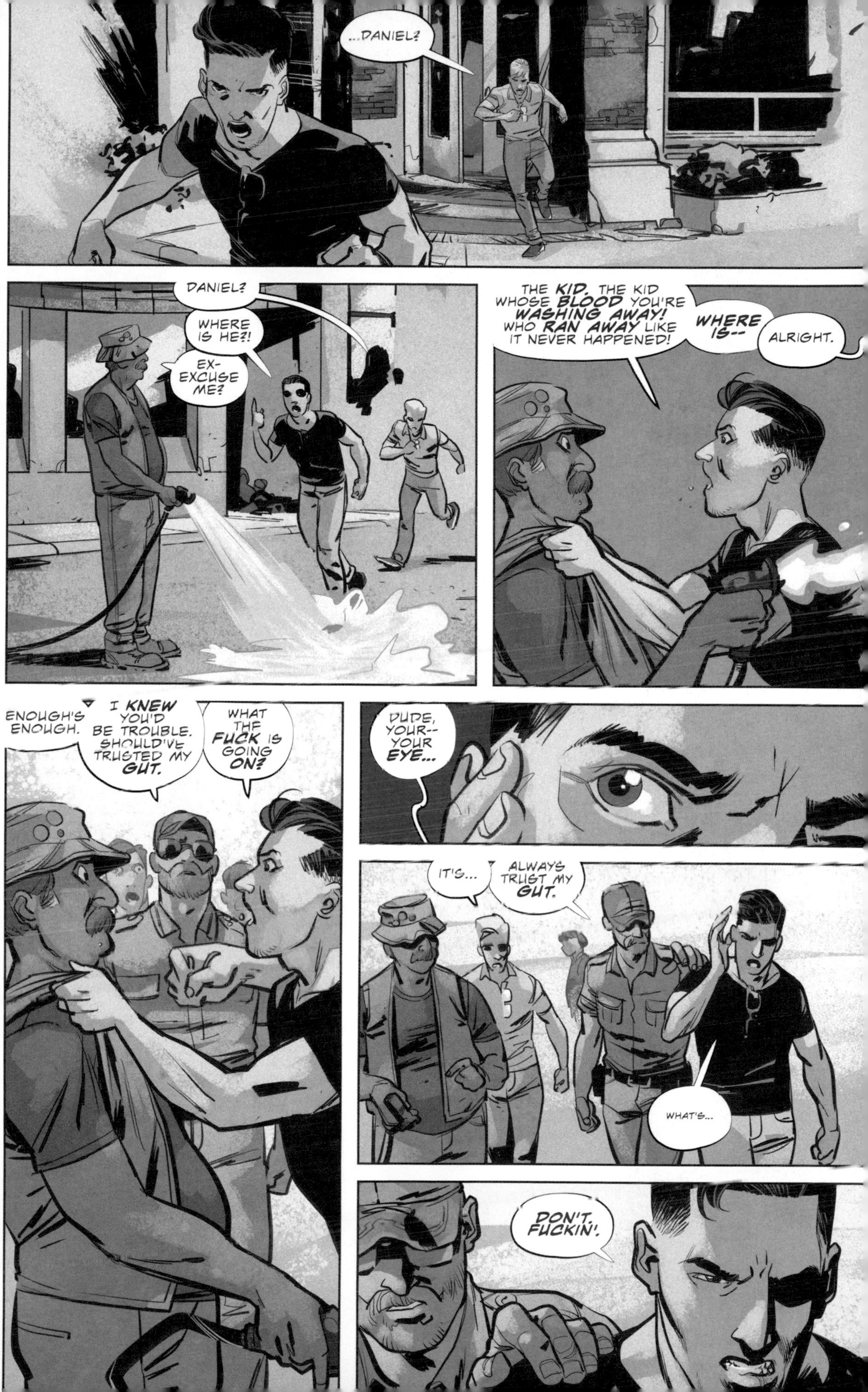
...DANIEL?
DANIEL?
WHERE IS HE?!
EX- EXCUSE ME?
THE KID. THE KID WHOSE BLOOD YOU'RE WASHING AWAY! WHO RAN AWAY LIKE IT NEVER HAPPENED!
WHERE IS--
ALRIGHT.
ENOUGH'S ENOUGH.
I KNEW YOU'D BE TROUBLE. SHOULD'VE TRUSTED MY GUT.
WHAT THE FUCK IS GOING ON?
DUDE, YOUR-- YOUR EYE...
IT'S...
ALWAYS TRUST MY GUT.
WHAT'S...
DON'T. FUCKIN'.

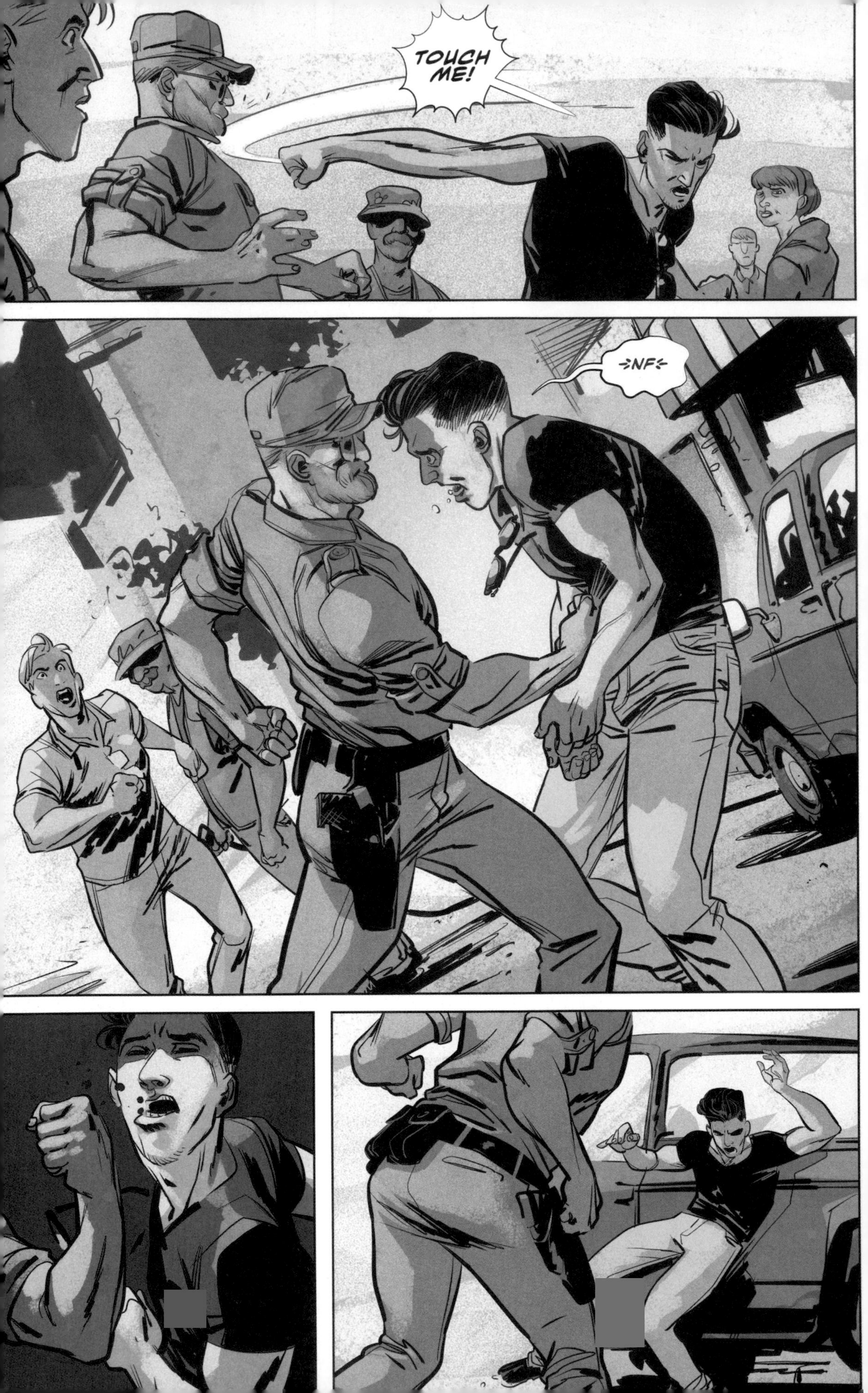
TOUCH ME!
NF

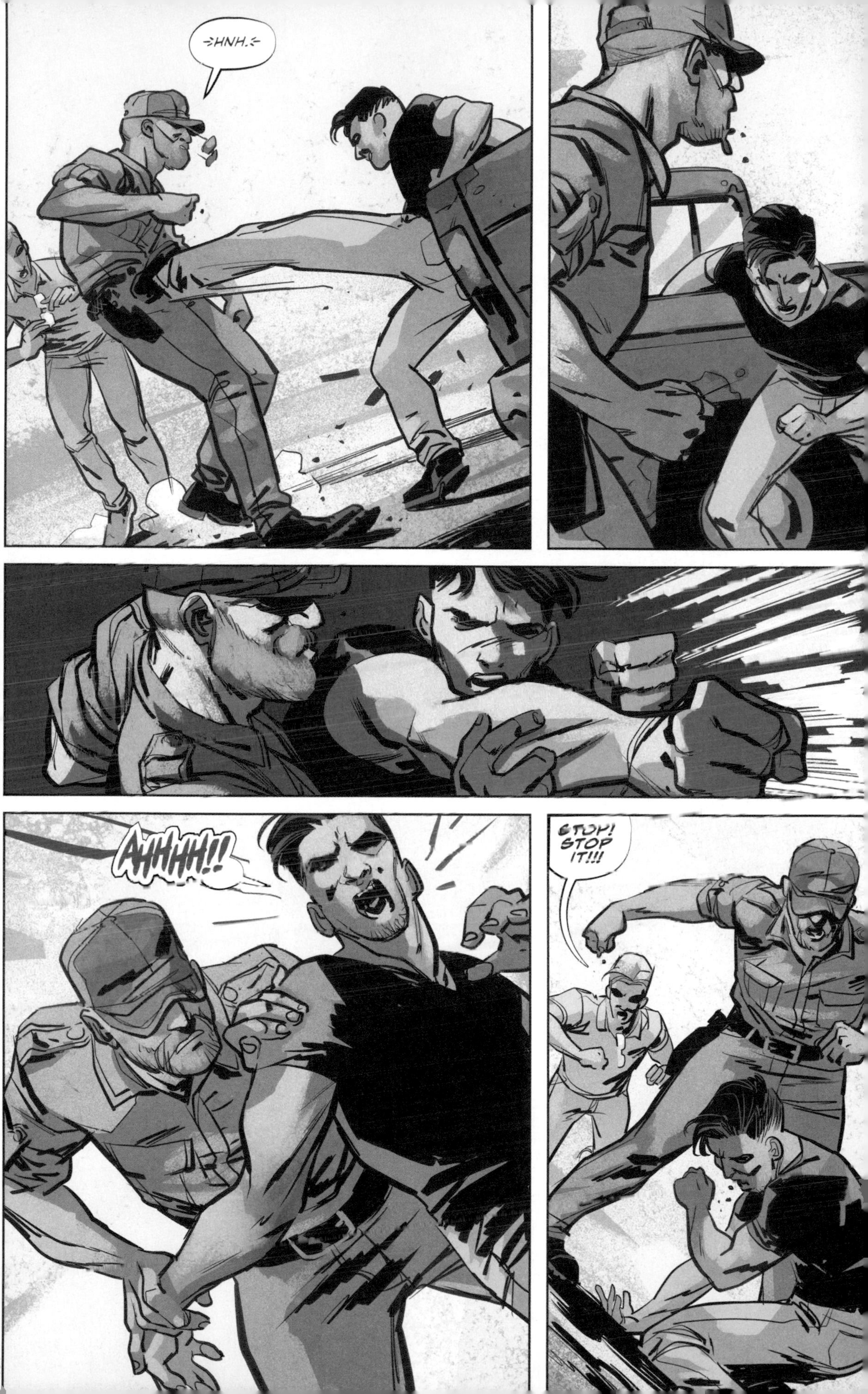
HNH.
AHHHH!!
STOP! STOP IT!!!

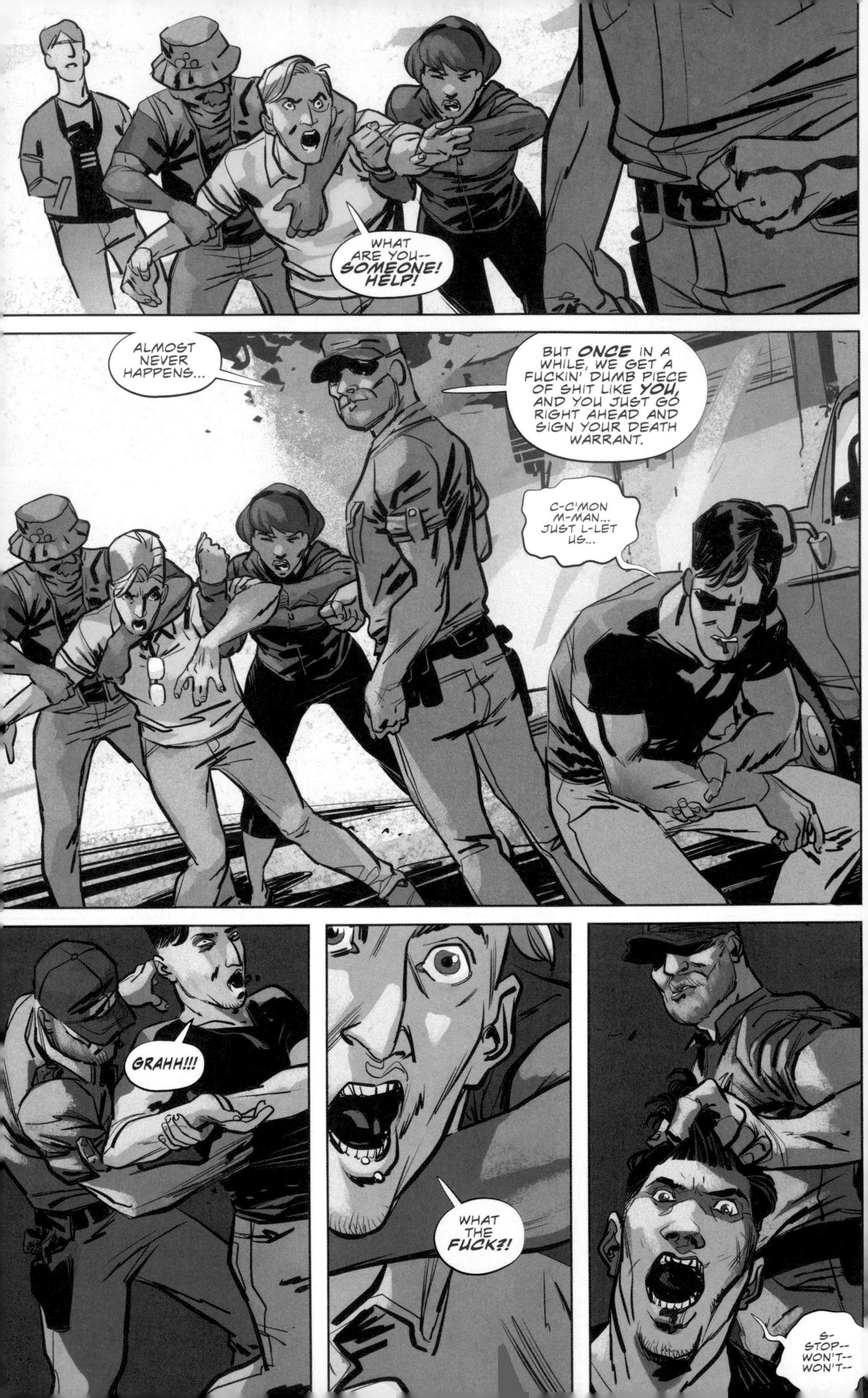
WHAT ARE YOU-- SOMEONE! HELP!
ALMOST NEVER HAPPENS...
BUT ONCE IN A WHILE, WE GET A FUCKIN' DUMB PIECE OF SHIT LIKE YOU, AND YOU JUST GO RIGHT AHEAD AND SIGN YOUR DEATH WARRANT.
C-C'MON M-MAN... JUST L-LET US...
GRAHH!!!
WHAT THE FUCK?!
S-STOP-- WON'T-- WON'T--

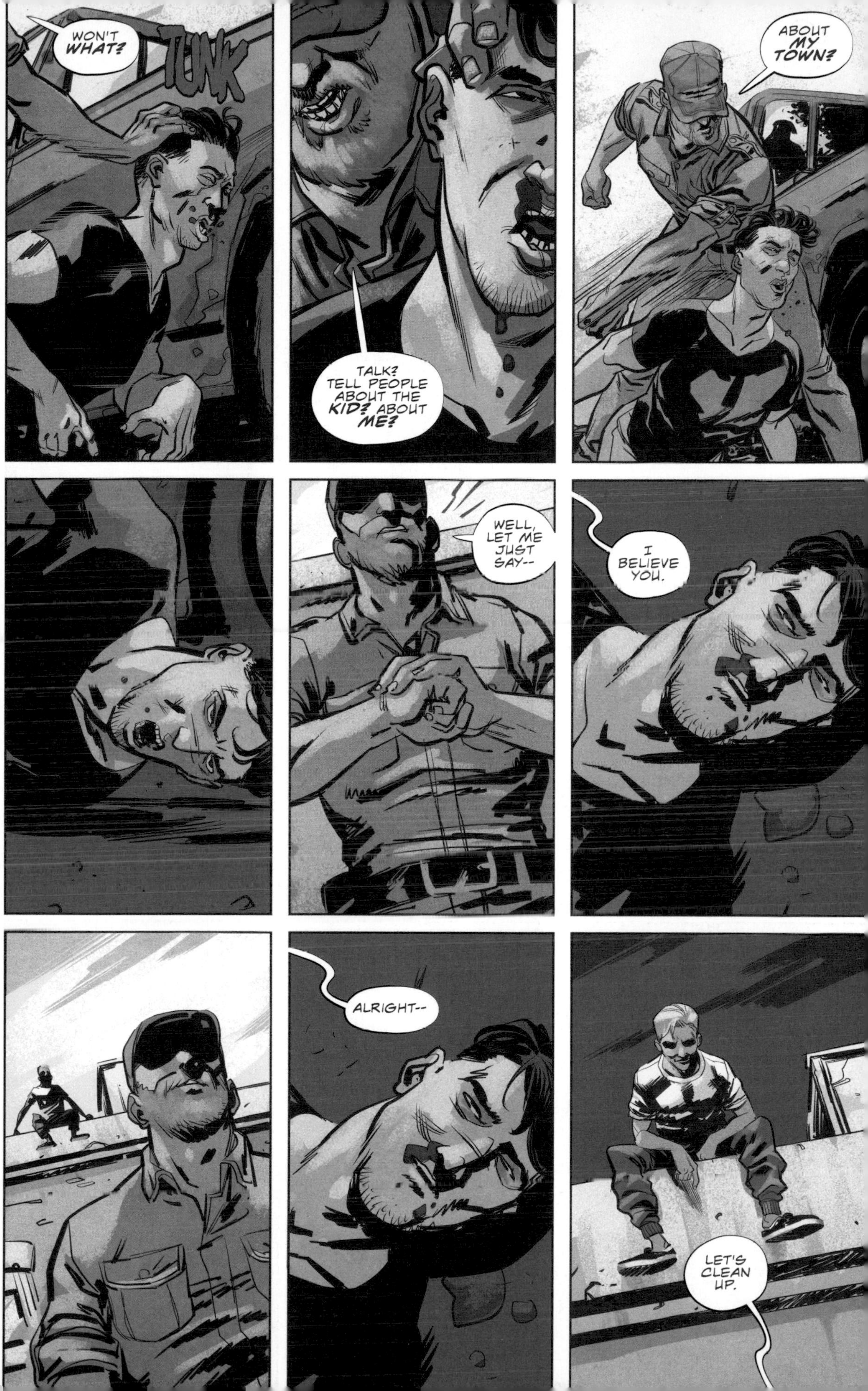
WON'T WHAT?
TUNK
TALK? TELL PEOPLE ABOUT THE KID? ABOUT ME?
ABOUT MY TOWN?
WELL, LET ME JUST SAY--
I BELIEVE YOU.
ALRIGHT--
LET'S CLEAN UP.

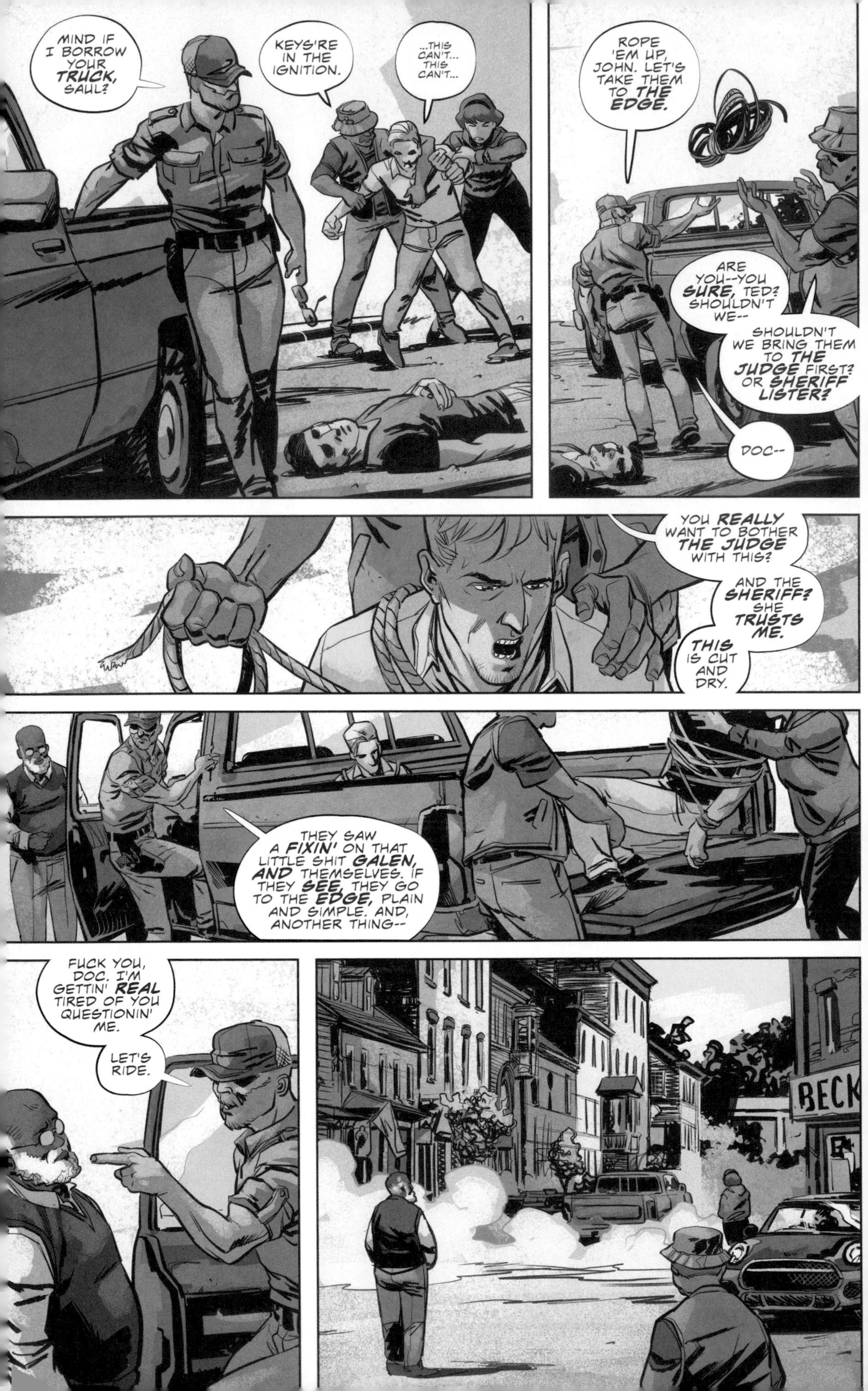
MIND IF I BORROW YOUR TRUCK, SAUL?
KEYS'RE IN THE IGNITION.
...THIS CAN'T... THIS CAN'T...
ROPE 'EM UP, JOHN. LET'S TAKE THEM TO THE EDGE.
ARE YOU--YOU SURE, TED? SHOULDN'T WE--
SHOULDN'T WE BRING THEM TO THE JUDGE FIRST? OR SHERIFF LISTER?
DOC--
YOU REALLY WANT TO BOTHER THE JUDGE WITH THIS?
AND THE SHERIFF? SHE TRUSTS ME.
THIS IS CUT AND DRY.
THEY SAW A FIXIN' ON THAT LITTLE SHIT GALEN, AND THEMSELVES. IF THEY SEE, THEY GO TO THE EDGE, PLAIN AND SIMPLE. AND, ANOTHER THING--
FUCK YOU, DOC. I'M GETTIN' REAL TIRED OF YOU QUESTIONIN' ME.
LET'S RIDE.
BECK

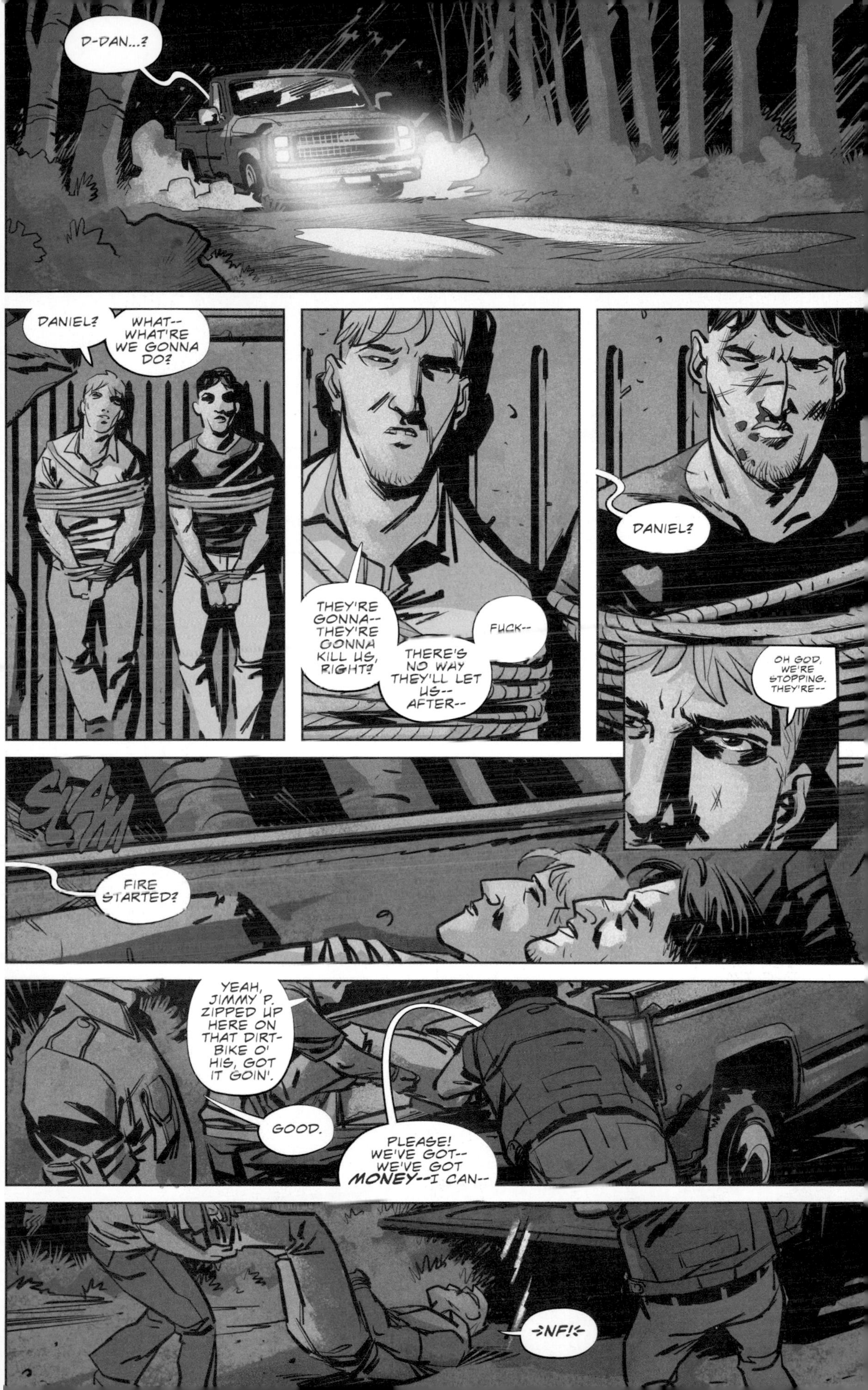
D-DAN...?
DANIEL?
WHAT-- WHAT'RE WE GONNA DO?
THEY'RE GONNA-- THEY'RE GONNA KILL US, RIGHT?
FUCK--
THERE'S NO WAY THEY'LL LET US-- AFTER--
DANIEL?
OH GOD, WE'RE STOPPING. THEY'RE--
SLAM
FIRE STARTED?
YEAH, JIMMY P. ZIPPED UP HERE ON THAT DIRT-BIKE O' HIS, GOT IT GOIN'.
GOOD.
PLEASE! WE'VE GOT-- WE'VE GOT MONEY--I CAN--
NF!

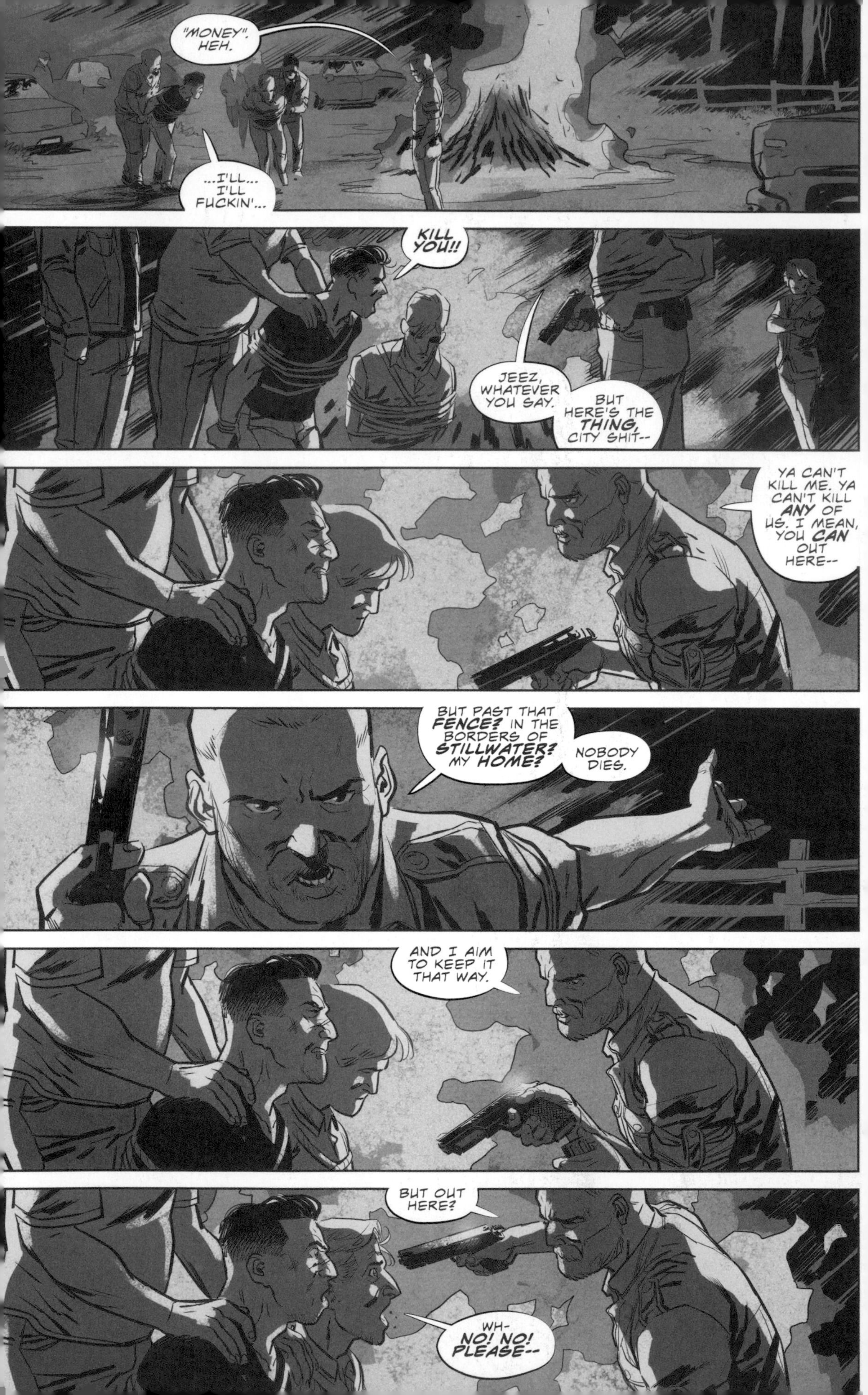
"MONEY". HEH.
...I'LL... I'LL FUCKIN'...
KILL YOU!!
JEEZ, WHATEVER YOU SAY.
BUT HERE'S THE THING, CITY SHIT--
YA CAN'T KILL ME. YA CAN'T KILL ANY OF US. I MEAN, YOU CAN OUT HERE--
BUT PAST THAT FENCE? IN THE BORDERS OF STILLWATER? MY HOME?
NOBODY DIES.
AND I AIM TO KEEP IT THAT WAY.
BUT OUT HERE?
WH- NO! NO! PLEASE--

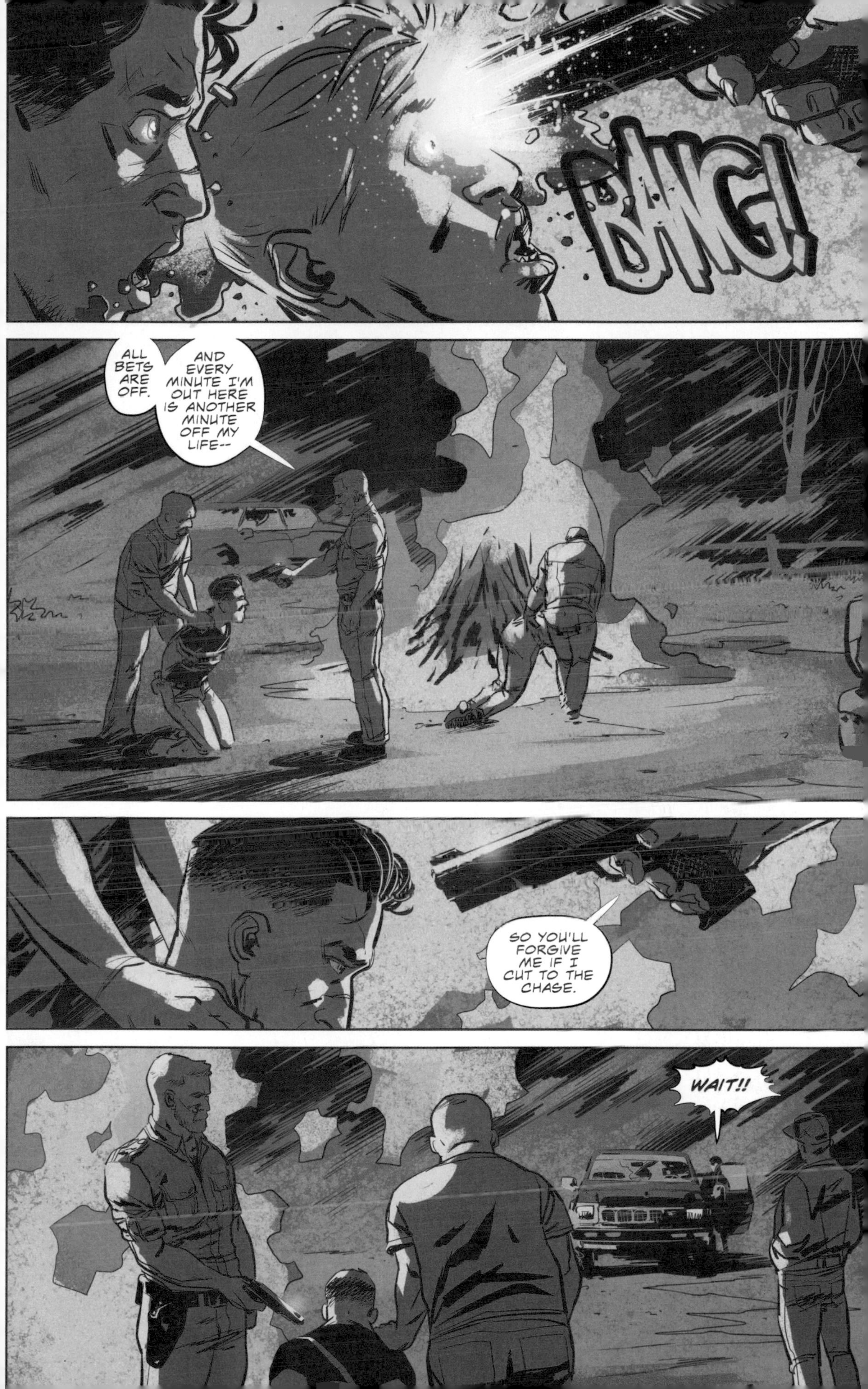
BANG!
ALL BETS ARE OFF.
AND EVERY MINUTE I'M OUT HERE IS ANOTHER MINUTE OFF MY LIFE--
SO YOU'LL FORGIVE ME IF I CUT TO THE CHASE.
WAIT!!

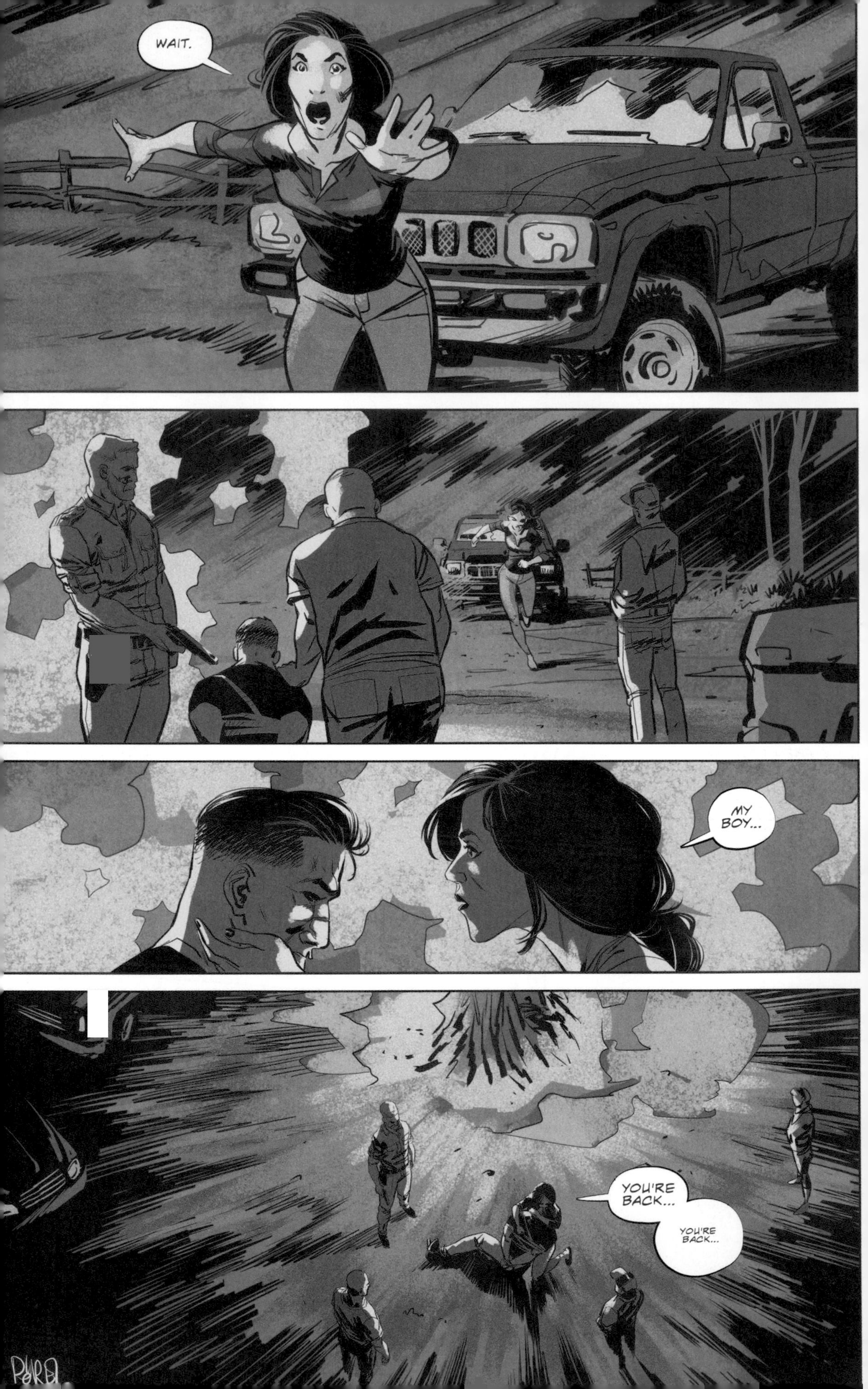
WAIT.
MY BOY...
YOU'RE BACK...
YOU'RE BACK...

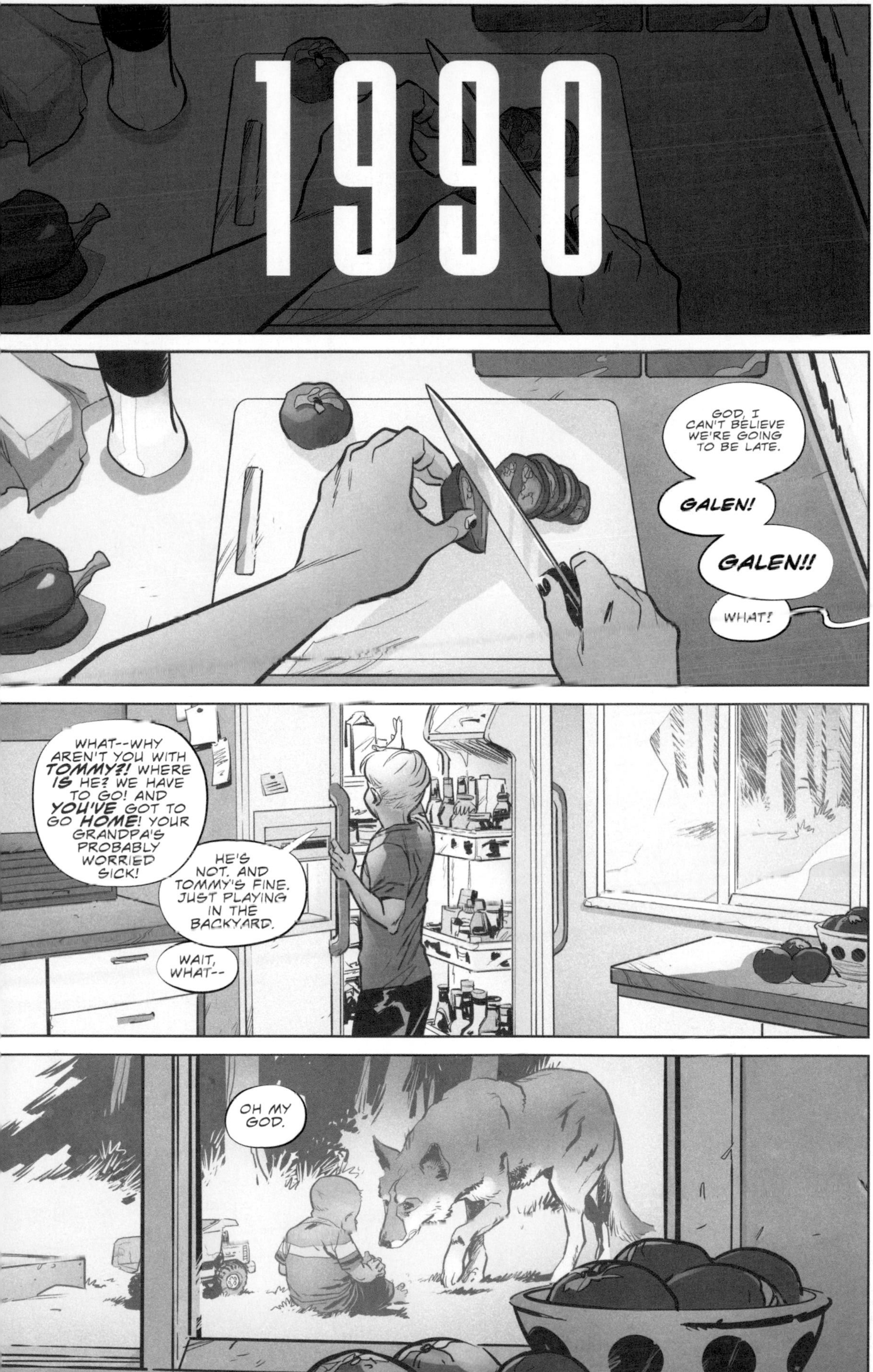
1990
GOD, I CAN'T BELIEVE WE'RE GOING TO BE LATE.
GALEN!
GALEN!!
WHAT!
WHAT--WHY AREN'T YOU WITH TOMMY?! WHERE IS HE? WE HAVE TO GO! AND YOU'VE GOT TO GO HOME! YOUR GRANDPA'S PROBABLY WORRIED SICK!
HE'S NOT. AND TOMMY'S FINE. JUST PLAYING IN THE BACKYARD.
WAIT, WHAT--
OH MY GOD.

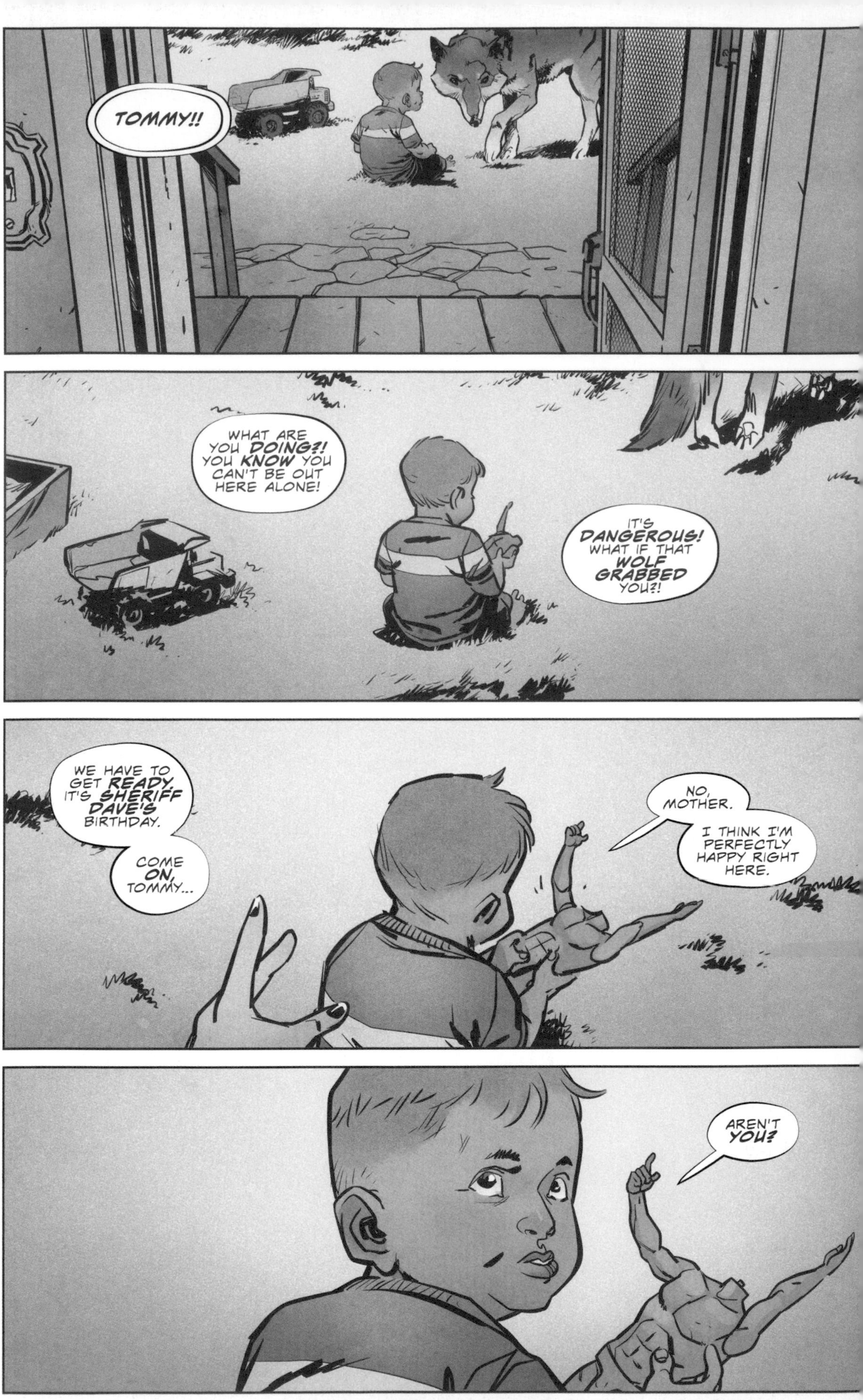
TOMMY!!
WHAT ARE YOU DOING?! YOU KNOW YOU CAN'T BE OUT HERE ALONE!
IT'S DANGEROUS! WHAT IF THAT WOLF GRABBED YOU?!
WE HAVE TO GET READY. IT'S SHERIFF DAVE'S BIRTHDAY.
COME ON, TOMMY...
NO, MOTHER.
I THINK I'M PERFECTLY HAPPY RIGHT HERE.
AREN'T YOU?

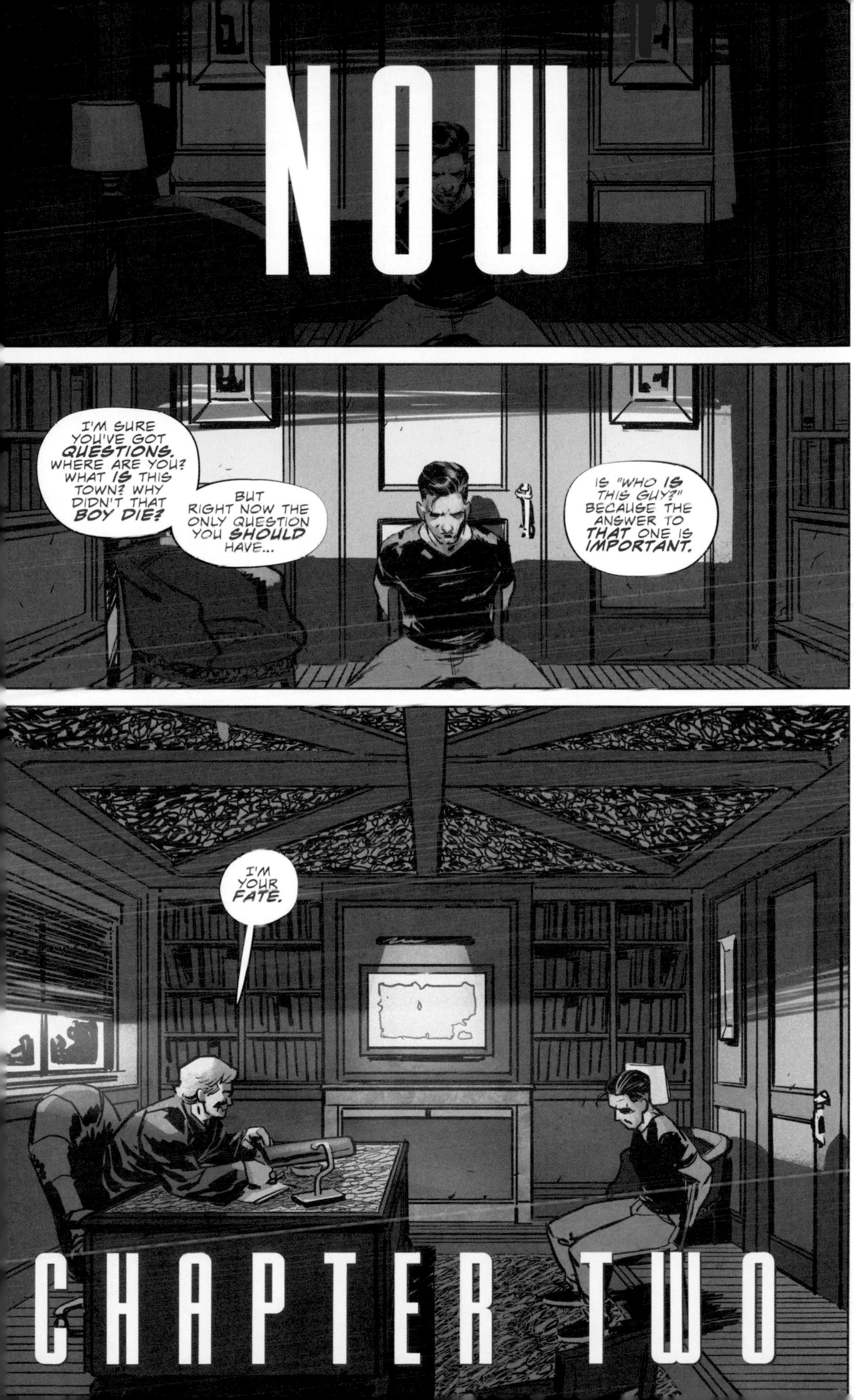
NOW
I'M SURE YOU'VE GOT QUESTIONS. WHERE ARE YOU? WHAT IS THIS TOWN? WHY DIDN'T THAT BOY DIE?
BUT RIGHT NOW THE ONLY QUESTION YOU SHOULD HAVE...
IS "WHO IS THIS GUY?" BECAUSE THE ANSWER TO THAT ONE IS IMPORTANT.
I'M YOUR FATE.
CHAPTER TWO

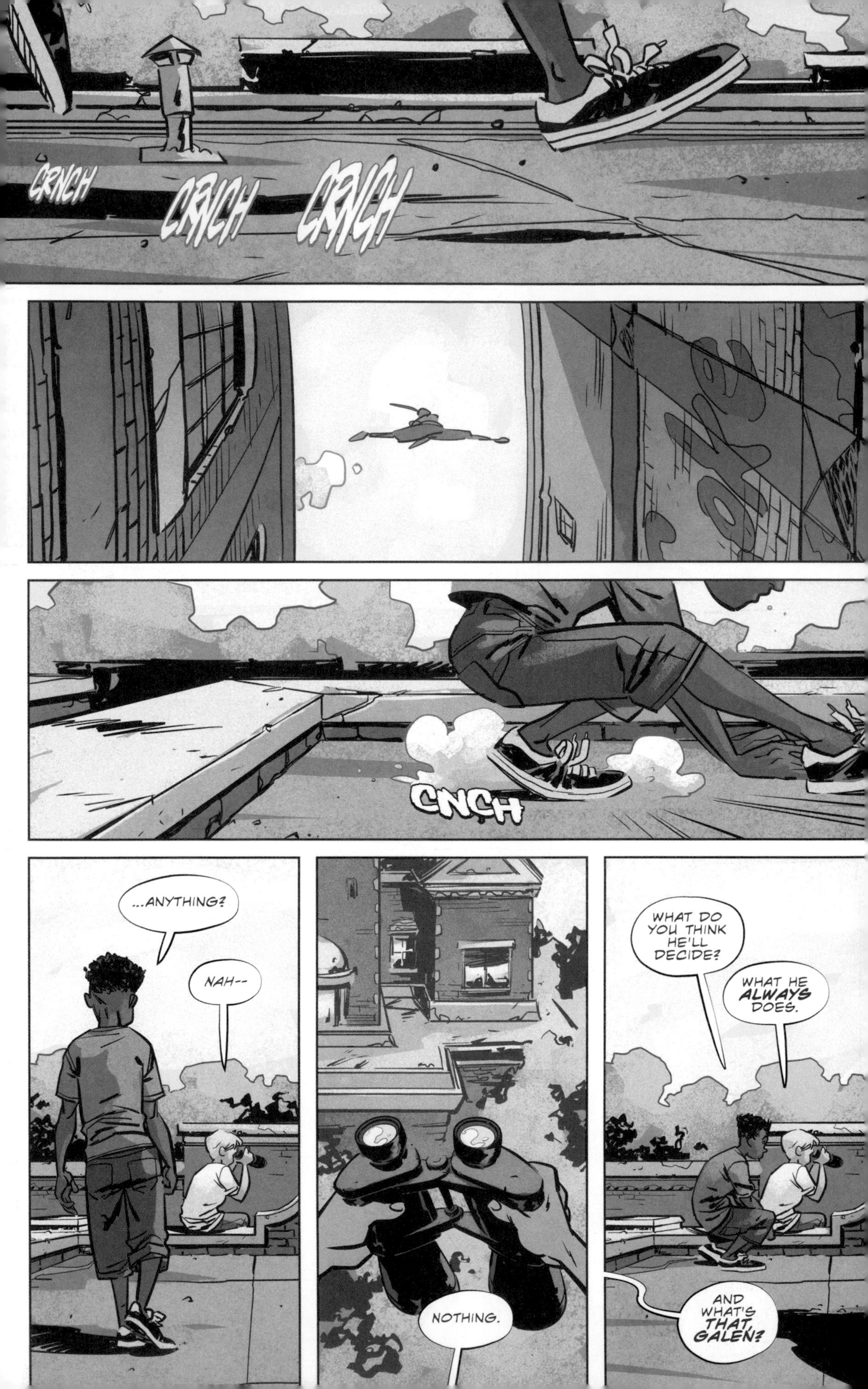
CRNCH
CRNCH
CRNCH
CNCH
...ANYTHING?
NAH--
NOTHING.
WHAT DO YOU THINK HE'LL DECIDE?
WHAT HE ALWAYS DOES.
AND WHAT'S THAT, GALEN?

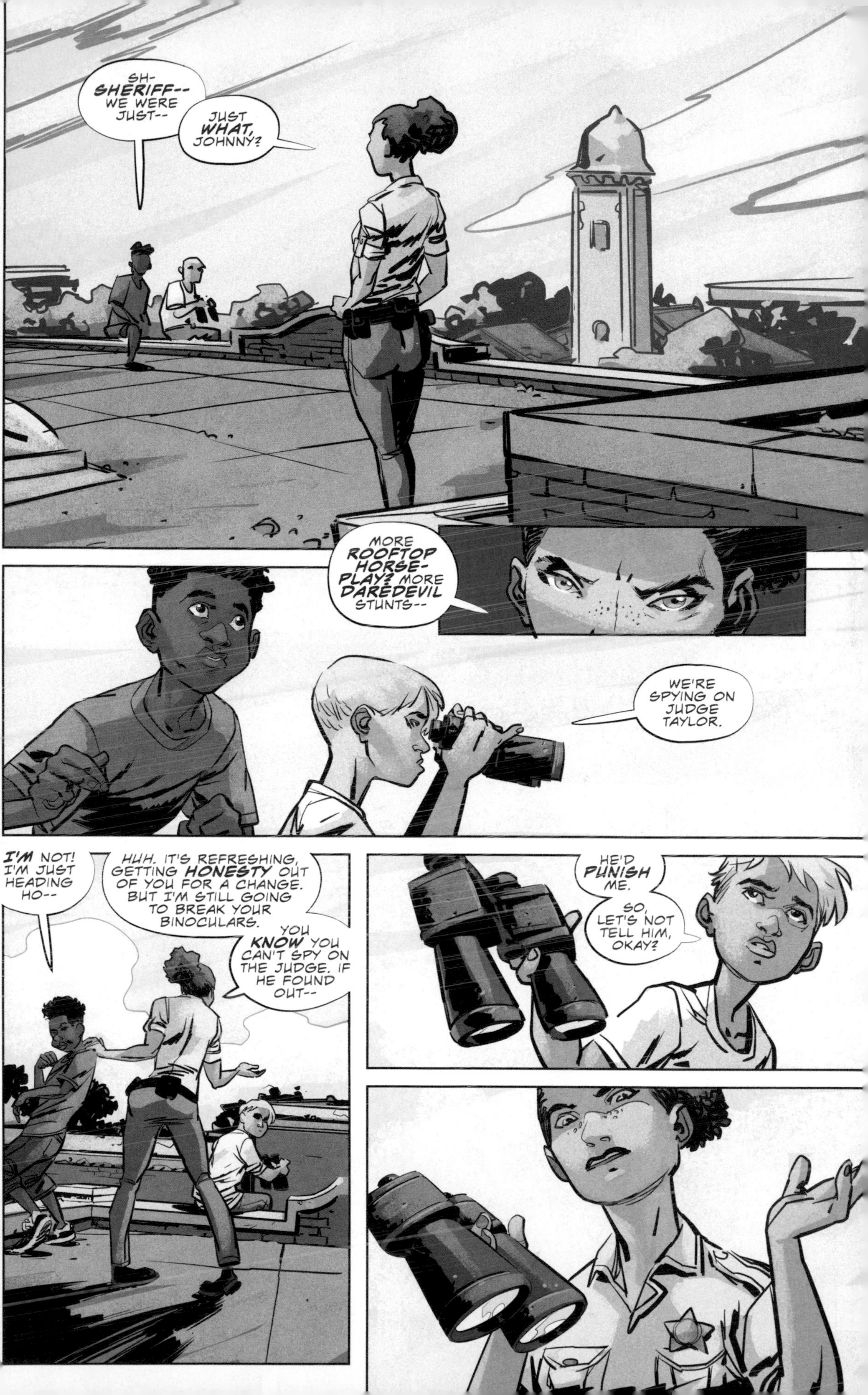
SH- SHERIFF-- WE WERE JUST--
JUST WHAT, JOHNNY?
MORE ROOFTOP HORSE-PLAY? MORE DAREDEVIL STUNTS--
WE'RE SPYING ON JUDGE TAYLOR.
I'M NOT! I'M JUST HEADING HO--
HUH. IT'S REFRESHING, GETTING HONESTY OUT OF YOU FOR A CHANGE. BUT I'M STILL GOING TO BREAK YOUR BINOCULARS.
YOU KNOW YOU CAN'T SPY ON THE JUDGE. IF HE FOUND OUT--
HE'D PUNISH ME.
SO, LET'S NOT TELL HIM, OKAY?

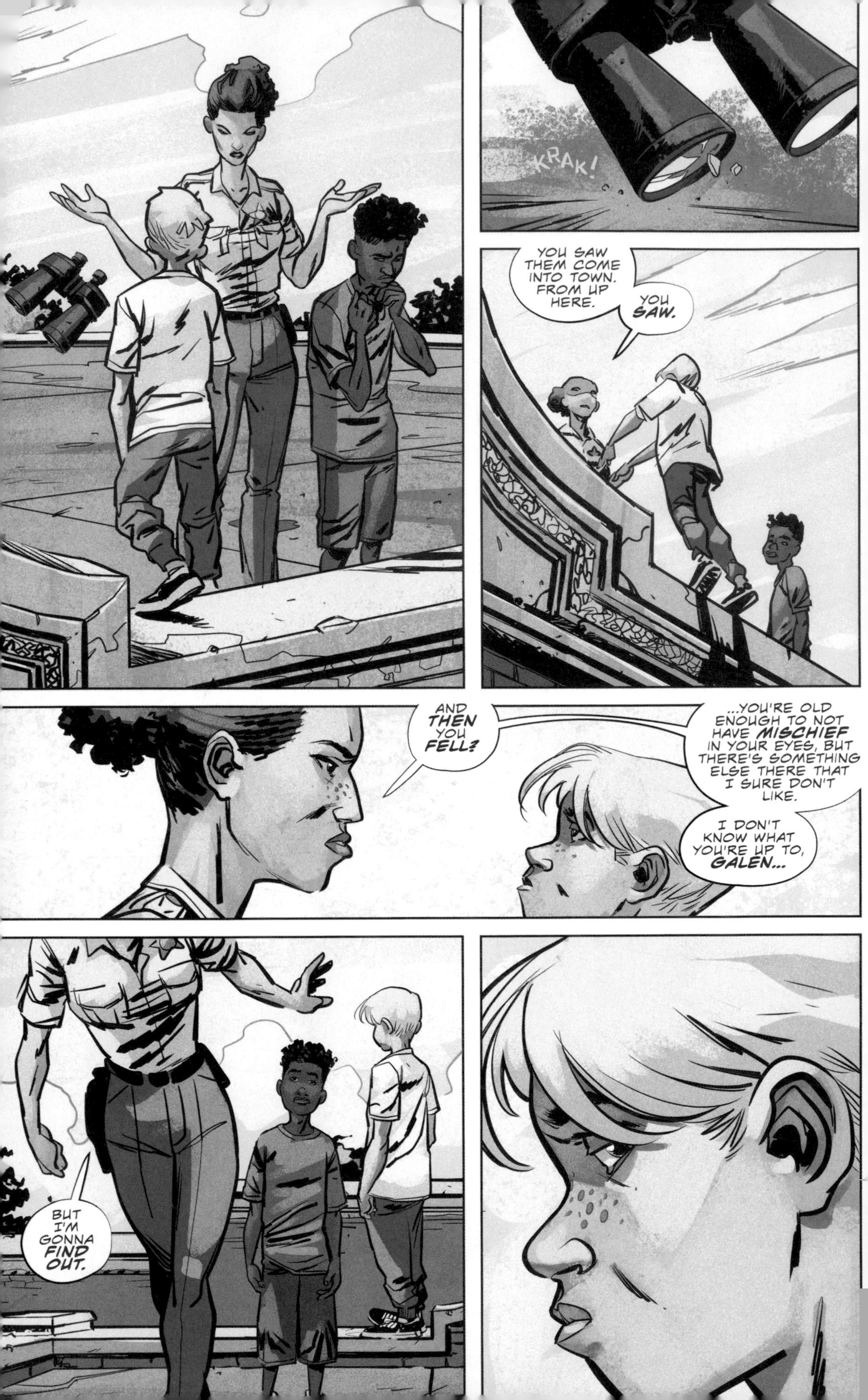
KRAK!
YOU SAW THEM COME INTO TOWN. FROM UP HERE.
YOU SAW.
AND THEN YOU FELL?
...YOU'RE OLD ENOUGH TO NOT HAVE MISCHIEF IN YOUR EYES, BUT THERE'S SOMETHING ELSE THERE THAT I SURE DON'T LIKE.
I DON'T KNOW WHAT YOU'RE UP TO, GALEN...
BUT I'M GONNA FIND OUT.

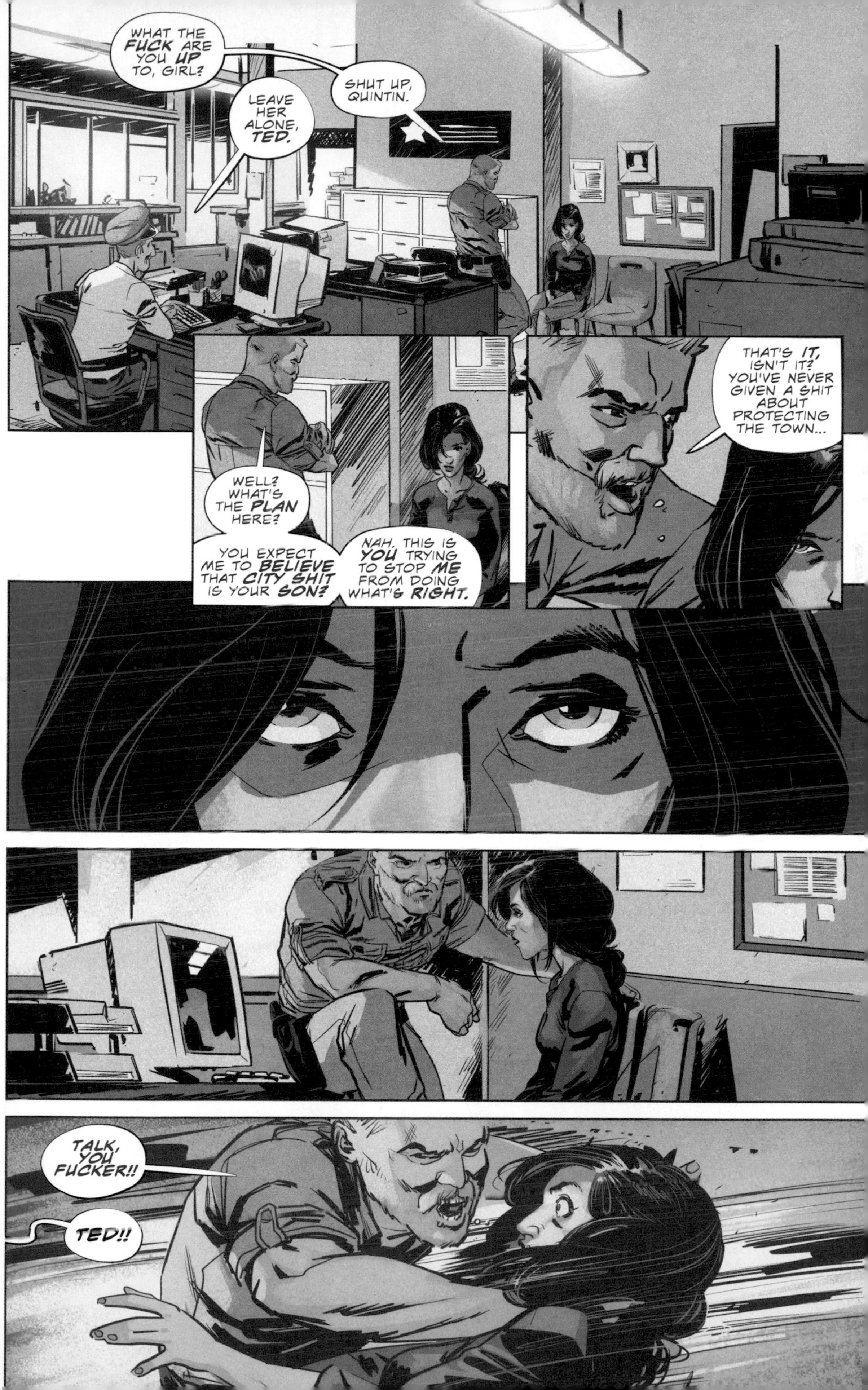

WHAT THE FUCK ARE YOU UP TO, GIRL?
SHUT UP, QUINTIN.
LEAVE HER ALONE, TED.
WELL? WHAT'S THE PLAN HERE?
YOU EXPECT ME TO BELIEVE THAT CITY SHIT IS YOUR SON?
NAH. THIS IS YOU TRYING TO STOP ME FROM DOING WHAT'S RIGHT.
THAT'S IT, ISN'T IT? YOU'VE NEVER GIVEN A SHIT ABOUT PROTECTING THE TOWN...
TALK, YOU FUCKER!!
TED!!

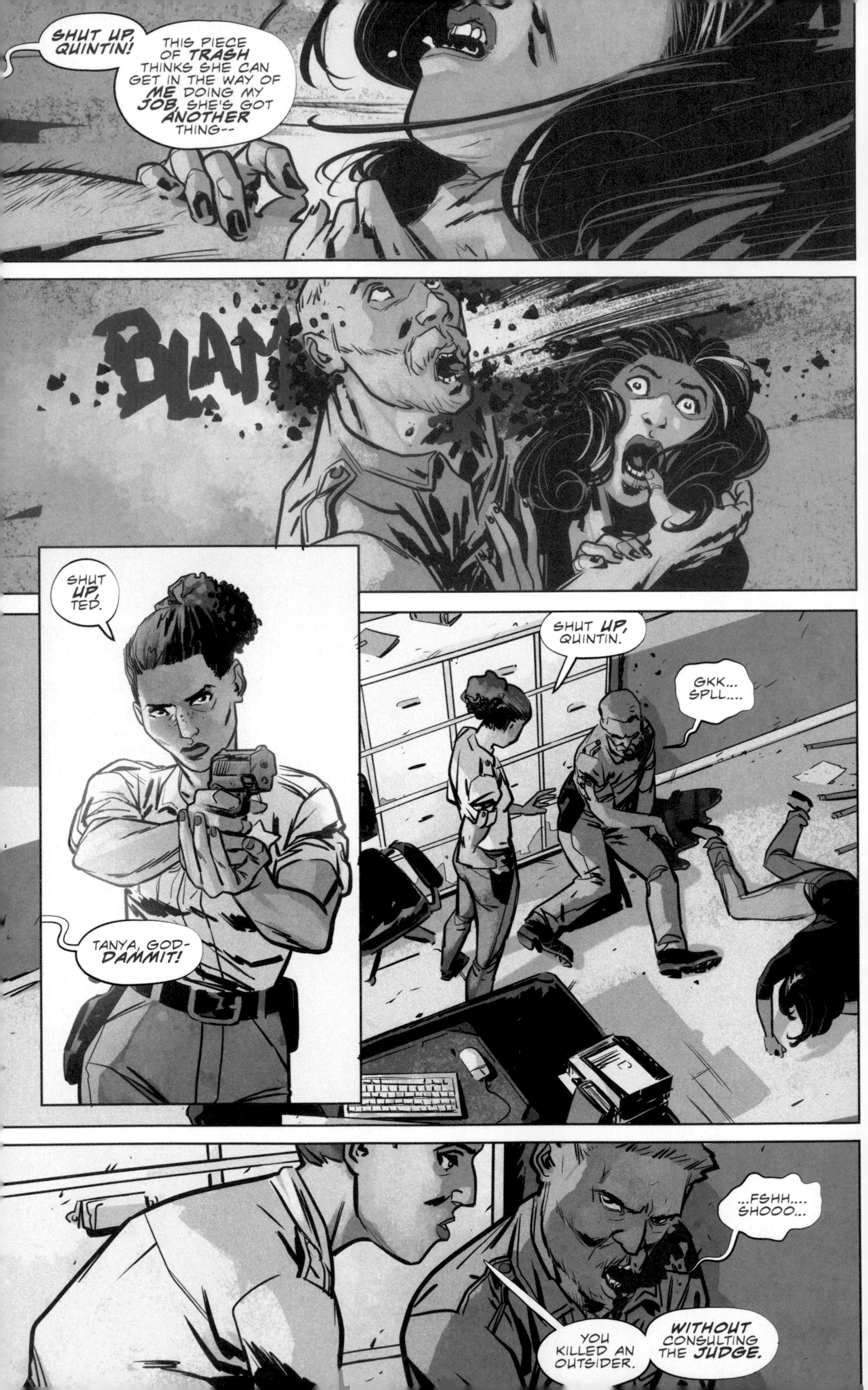
SHUT UP, QUINTIN!
THIS PIECE OF TRASH THINKS SHE CAN GET IN THE WAY OF ME DOING MY JOB, SHE'S GOT ANOTHER THING--
BLAM
SHUT UP, TED.
TANYA, GOD-DAMMIT!
SHUT UP, QUINTIN.
GKK... SPLL....
...FSHH.... SHOOO...
YOU KILLED AN OUTSIDER.
WITHOUT CONSULTING THE JUDGE.

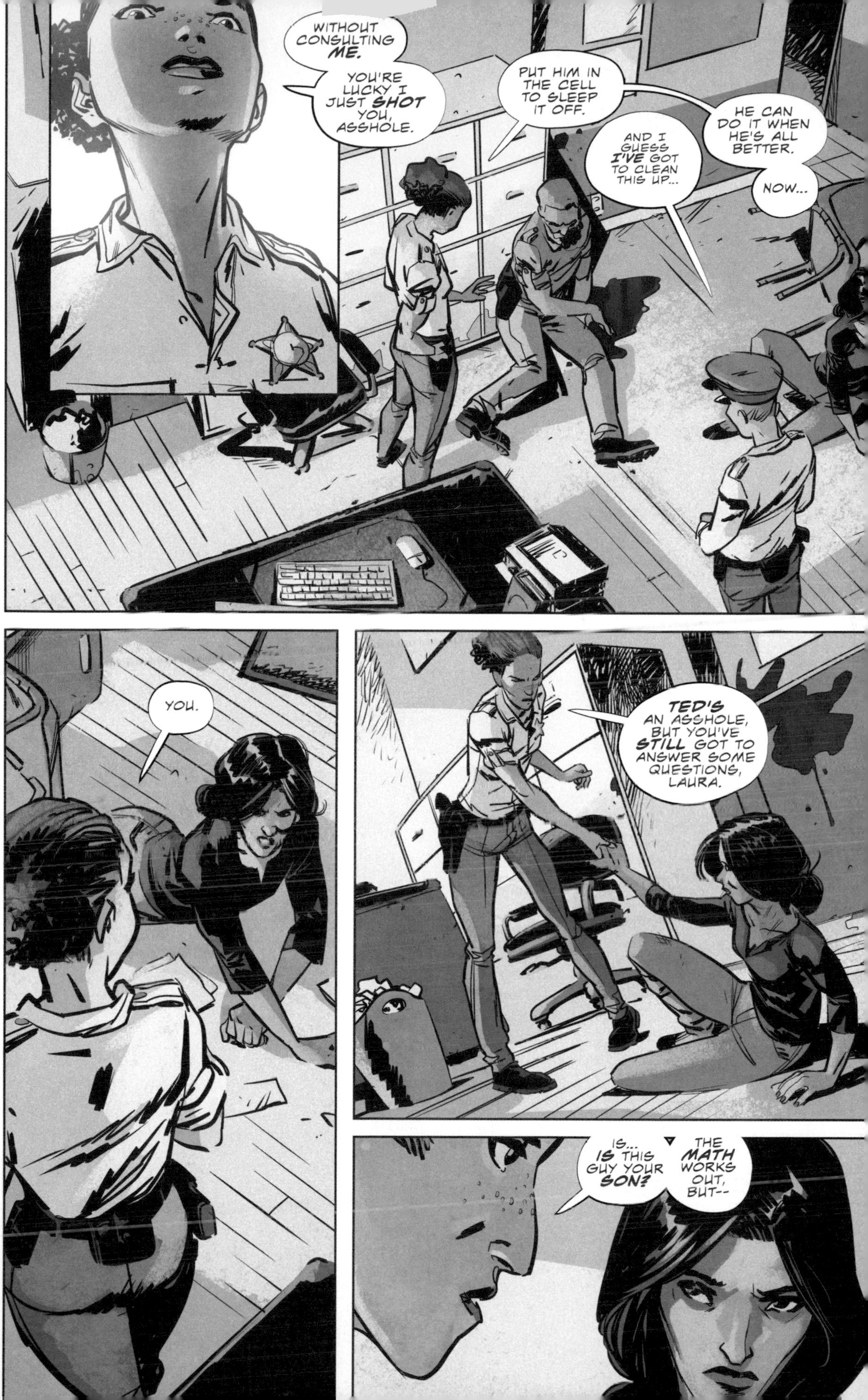
WITHOUT CONSULTING ME.
YOU'RE LUCKY I JUST SHOT YOU, ASSHOLE.
PUT HIM IN THE CELL TO SLEEP IT OFF.
AND I GUESS I'VE GOT TO CLEAN THIS UP...
HE CAN DO IT WHEN HE'S ALL BETTER.
NOW...
YOU.
TED'S AN ASSHOLE, BUT YOU'VE STILL GOT TO ANSWER SOME QUESTIONS, LAURA.
IS... IS THIS GUY YOUR SON?
THE MATH WORKS OUT, BUT--

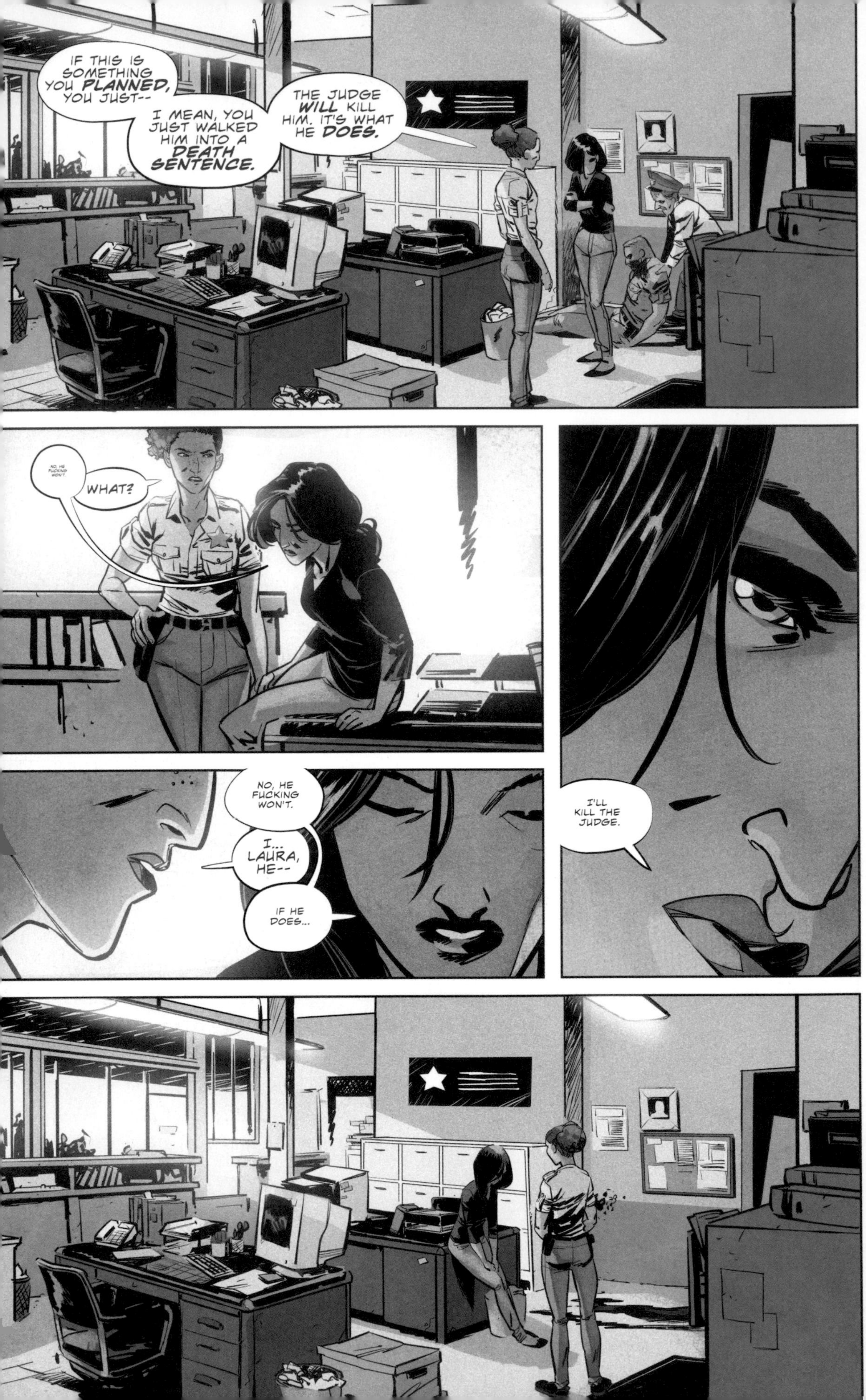
IF THIS IS SOMETHING YOU PLANNED, YOU JUST--
I MEAN, YOU JUST WALKED HIM INTO A DEATH SENTENCE.
THE JUDGE WILL KILL HIM. IT'S WHAT HE DOES.
WHAT?
NO, HE FUCKING WON'T.
I... LAURA, HE--
IF HE DOES...
I'LL KILL THE JUDGE.

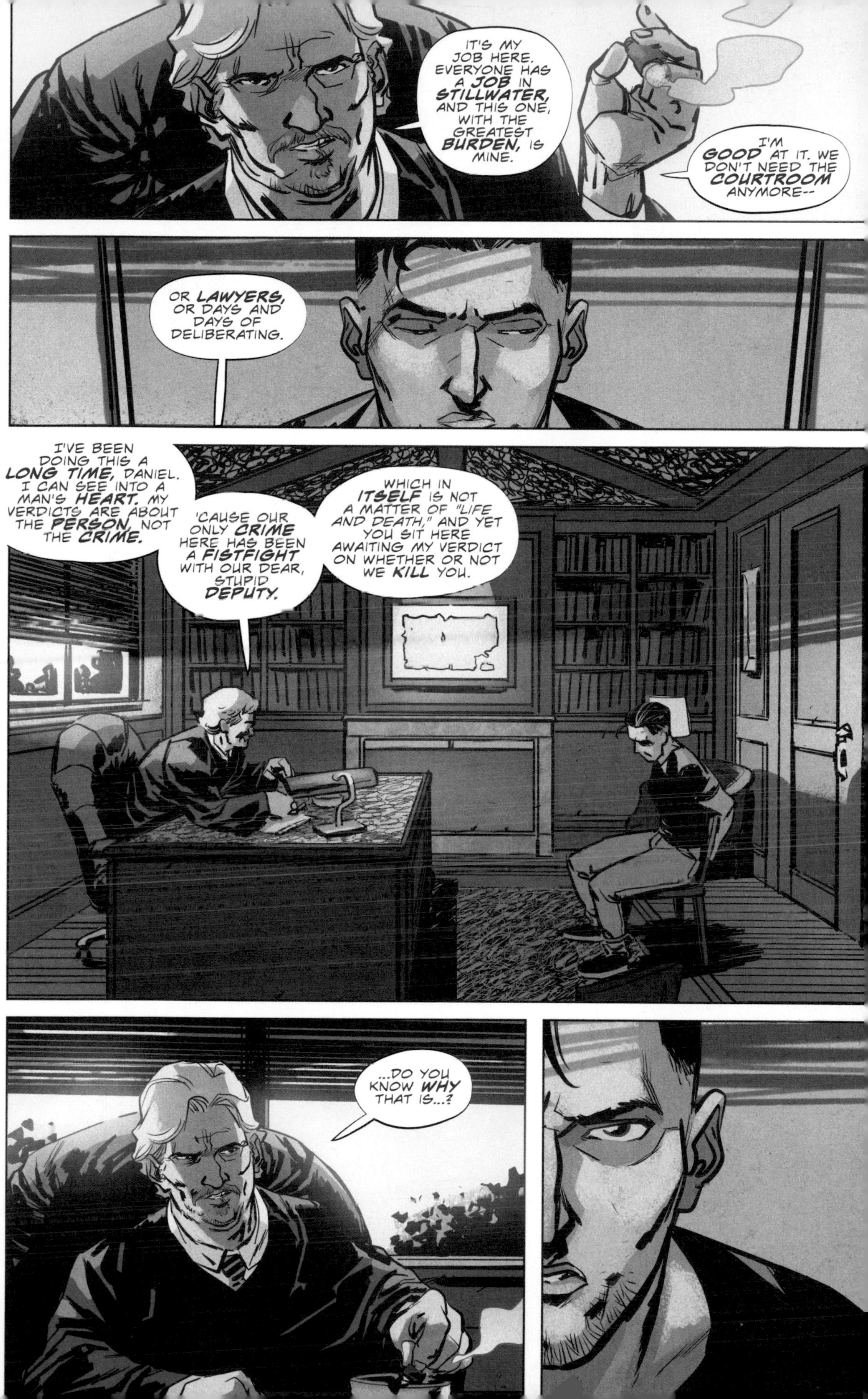
IT'S MY JOB HERE. EVERYONE HAS A JOB IN STILLWATER, AND THIS ONE, WITH THE GREATEST BURDEN, IS MINE.
I'M GOOD AT IT. WE DON'T NEED THE COURTROOM ANYMORE--
OR LAWYERS, OR DAYS AND DAYS OF DELIBERATING.
I'VE BEEN DOING THIS A LONG TIME, DANIEL. I CAN SEE INTO A MAN'S HEART. MY VERDICTS ARE ABOUT THE PERSON, NOT THE CRIME.
'CAUSE OUR ONLY CRIME HERE HAS BEEN A FISTFIGHT WITH OUR DEAR, STUPID DEPUTY.
WHICH IN ITSELF IS NOT A MATTER OF "LIFE AND DEATH," AND YET YOU SIT HERE AWAITING MY VERDICT ON WHETHER OR NOT WE KILL YOU.
...DO YOU KNOW WHY THAT IS...?

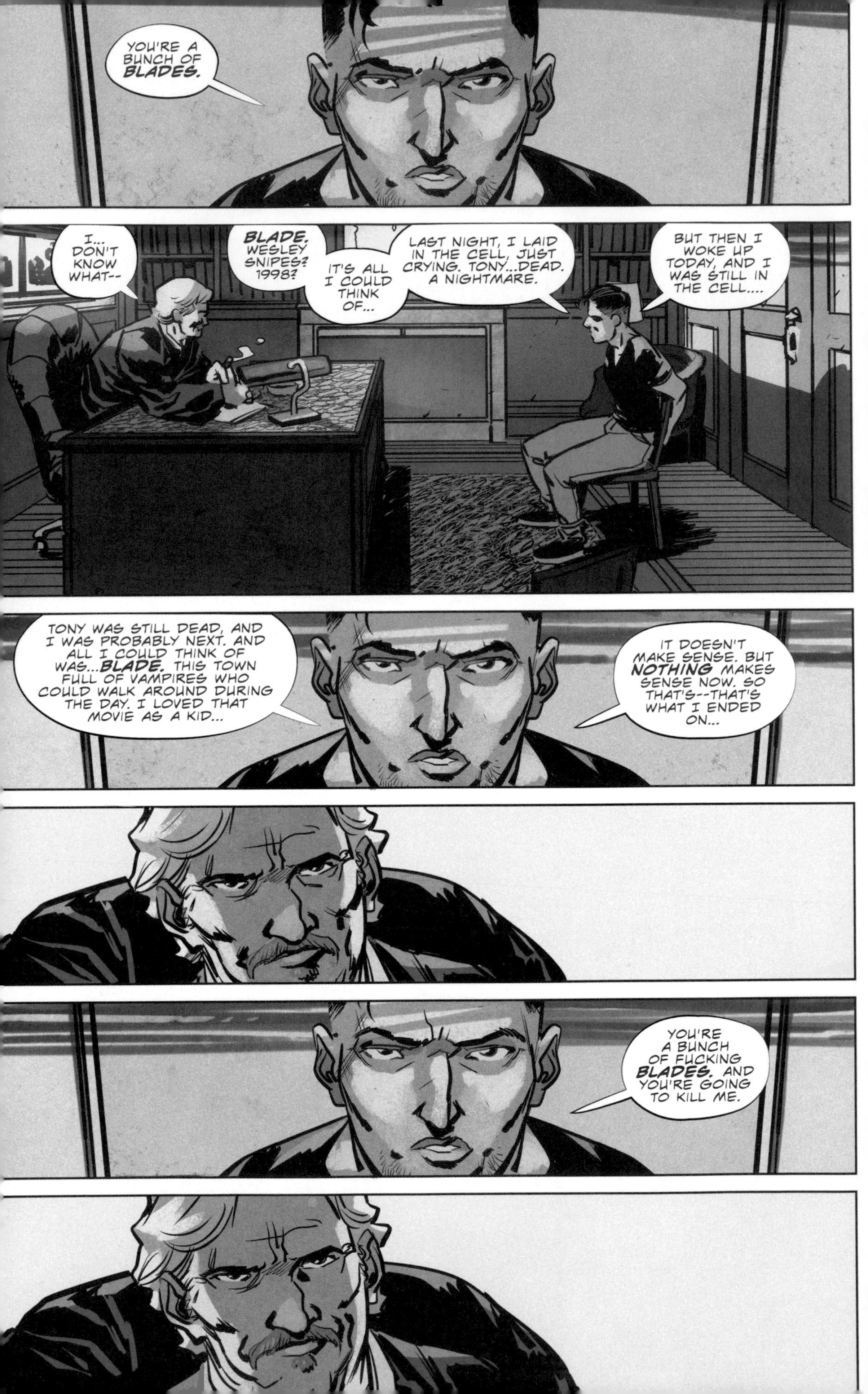
YOU'RE A BUNCH OF BLADES.
I... DON'T KNOW WHAT--
BLADE. WESLEY SNIPES? 1998?
IT'S ALL I COULD THINK OF...
LAST NIGHT, I LAID IN THE CELL, JUST CRYING. TONY...DEAD. A NIGHTMARE.
BUT THEN I WOKE UP TODAY, AND I WAS STILL IN THE CELL....
TONY WAS STILL DEAD, AND I WAS PROBABLY NEXT. AND ALL I COULD THINK OF WAS...BLADE. THIS TOWN FULL OF VAMPIRES WHO COULD WALK AROUND DURING THE DAY. I LOVED THAT MOVIE AS A KID...
IT DOESN'T MAKE SENSE. BUT NOTHING MAKES SENSE NOW. SO THAT'S--THAT'S WHAT I ENDED ON...
YOU'RE A BUNCH OF FUCKING BLADES. AND YOU'RE GOING TO KILL ME.

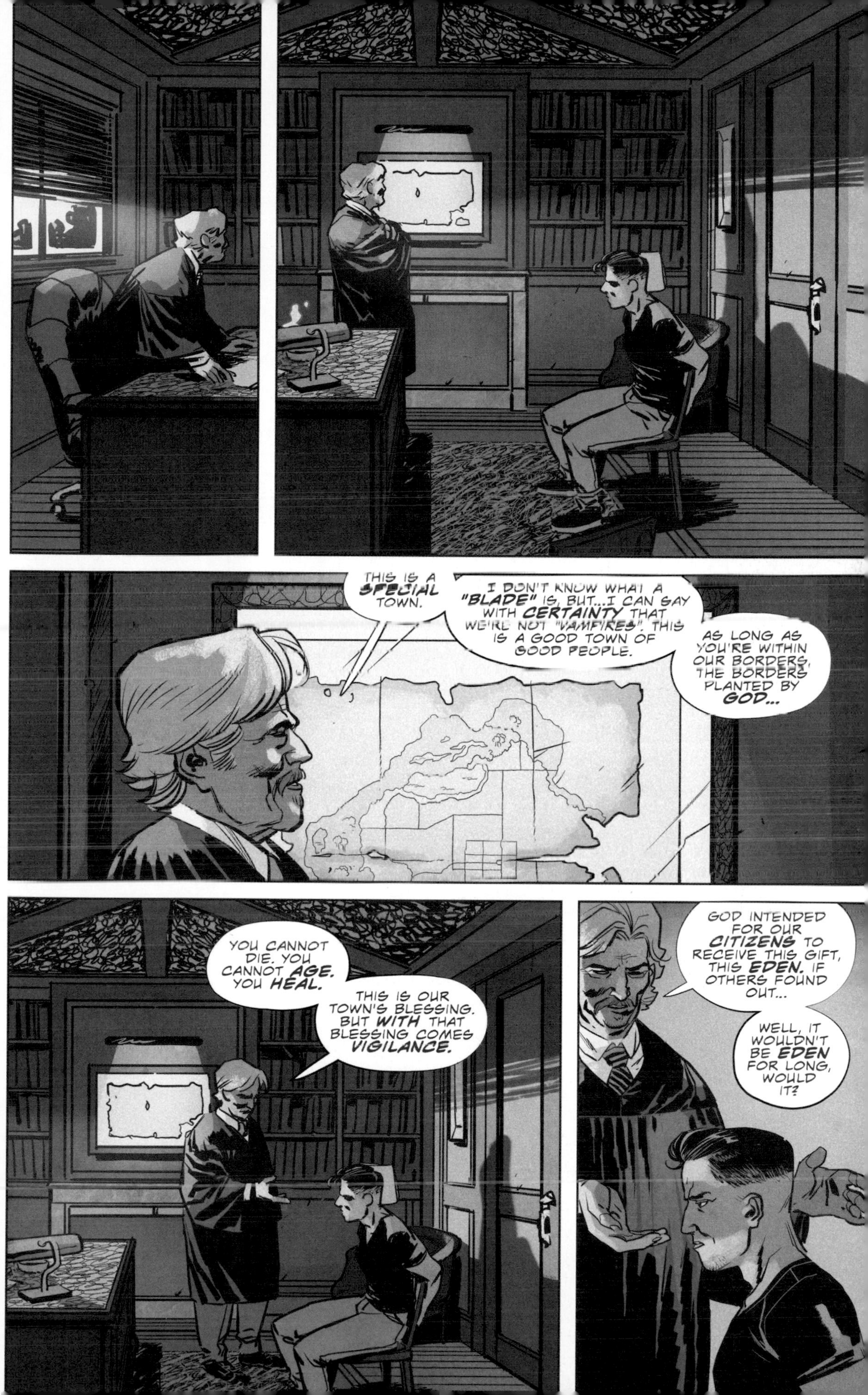
THIS IS A SPECIAL TOWN.
I DON'T KNOW WHAT A "BLADE" IS, BUT...I CAN SAY WITH CERTAINTY THAT WE'RE NOT "VAMPIRES". THIS IS A GOOD TOWN OF GOOD PEOPLE.
AS LONG AS YOU'RE WITHIN OUR BORDERS, THE BORDERS PLANTED BY GOD...
YOU CANNOT DIE. YOU CANNOT AGE. YOU HEAL.
THIS IS OUR TOWN'S BLESSING. BUT WITH THAT BLESSING COMES VIGILANCE.
GOD INTENDED FOR OUR CITIZENS TO RECEIVE THIS GIFT, THIS EDEN. IF OTHERS FOUND OUT...
WELL, IT WOULDN'T BE EDEN FOR LONG, WOULD IT?

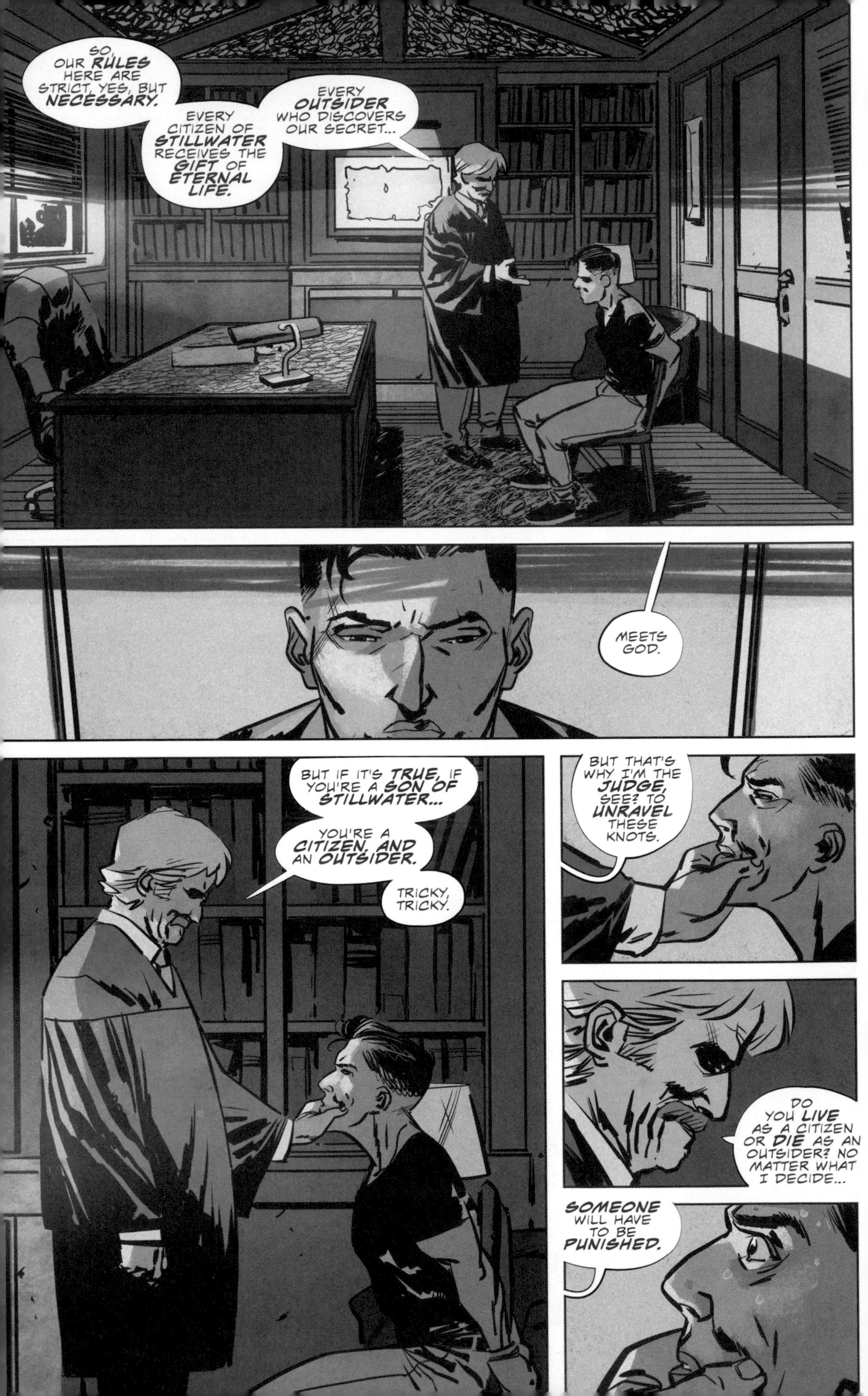
SO, OUR RULES HERE ARE STRICT, YES, BUT NECESSARY.
EVERY CITIZEN OF STILLWATER RECEIVES THE GIFT OF ETERNAL LIFE.
EVERY OUTSIDER WHO DISCOVERS OUR SECRET...
MEETS GOD.
BUT IF IT'S TRUE, IF YOU'RE A SON OF STILLWATER...
YOU'RE A CITIZEN, AND AN OUTSIDER.
TRICKY, TRICKY.
BUT THAT'S WHY I'M THE JUDGE, SEE? TO UNRAVEL THESE KNOTS.
DO YOU LIVE AS A CITIZEN OR DIE AS AN OUTSIDER? NO MATTER WHAT I DECIDE...
SOMEONE WILL HAVE TO BE PUNISHED.

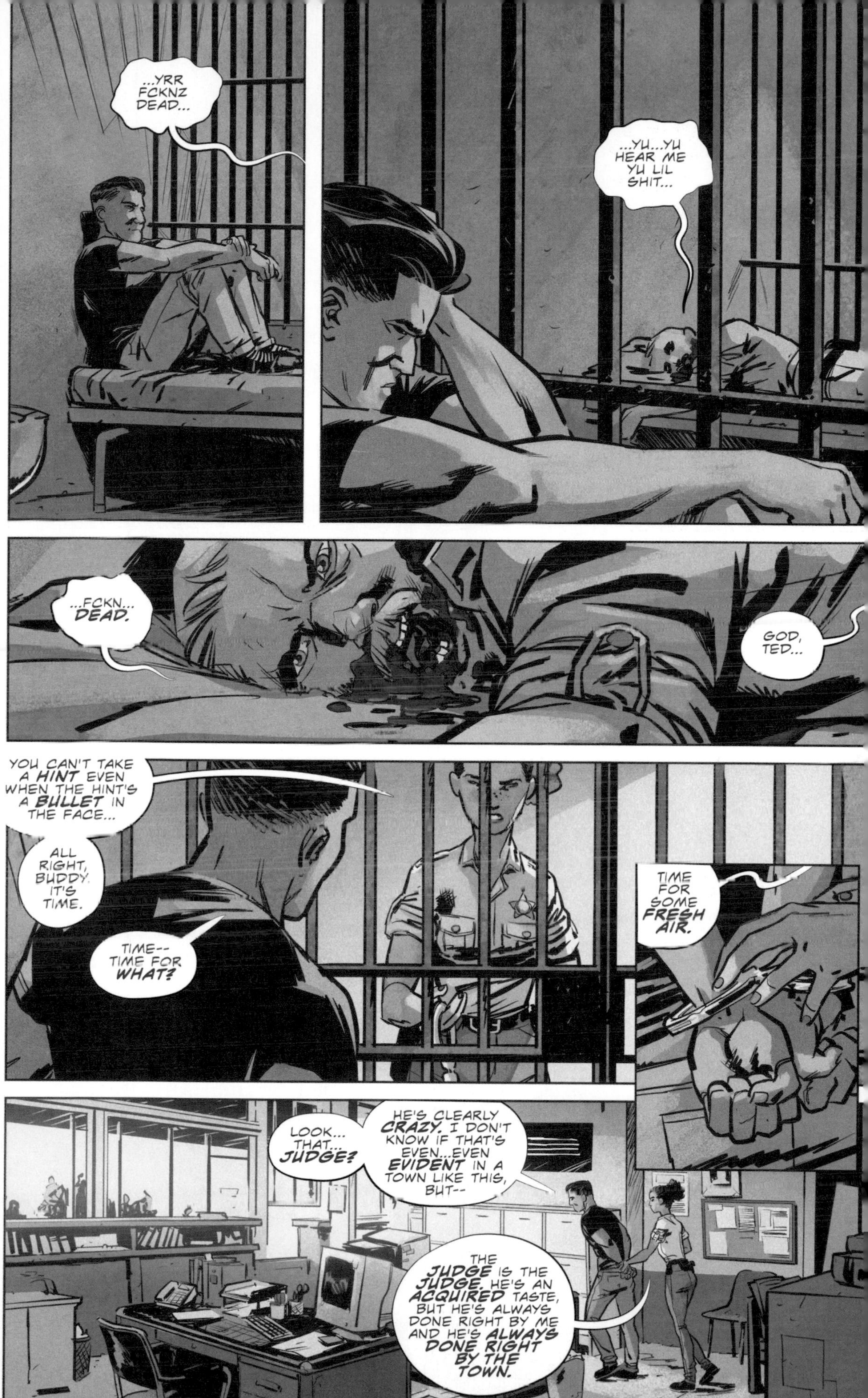
...YRR FCKNZ DEAD...
...YU...YU HEAR ME YU LIL SHIT...
...FCKN... DEAD.
GOD, TED...
YOU CAN'T TAKE A HINT EVEN WHEN THE HINT'S A BULLET IN THE FACE...
ALL RIGHT, BUDDY. IT'S TIME.
TIME-- TIME FOR WHAT?
TIME FOR SOME FRESH AIR.
LOOK... THAT... JUDGE?
HE'S CLEARLY CRAZY. I DON'T KNOW IF THAT'S EVEN...EVEN EVIDENT IN A TOWN LIKE THIS, BUT--
THE JUDGE IS THE JUDGE. HE'S AN ACQUIRED TASTE, BUT HE'S ALWAYS DONE RIGHT BY ME AND HE'S ALWAYS DONE RIGHT BY THE TOWN.

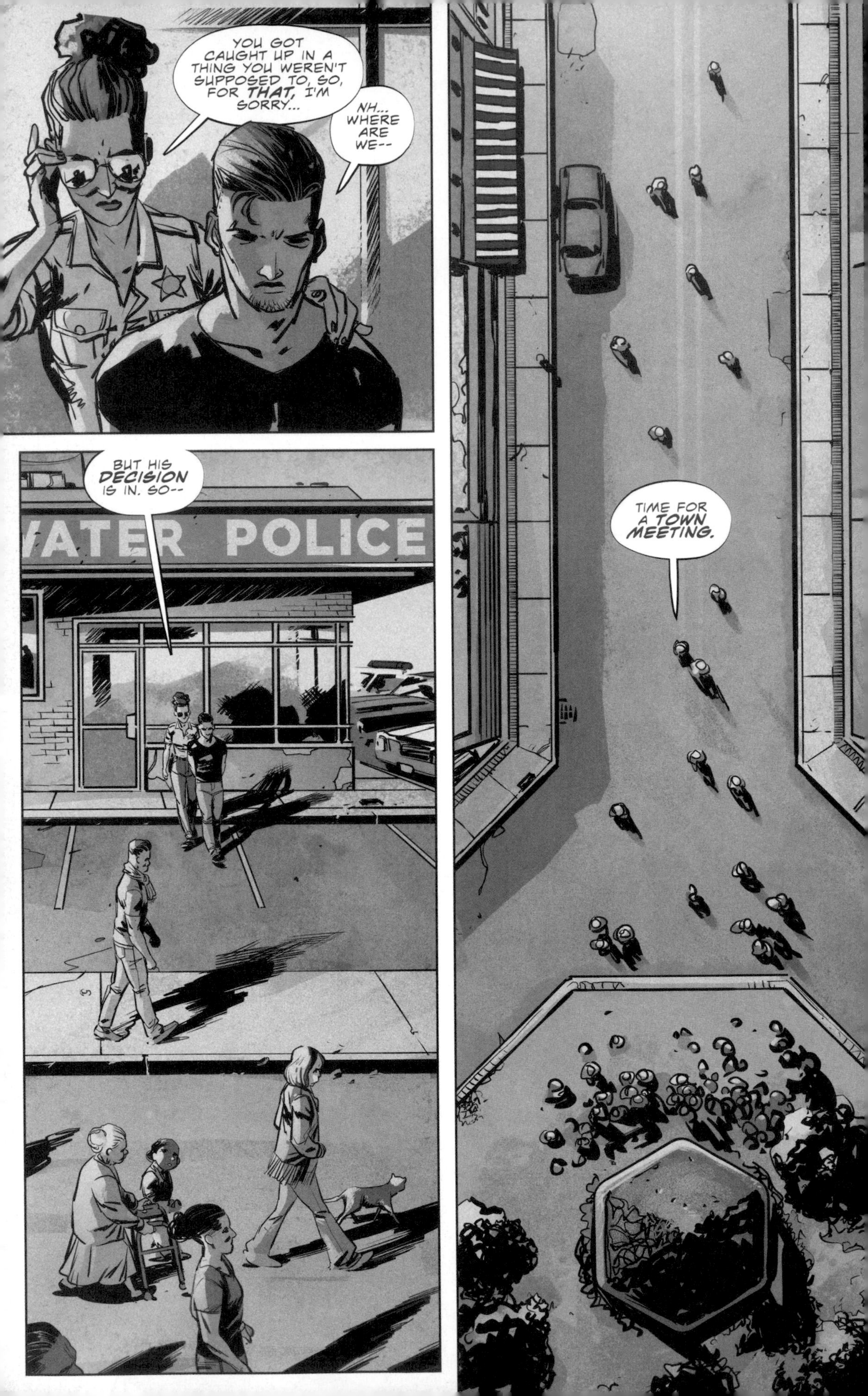
YOU GOT CAUGHT UP IN A THING YOU WEREN'T SUPPOSED TO, SO, FOR THAT, I'M SORRY...
NH... WHERE ARE WE--
BUT HIS DECISION IS IN. SO--
VATER POLICE
TIME FOR A TOWN MEETING.

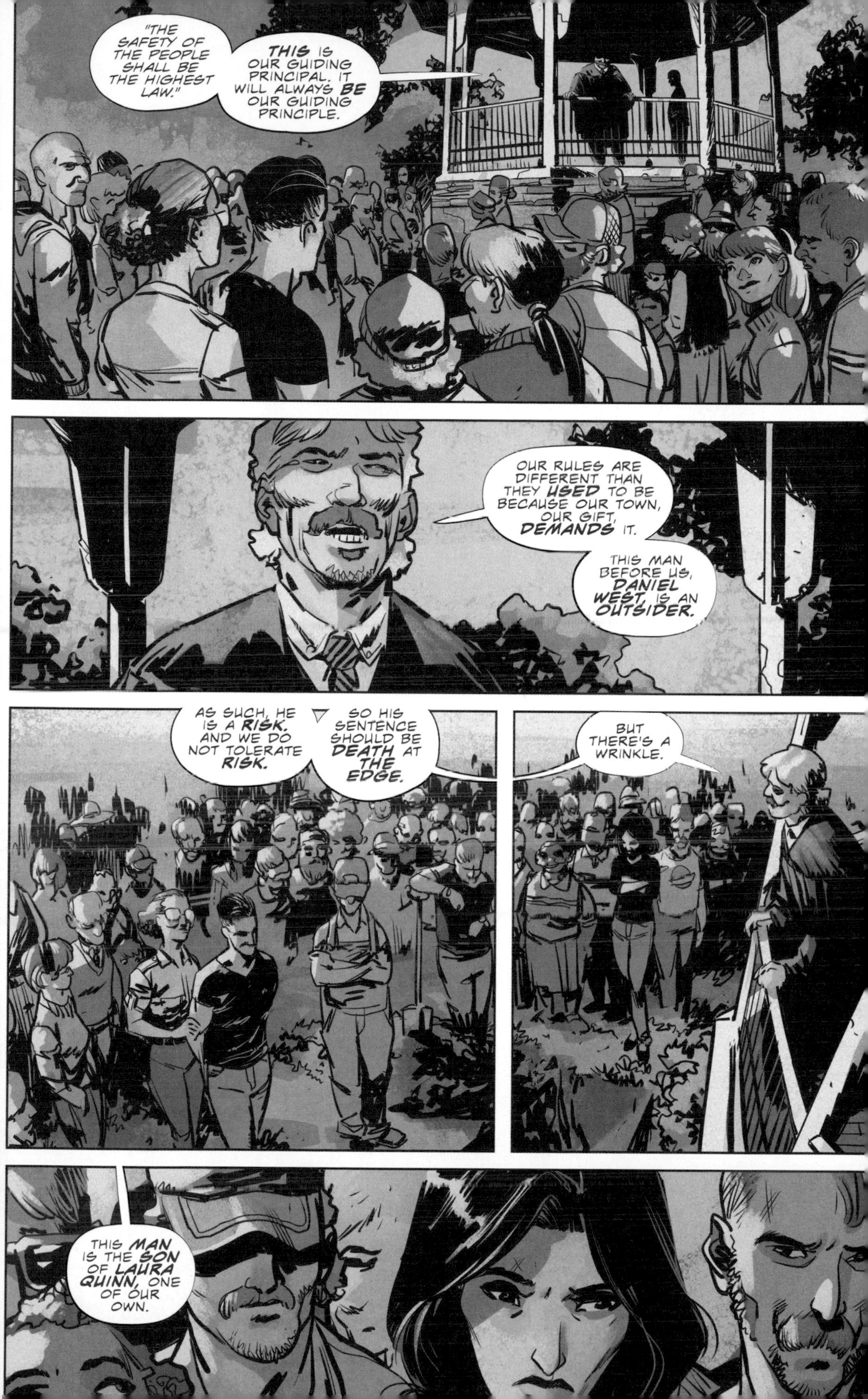
"THE SAFETY OF THE PEOPLE SHALL BE THE HIGHEST LAW."
THIS IS OUR GUIDING PRINCIPAL. IT WILL ALWAYS BE OUR GUIDING PRINCIPLE.
OUR RULES ARE DIFFERENT THAN THEY USED TO BE BECAUSE OUR TOWN, OUR GIFT, DEMANDS IT.
THIS MAN BEFORE US, DANIEL WEST, IS AN OUTSIDER.
AS SUCH, HE IS A RISK. AND WE DO NOT TOLERATE RISK.
SO HIS SENTENCE SHOULD BE DEATH AT THE EDGE.
BUT THERE'S A WRINKLE.
THIS MAN IS THE SON OF LAURA QUINN, ONE OF OUR OWN.

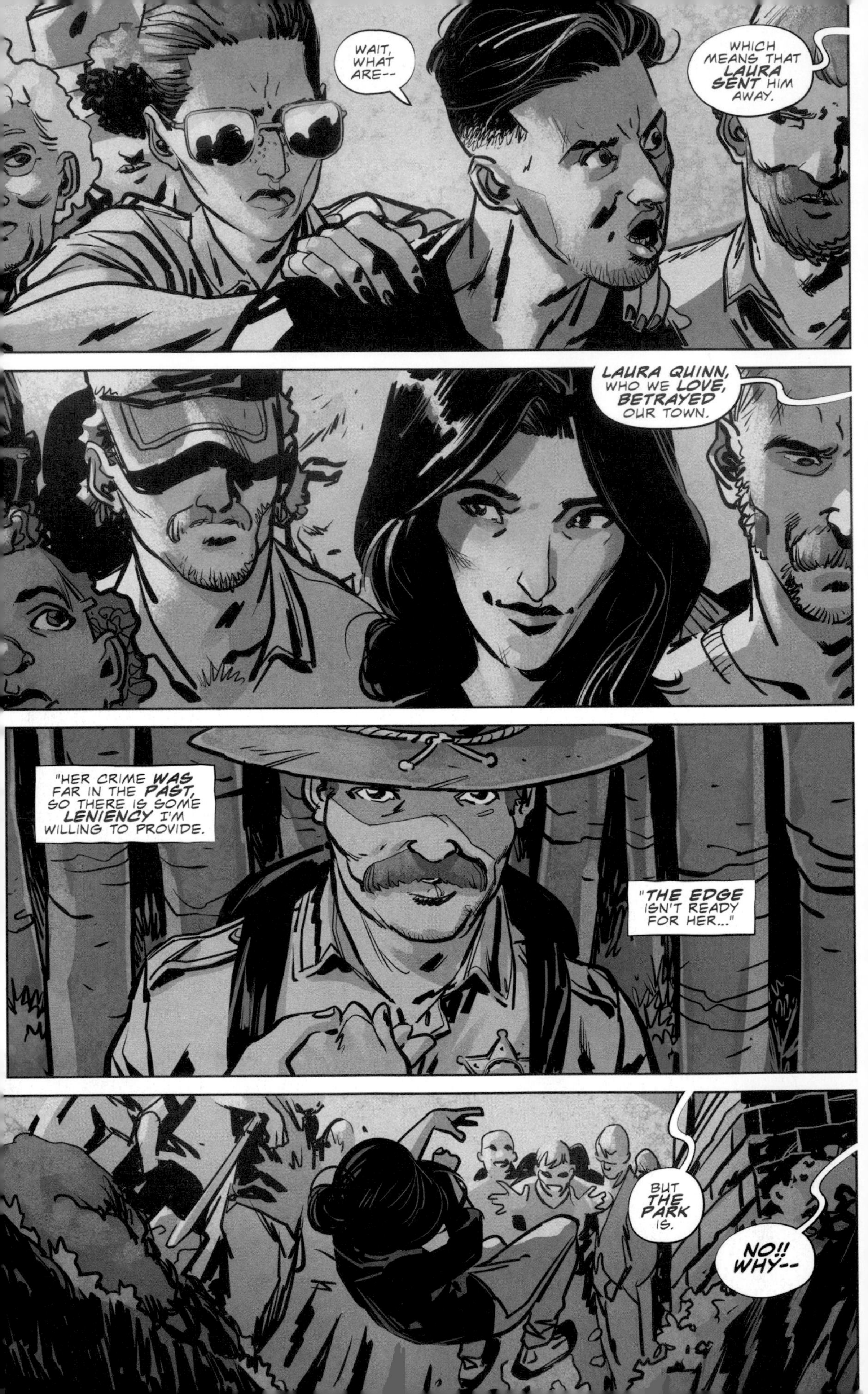
WAIT, WHAT ARE--
WHICH MEANS THAT LAURA SENT HIM AWAY.
LAURA QUINN, WHO WE LOVE, BETRAYED OUR TOWN.
"HER CRIME WAS FAR IN THE PAST, SO THERE IS SOME LENIENCY I'M WILLING TO PROVIDE.
"THE EDGE ISN'T READY FOR HER..."
BUT THE PARK IS.
NO!! WHY--

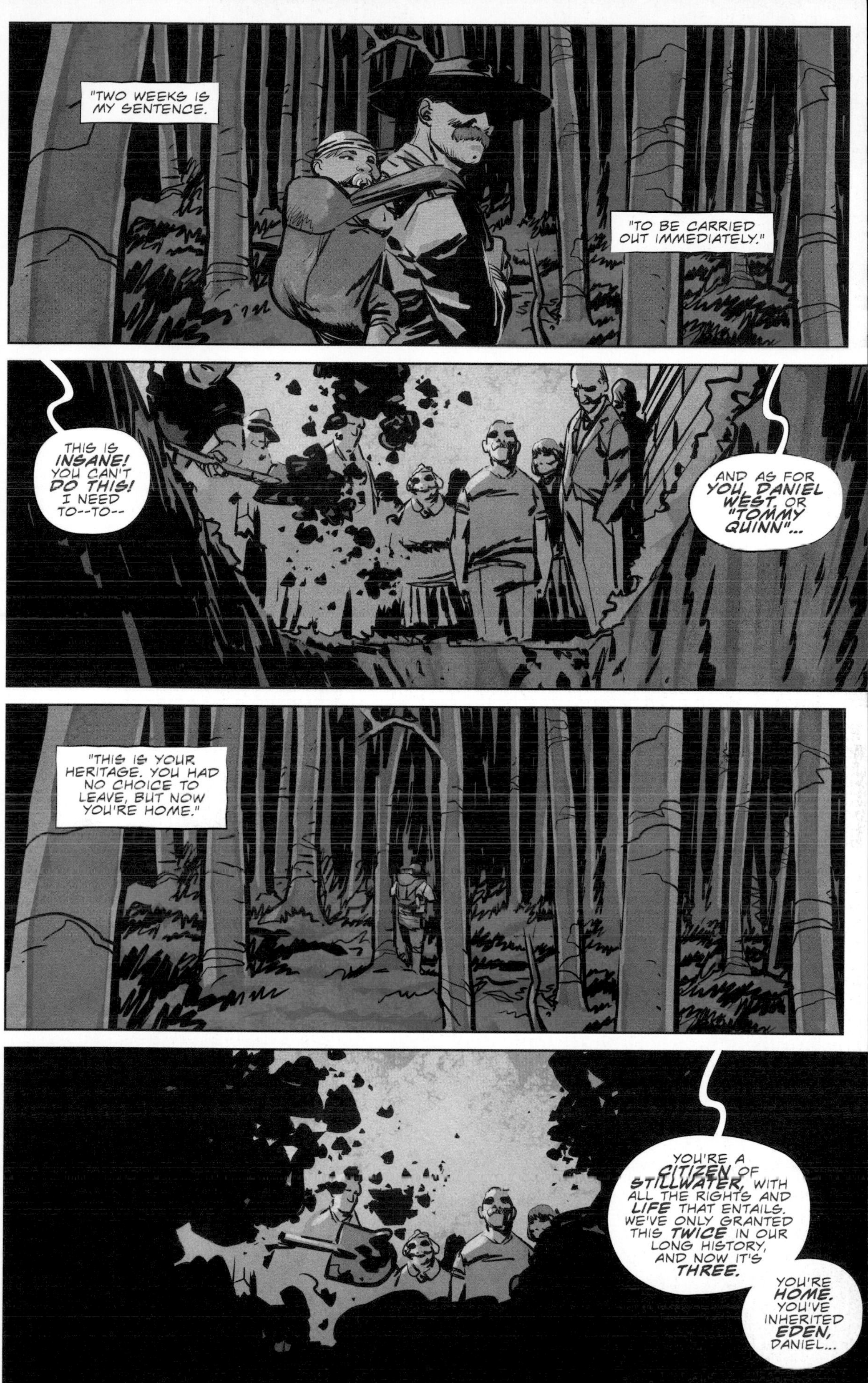
"TWO WEEKS IS MY SENTENCE.
"TO BE CARRIED OUT IMMEDIATELY."
THIS IS INSANE! YOU CAN'T DO THIS! I NEED TO--TO--
AND AS FOR YOU, DANIEL WEST, OR "TOMMY QUINN"...
"THIS IS YOUR HERITAGE. YOU HAD NO CHOICE TO LEAVE, BUT NOW YOU'RE HOME."
YOU'RE A CITIZEN OF STILLWATER, WITH ALL THE RIGHTS AND LIFE THAT ENTAILS. WE'VE ONLY GRANTED THIS TWICE IN OUR LONG HISTORY, AND NOW IT'S THREE.
YOU'RE HOME. YOU'VE INHERITED EDEN, DANIEL...

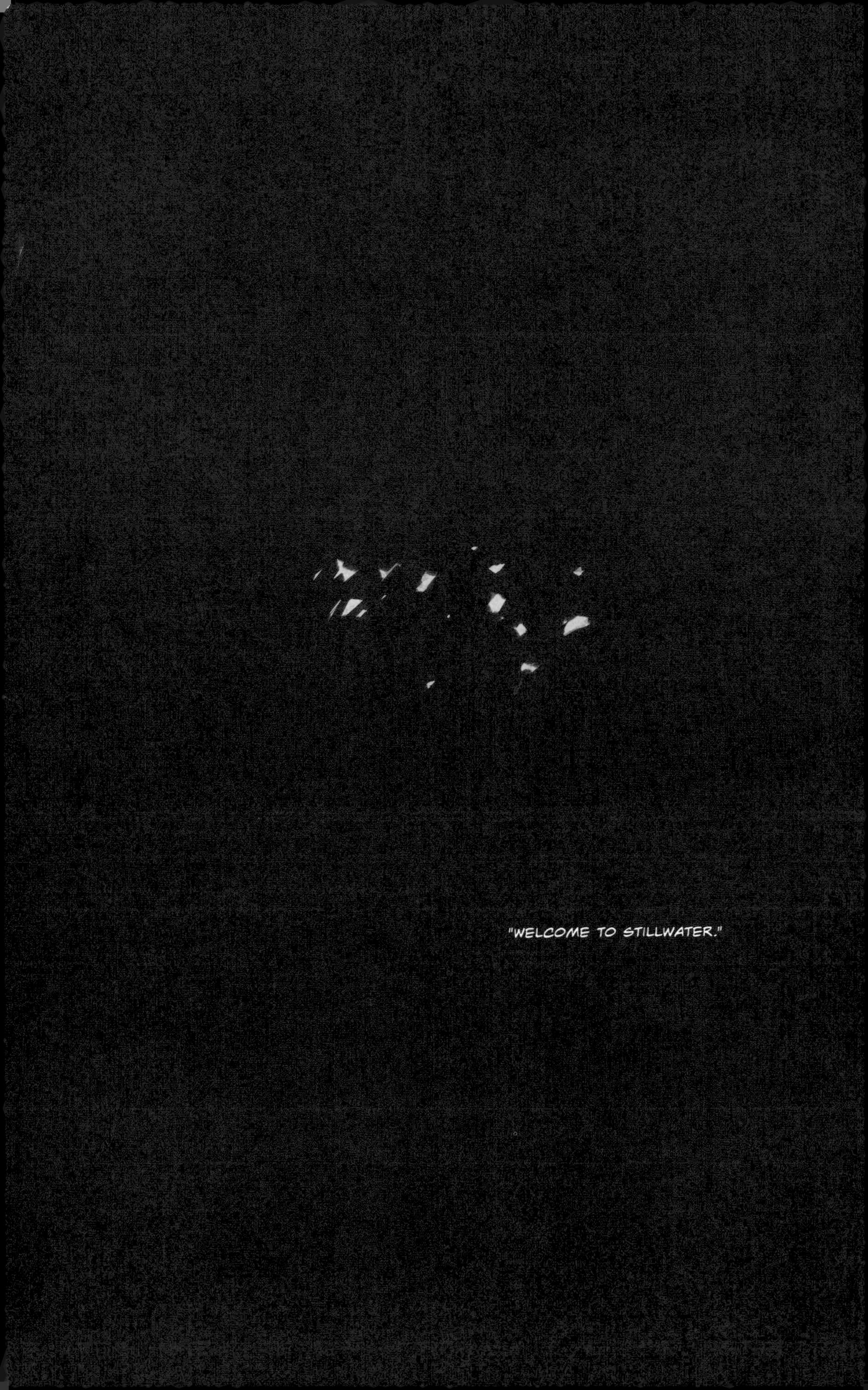
"WELCOME TO STILLWATER."

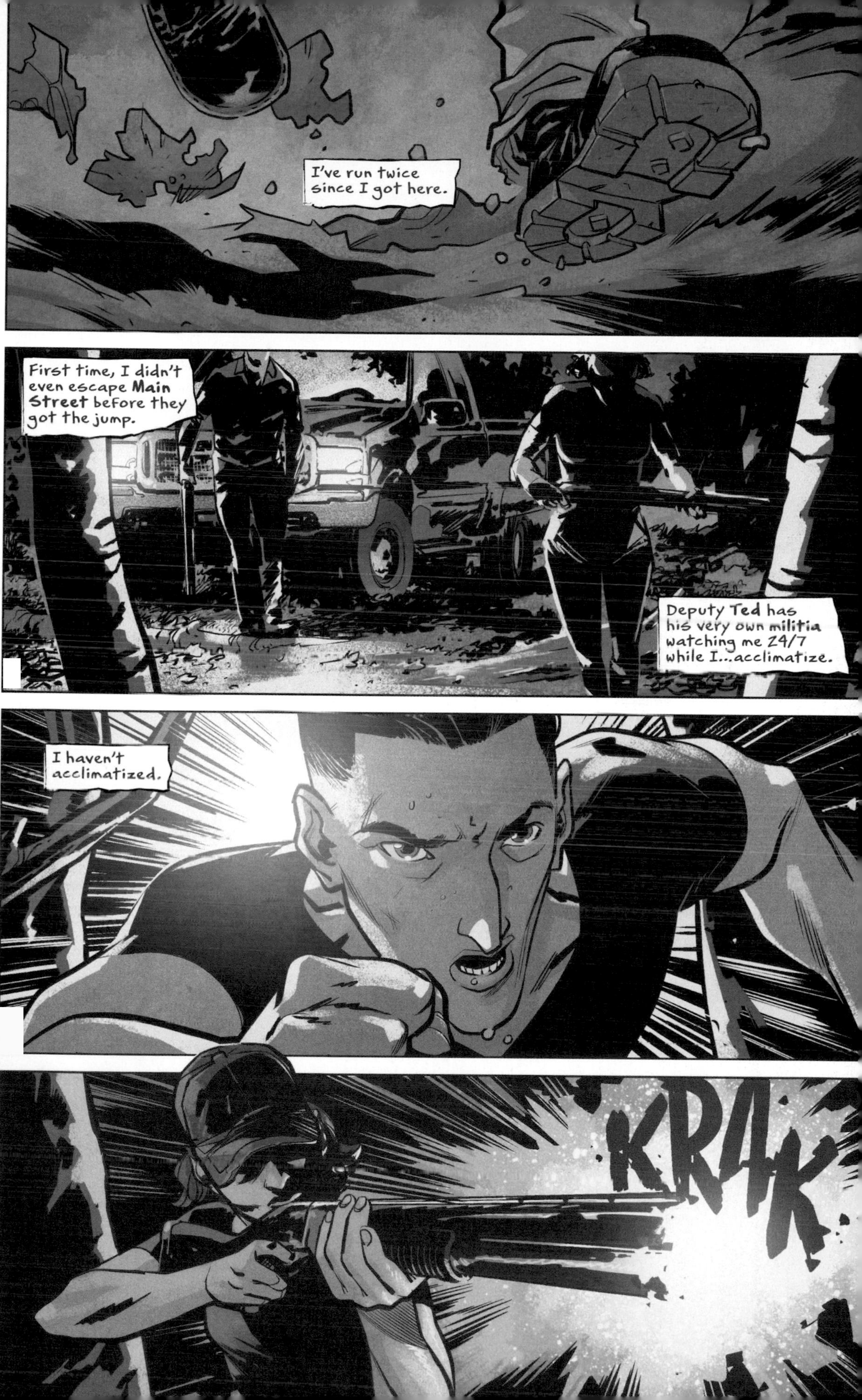
I've run twice since I got here.
First time, I didn't even escape Main Street before they got the jump.
Deputy Ted has his very own militia watching me 24/7 while I...acclimatize.
I haven't acclimatized.
KRAK

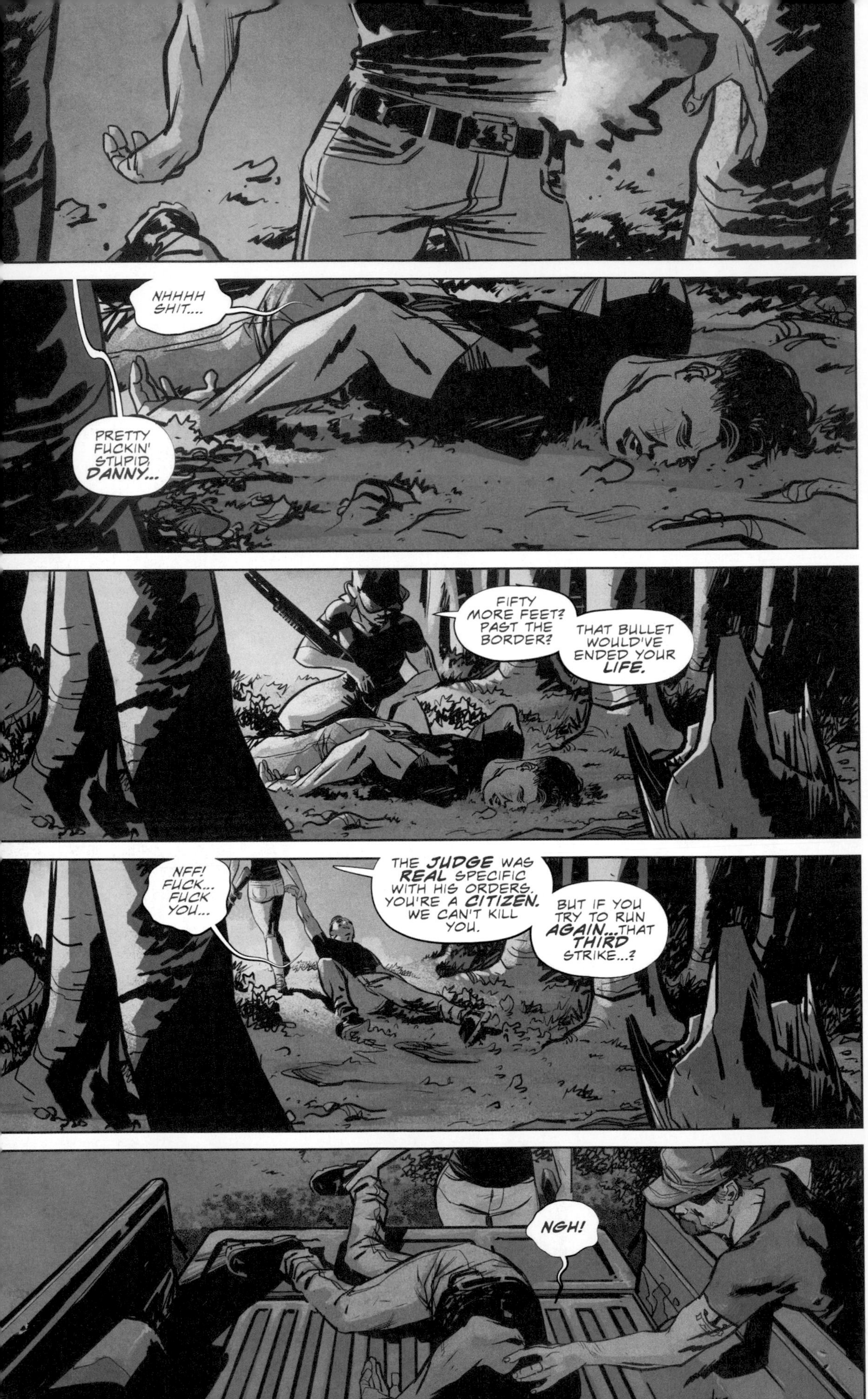
NHHHH SHIT....
PRETTY FUCKIN' STUPID, DANNY...
FIFTY MORE FEET? PAST THE BORDER?
THAT BULLET WOULD'VE ENDED YOUR LIFE.
NFF! FUCK... FUCK YOU...
THE JUDGE WAS REAL SPECIFIC WITH HIS ORDERS. YOU'RE A CITIZEN. WE CAN'T KILL YOU.
BUT IF YOU TRY TO RUN AGAIN...THAT THIRD STRIKE...?
NGH!

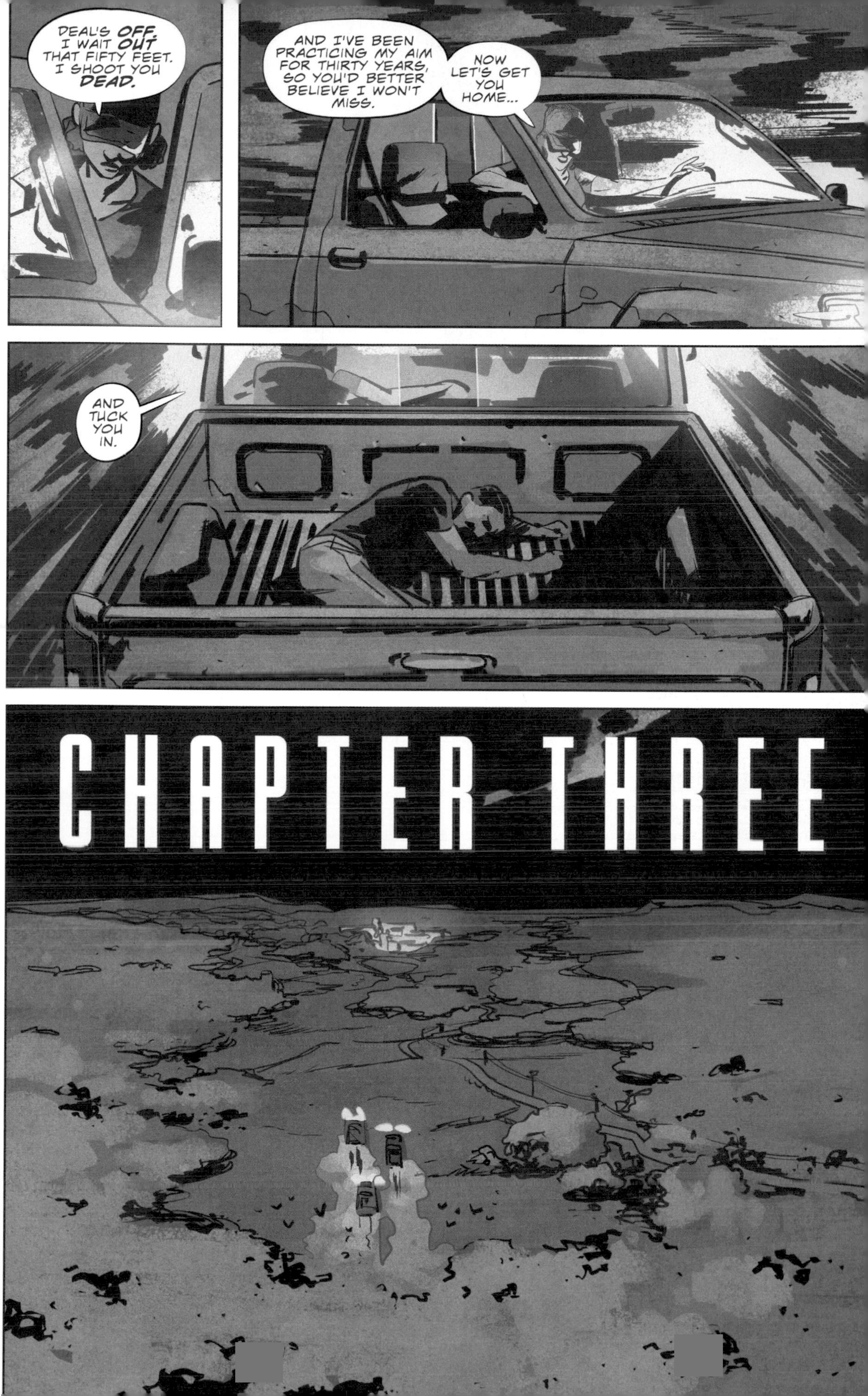
DEAL'S OFF. I WAIT OUT THAT FIFTY FEET. I SHOOT YOU DEAD.
AND I'VE BEEN PRACTICING MY AIM FOR THIRTY YEARS, SO YOU'D BETTER BELIEVE I WON'T MISS.
NOW LET'S GET YOU HOME...
AND TUCK YOU IN.
CHAPTER THREE

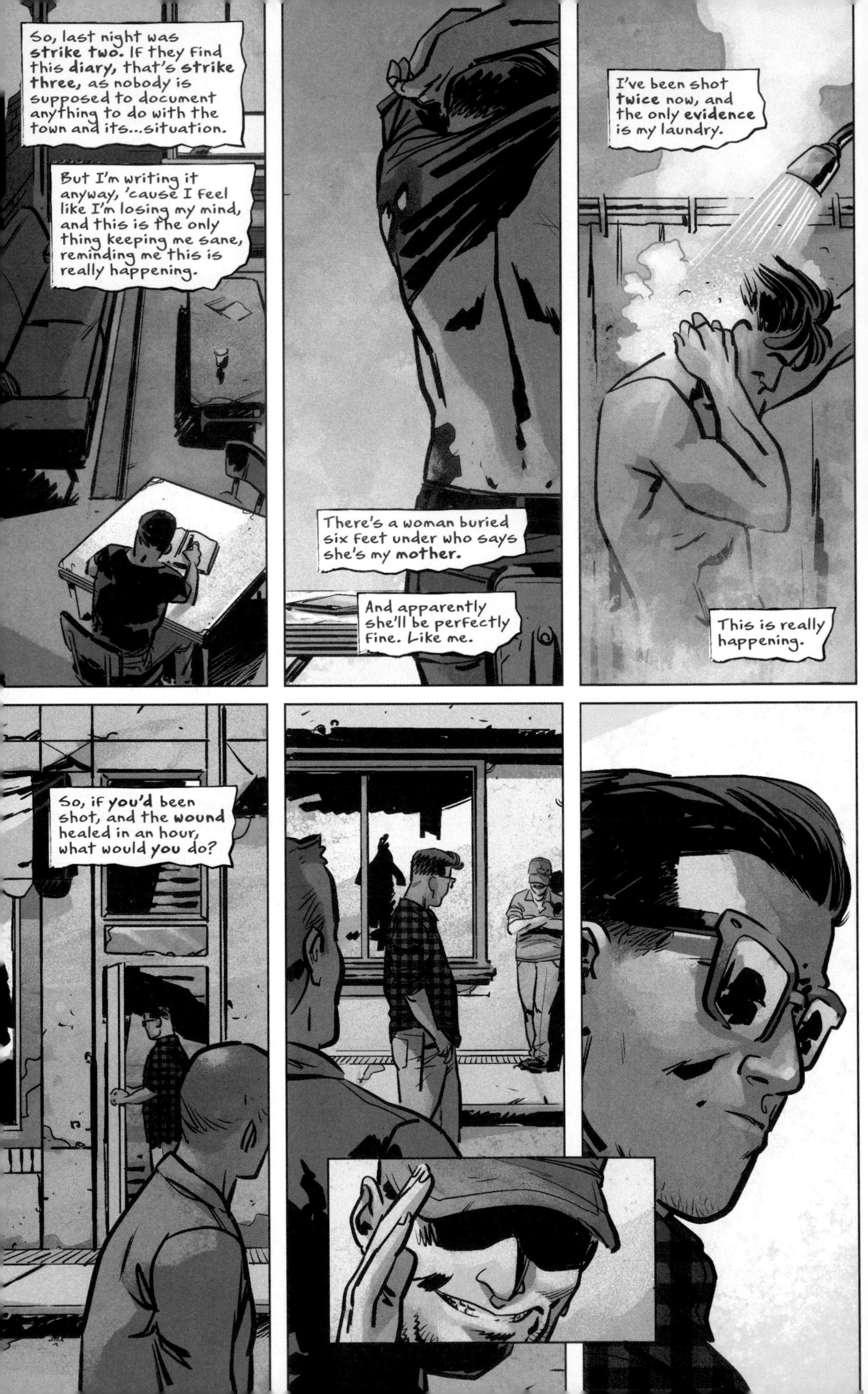
So, last night was strike two. If they find this diary, that's strike three, as nobody is supposed to document anything to do with the town and its...situation.
But I'm writing it anyway, 'cause I feel like I'm losing my mind, and this is the only thing keeping me sane, reminding me this is really happening.
There's a woman buried six feet under who says she's my mother.
And apparently she'll be perfectly fine. Like me.
I've been shot twice now, and the only evidence is my laundry.
This is really happening.
So, if you'd been shot, and the wound healed in an hour, what would you do?

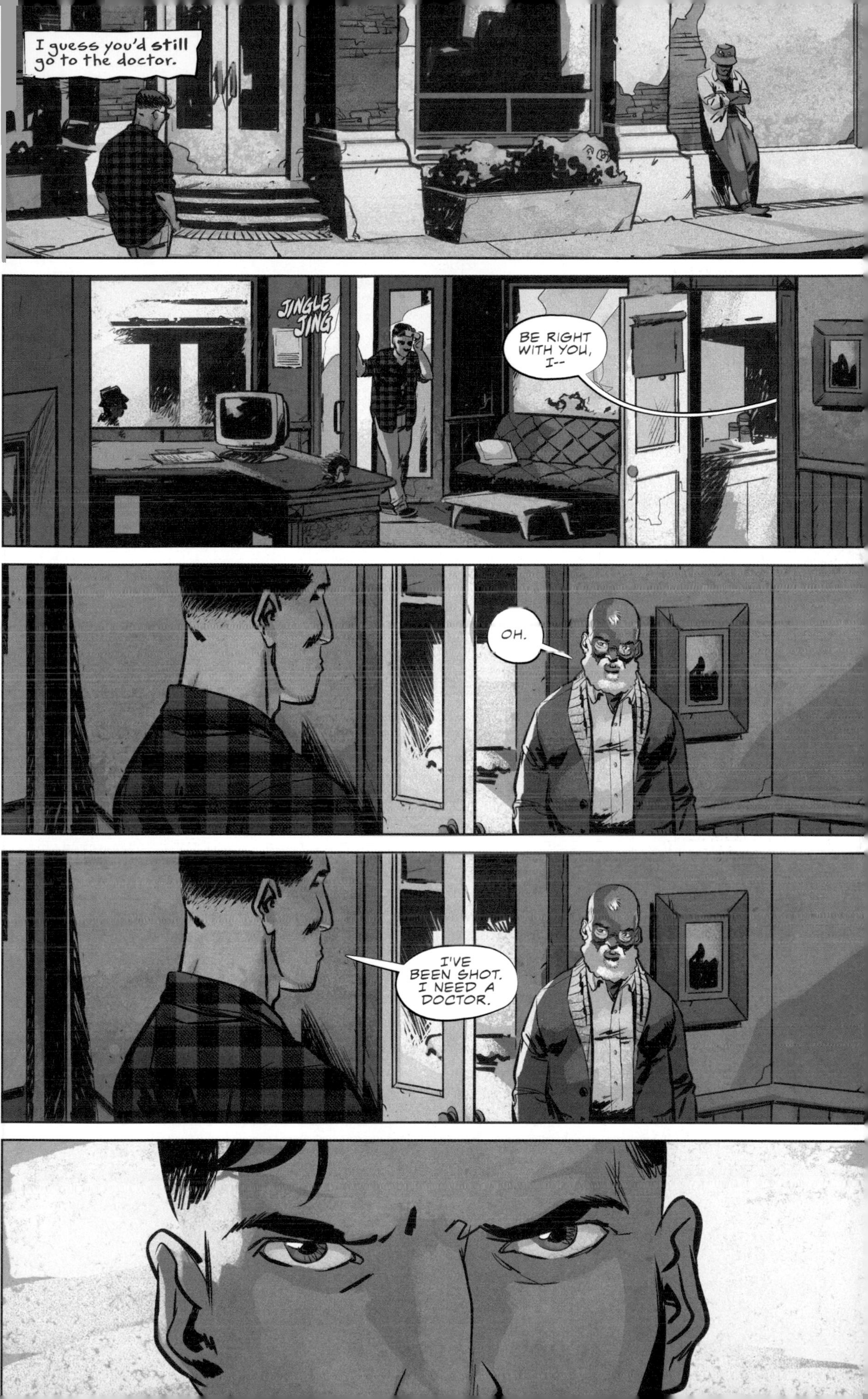
I guess you'd still go to the doctor.
JINGLE JING
BE RIGHT WITH YOU, I--
OH.
I'VE BEEN SHOT. I NEED A DOCTOR.

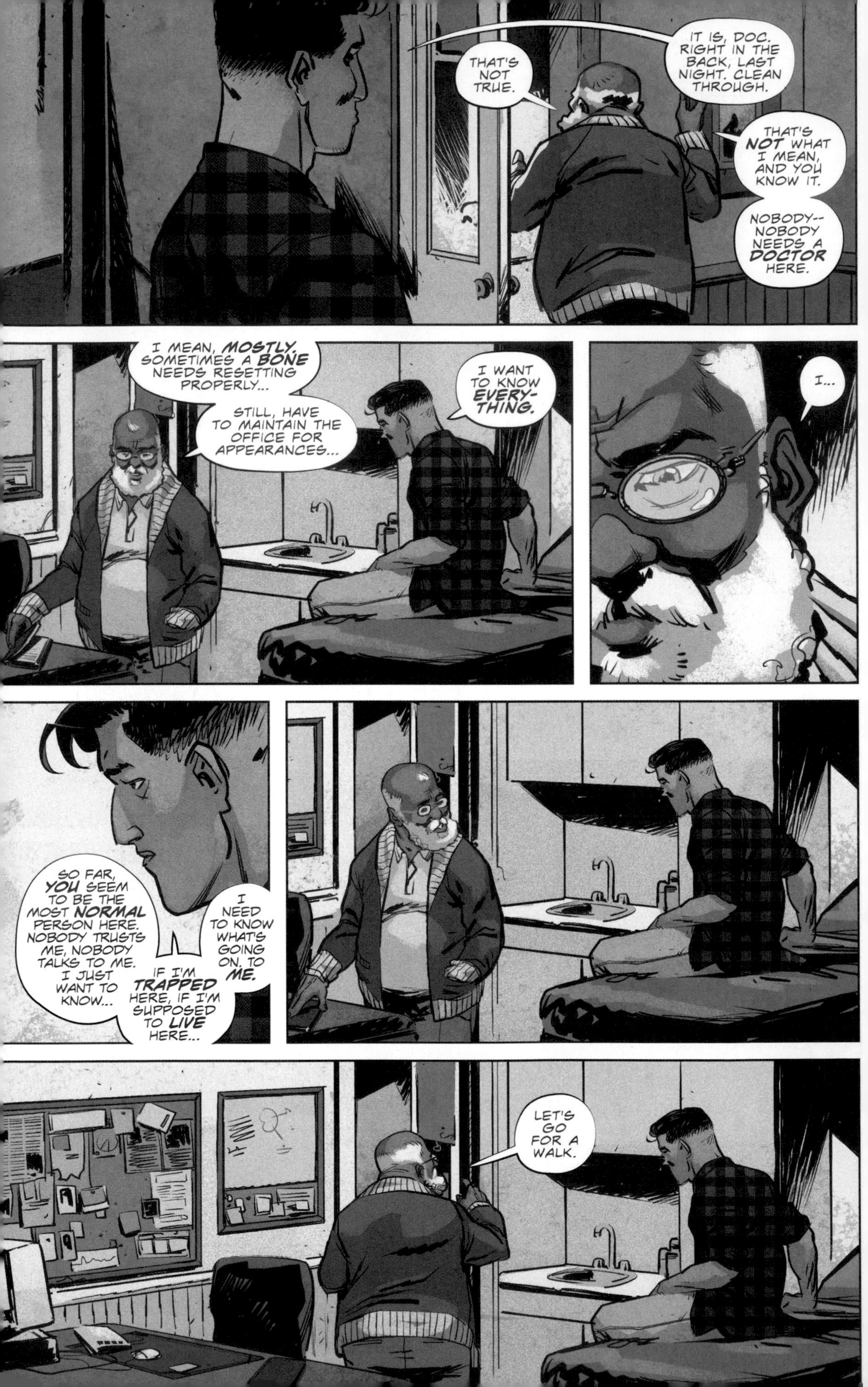
IT IS, DOC. RIGHT IN THE BACK, LAST NIGHT. CLEAN THROUGH.
THAT'S NOT TRUE.
THAT'S NOT WHAT I MEAN, AND YOU KNOW IT.
NOBODY-- NOBODY NEEDS A DOCTOR HERE.
I MEAN, MOSTLY. SOMETIMES A BONE NEEDS RESETTING PROPERLY...
STILL, HAVE TO MAINTAIN THE OFFICE FOR APPEARANCES...
I WANT TO KNOW EVERYTHING.
I...
SO FAR, YOU SEEM TO BE THE MOST NORMAL PERSON HERE. NOBODY TRUSTS ME, NOBODY TALKS TO ME. I JUST WANT TO KNOW...
IF I'M TRAPPED HERE, IF I'M SUPPOSED TO LIVE HERE...
I NEED TO KNOW WHAT'S GOING ON. TO ME.
LET'S GO FOR A WALK.

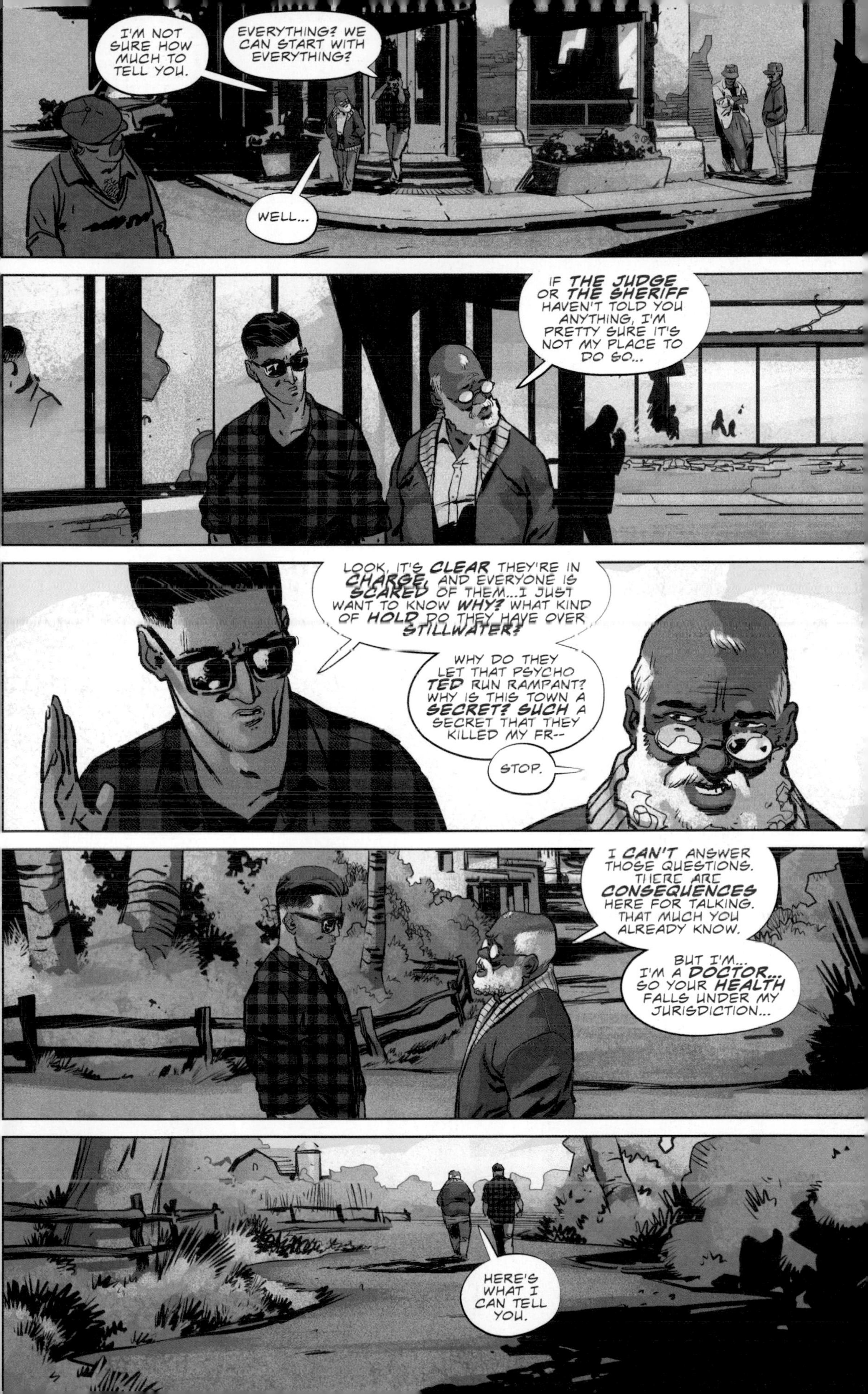

I'M NOT SURE HOW MUCH TO TELL YOU.
EVERYTHING? WE CAN START WITH EVERYTHING?
WELL...
IF THE JUDGE OR THE SHERIFF HAVEN'T TOLD YOU ANYTHING, I'M PRETTY SURE IT'S NOT MY PLACE TO DO SO...
LOOK, IT'S CLEAR THEY'RE IN CHARGE, AND EVERYONE IS SCARED OF THEM...I JUST WANT TO KNOW WHY? WHAT KIND OF HOLD DO THEY HAVE OVER STILLWATER?
WHY DO THEY LET THAT PSYCHO TED RUN RAMPANT? WHY IS THIS TOWN A SECRET? SUCH A SECRET THAT THEY KILLED MY FR--
STOP.
I CAN'T ANSWER THOSE QUESTIONS. THERE ARE CONSEQUENCES HERE FOR TALKING. THAT MUCH YOU ALREADY KNOW.
BUT I'M... I'M A DOCTOR... SO YOUR HEALTH FALLS UNDER MY JURISDICTION...
HERE'S WHAT I CAN TELL YOU.

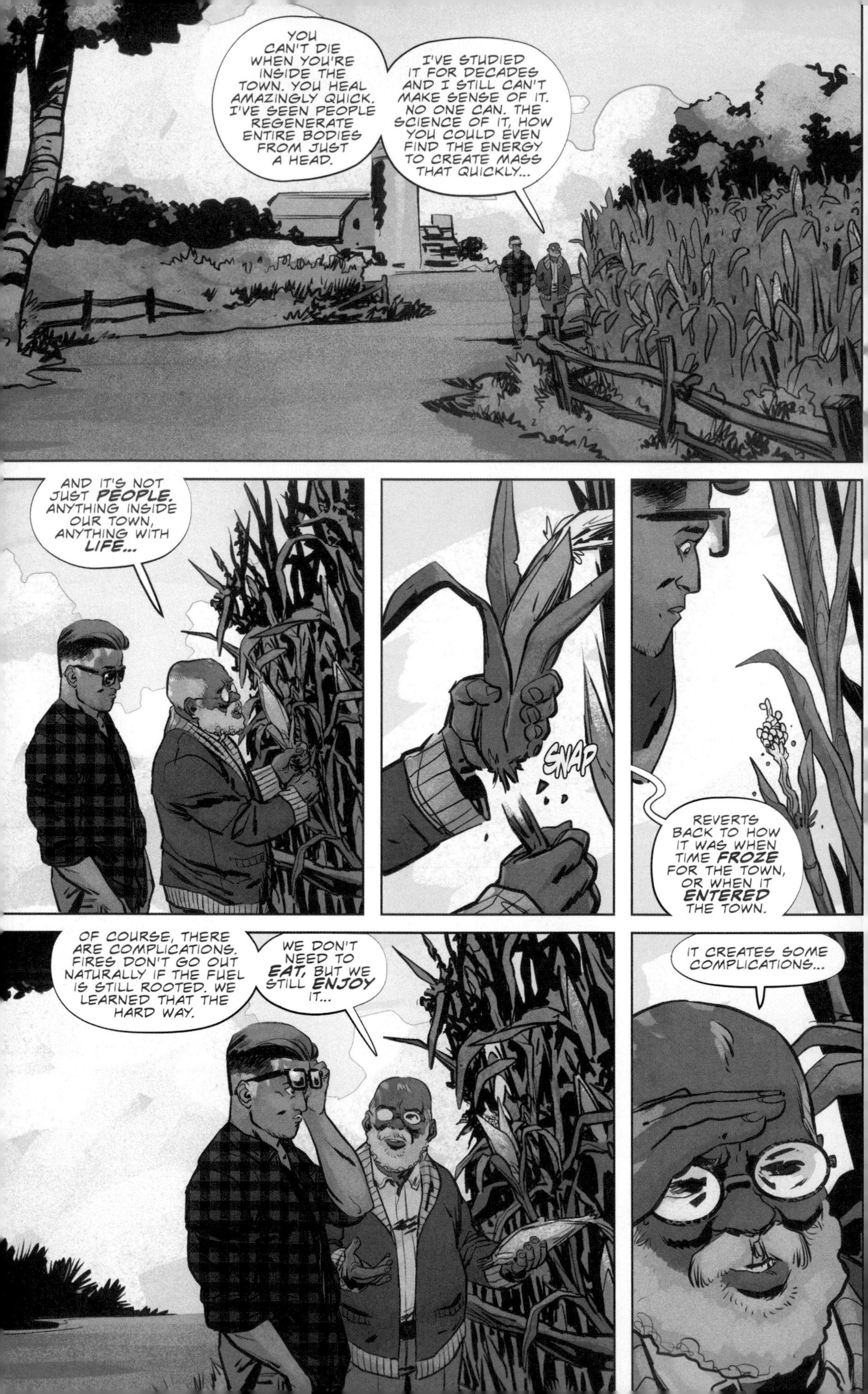
YOU CAN'T DIE WHEN YOU'RE INSIDE THE TOWN. YOU HEAL AMAZINGLY QUICK. I'VE SEEN PEOPLE REGENERATE ENTIRE BODIES FROM JUST A HEAD.
I'VE STUDIED IT FOR DECADES AND I STILL CAN'T MAKE SENSE OF IT. NO ONE CAN. THE SCIENCE OF IT, HOW YOU COULD EVEN FIND THE ENERGY TO CREATE MASS THAT QUICKLY...
AND IT'S NOT JUST PEOPLE. ANYTHING INSIDE OUR TOWN, ANYTHING WITH LIFE...
SNAP
REVERTS BACK TO HOW IT WAS WHEN TIME FROZE FOR THE TOWN, OR WHEN IT ENTERED THE TOWN.
OF COURSE, THERE ARE COMPLICATIONS. FIRES DON'T GO OUT NATURALLY IF THE FUEL IS STILL ROOTED. WE LEARNED THAT THE HARD WAY.
WE DON'T NEED TO EAT, BUT WE STILL ENJOY IT...
IT CREATES SOME COMPLICATIONS...

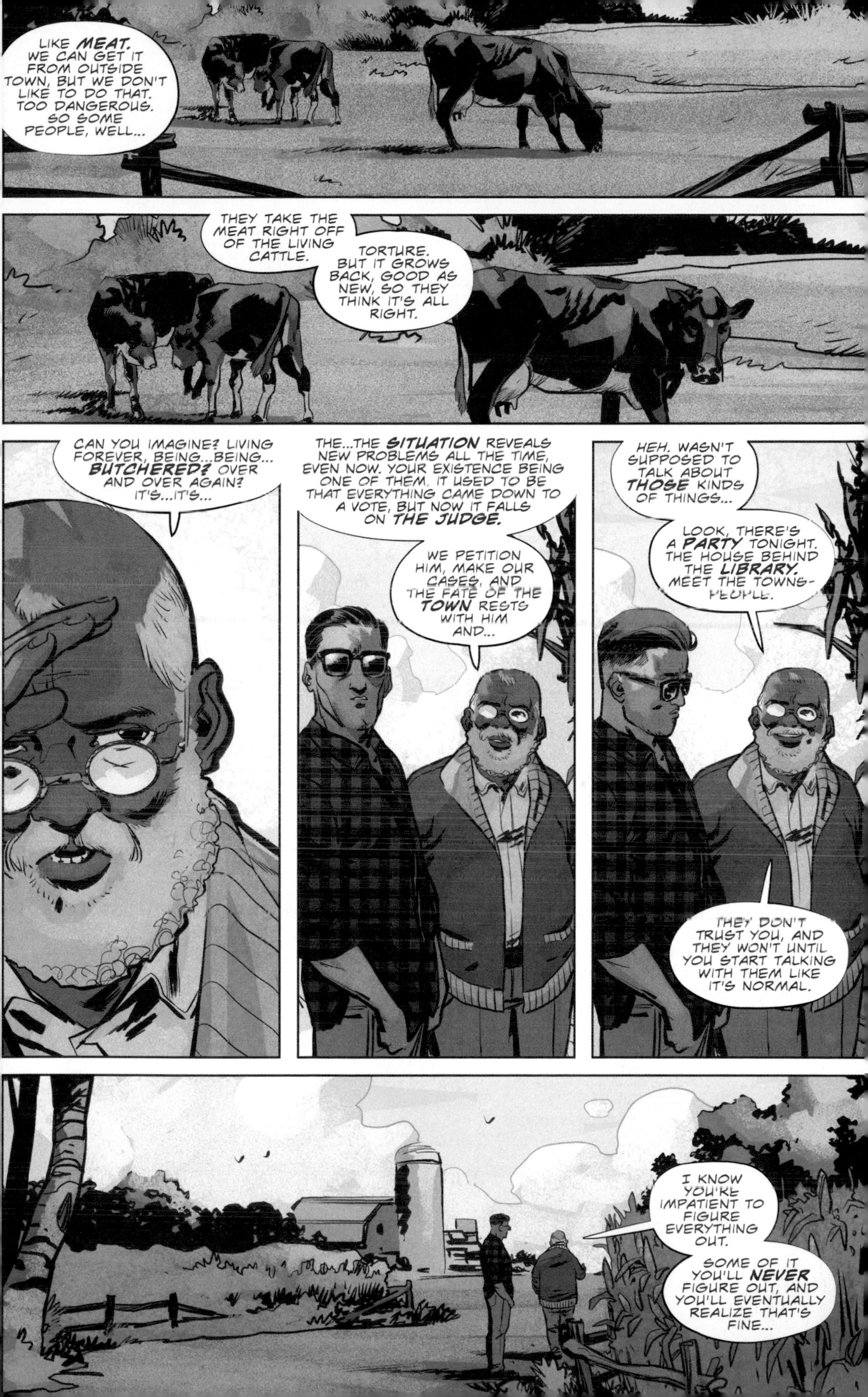
LIKE MEAT. WE CAN GET IT FROM OUTSIDE TOWN, BUT WE DON'T LIKE TO DO THAT. TOO DANGEROUS. SO SOME PEOPLE, WELL...
THEY TAKE THE MEAT RIGHT OFF OF THE LIVING CATTLE.
TORTURE. BUT IT GROWS BACK, GOOD AS NEW, SO THEY THINK IT'S ALL RIGHT.
CAN YOU IMAGINE? LIVING FOREVER, BEING...BEING... BUTCHERED? OVER AND OVER AGAIN? IT'S...IT'S...
THE...THE SITUATION REVEALS NEW PROBLEMS ALL THE TIME, EVEN NOW. YOUR EXISTENCE BEING ONE OF THEM. IT USED TO BE THAT EVERYTHING CAME DOWN TO A VOTE, BUT NOW IT FALLS ON THE JUDGE.
WE PETITION HIM, MAKE OUR CASES, AND THE FATE OF THE TOWN RESTS WITH HIM AND...
HEH. WASN'T SUPPOSED TO TALK ABOUT THOSE KINDS OF THINGS...
LOOK, THERE'S A PARTY TONIGHT. THE HOUSE BEHIND THE LIBRARY. MEET THE TOWNSPEOPLE.
THEY DON'T TRUST YOU, AND THEY WON'T UNTIL YOU START TALKING WITH THEM LIKE IT'S NORMAL.
I KNOW YOU'RE IMPATIENT TO FIGURE EVERYTHING OUT.
SOME OF IT YOU'LL NEVER FIGURE OUT, AND YOU'LL EVENTUALLY REALIZE THAT'S FINE...

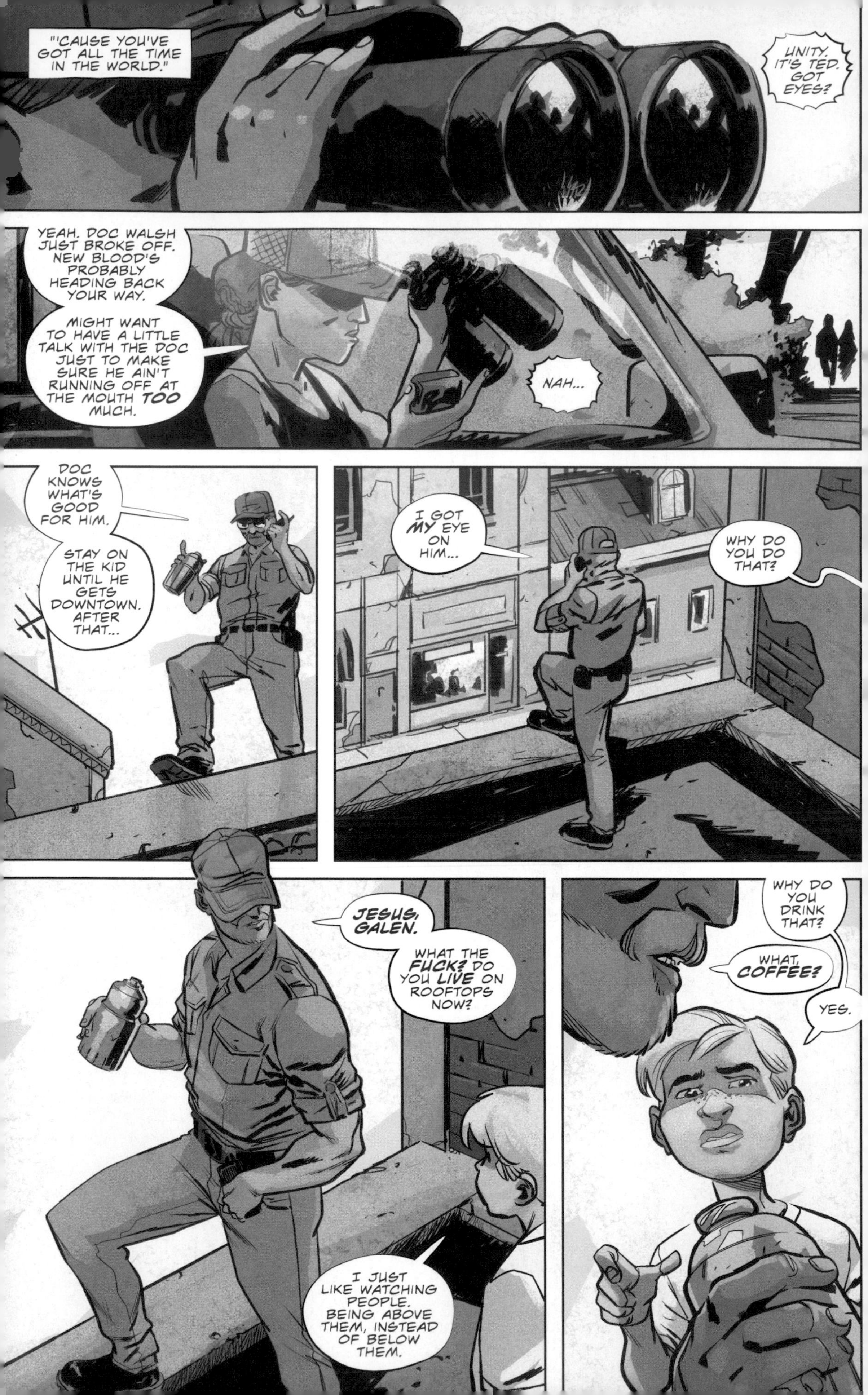
"'CAUSE YOU'VE GOT ALL THE TIME IN THE WORLD."
UNITY. IT'S TED. GOT EYES?
YEAH. DOC WALSH JUST BROKE OFF. NEW BLOOD'S PROBABLY HEADING BACK YOUR WAY.
MIGHT WANT TO HAVE A LITTLE TALK WITH THE DOC JUST TO MAKE SURE HE AIN'T RUNNING OFF AT THE MOUTH TOO MUCH.
NAH...
DOC KNOWS WHAT'S GOOD FOR HIM.
STAY ON THE KID UNTIL HE GETS DOWNTOWN. AFTER THAT...
I GOT MY EYE ON HIM...
WHY DO YOU DO THAT?
JESUS, GALEN.
WHAT THE FUCK? DO YOU LIVE ON ROOFTOPS NOW?
I JUST LIKE WATCHING PEOPLE. BEING ABOVE THEM, INSTEAD OF BELOW THEM.
WHY DO YOU DRINK THAT?
WHAT, COFFEE?
YES.

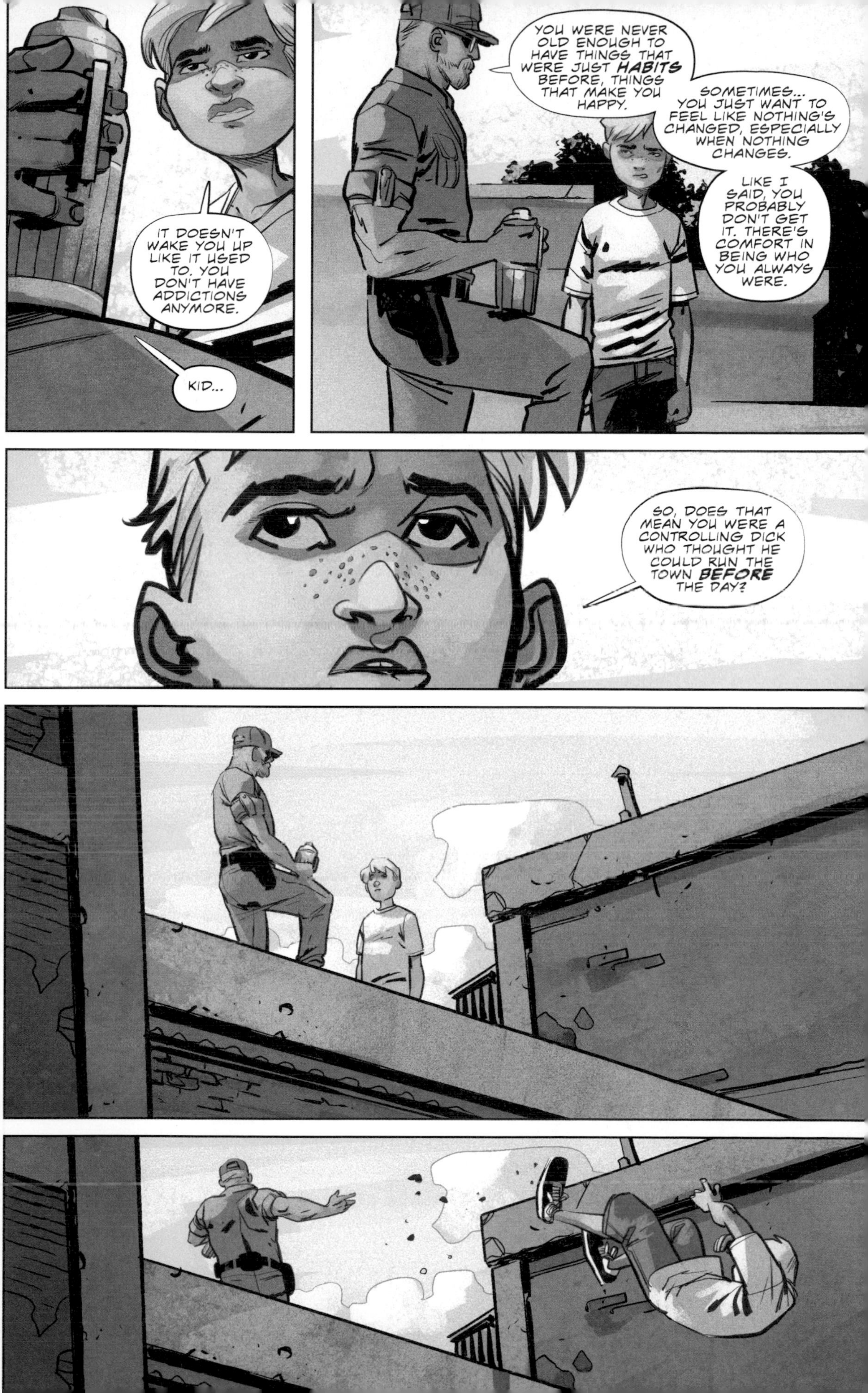
IT DOESN'T WAKE YOU UP LIKE IT USED TO. YOU DON'T HAVE ADDICTIONS ANYMORE.
KID...
YOU WERE NEVER OLD ENOUGH TO HAVE THINGS THAT WERE JUST HABITS BEFORE, THINGS THAT MAKE YOU HAPPY.
SOMETIMES... YOU JUST WANT TO FEEL LIKE NOTHING'S CHANGED, ESPECIALLY WHEN NOTHING CHANGES.
LIKE I SAID, YOU PROBABLY DON'T GET IT. THERE'S COMFORT IN BEING WHO YOU ALWAYS WERE.
SO, DOES THAT MEAN YOU WERE A CONTROLLING DICK WHO THOUGHT HE COULD RUN THE TOWN BEFORE THE DAY?

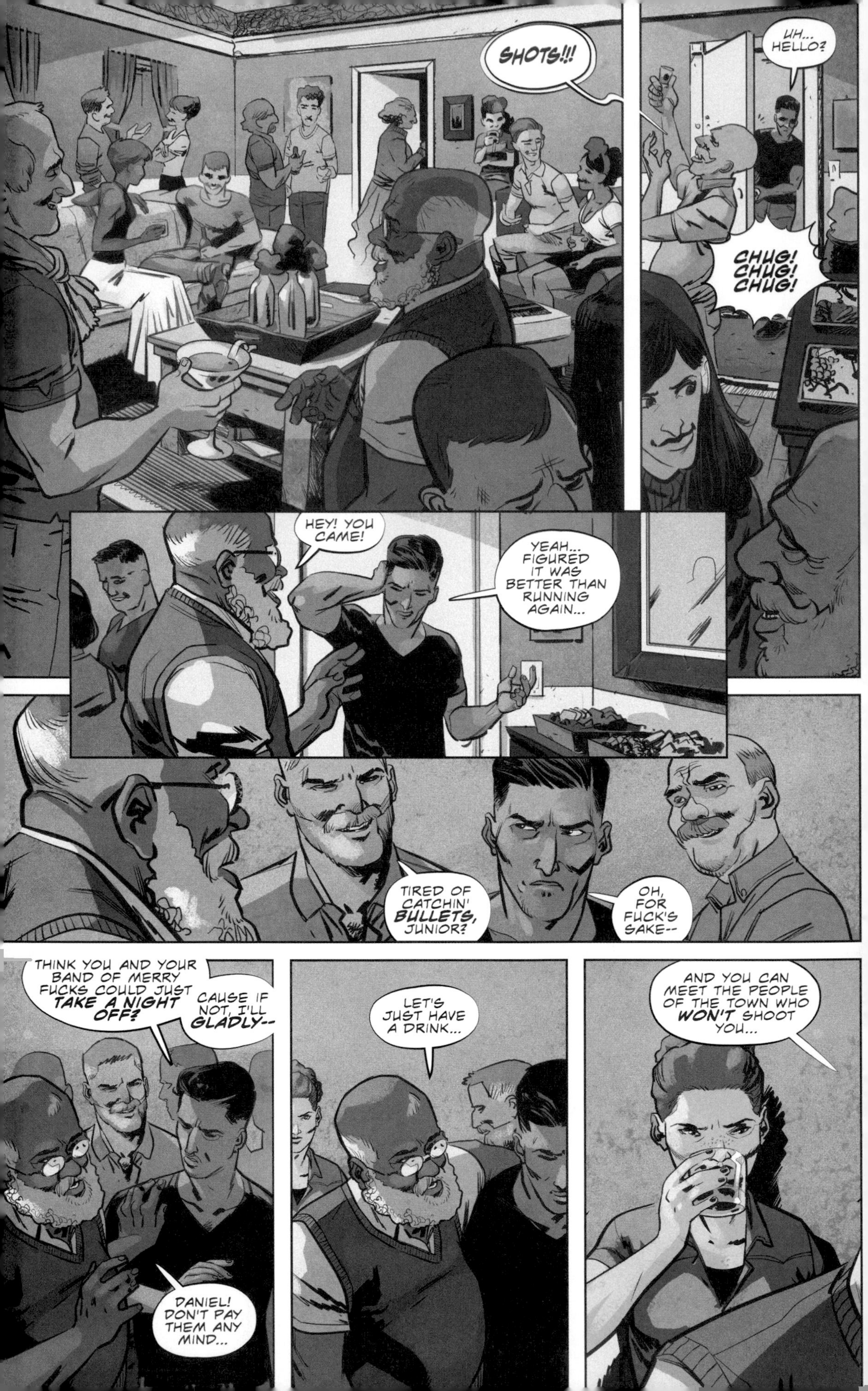

SHOTS!!!
UH... HELLO?
CHUG! CHUG! CHUG!
HEY! YOU CAME!
YEAH... FIGURED IT WAS BETTER THAN RUNNING AGAIN...
TIRED OF CATCHIN' BULLETS, JUNIOR?
OH, FOR FUCK'S SAKE--
THINK YOU AND YOUR BAND OF MERRY FUCKS COULD JUST TAKE A NIGHT OFF?
CAUSE IF NOT, I'LL GLADLY--
DANIEL! DON'T PAY THEM ANY MIND...
LET'S JUST HAVE A DRINK...
AND YOU CAN MEET THE PEOPLE OF THE TOWN WHO WON'T SHOOT YOU...

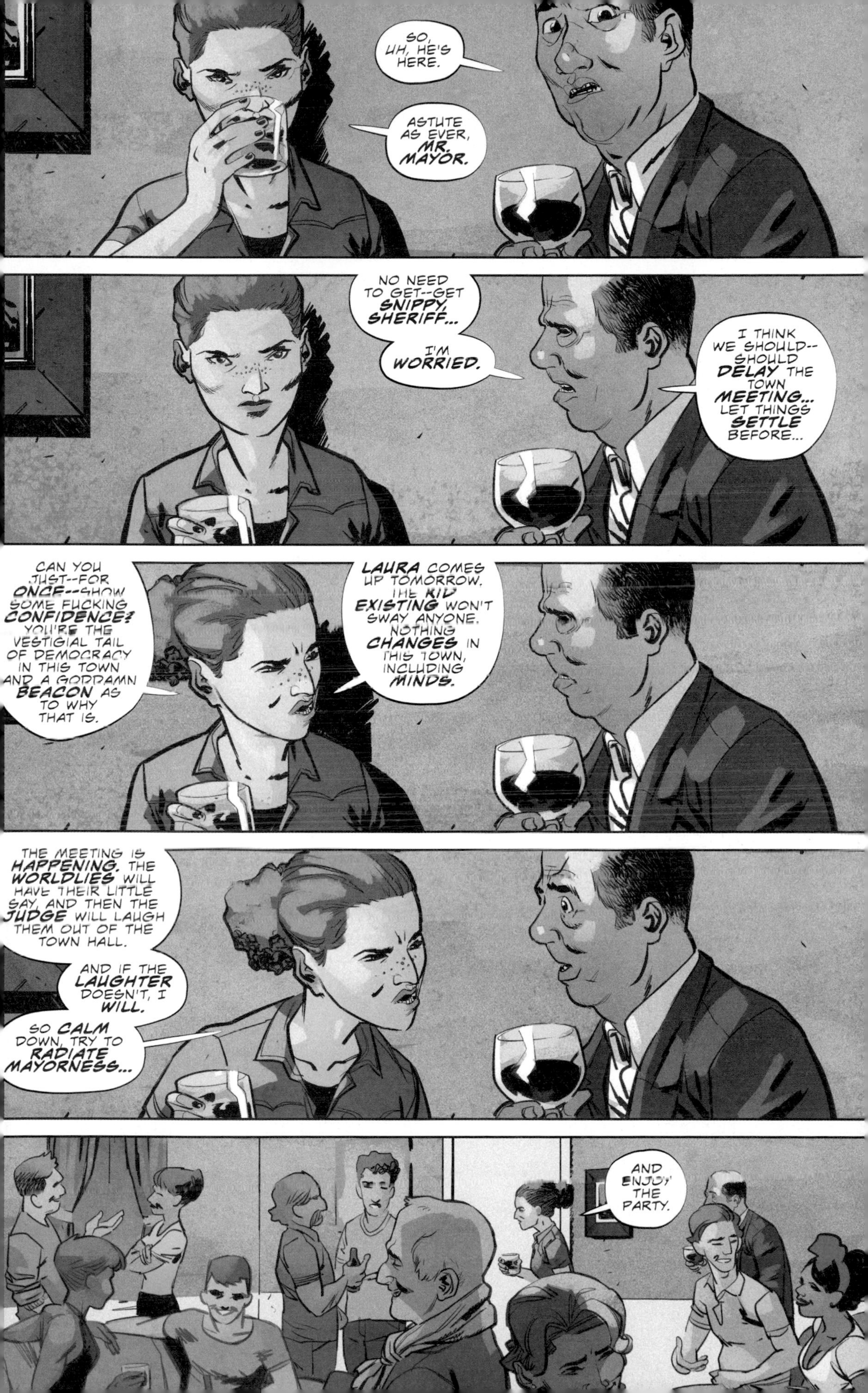

SO, UH, HE'S HERE.
ASTUTE AS EVER, MR. MAYOR.
NO NEED TO GET--GET SNIPPY, SHERIFF...
I'M WORRIED.
I THINK WE SHOULD--SHOULD DELAY THE TOWN MEETING... LET THINGS SETTLE BEFORE...
LAURA COMES UP TOMORROW. THE KID EXISTING WON'T SWAY ANYONE. NOTHING CHANGES IN THIS TOWN, INCLUDING MINDS.
CAN YOU JUST--FOR ONCE--SHOW SOME FUCKING CONFIDENCE? YOU'RE THE VESTIGIAL TAIL OF DEMOCRACY IN THIS TOWN AND A GODDAMN BEACON AS TO WHY THAT IS.
THE MEETING IS HAPPENING. THE WORLDLIES WILL HAVE THEIR LITTLE SAY, AND THEN THE JUDGE WILL LAUGH THEM OUT OF THE TOWN HALL.
AND IF THE LAUGHTER DOESN'T, I WILL.
SO CALM DOWN, TRY TO RADIATE MAYORNESS...
AND ENJOY THE PARTY.

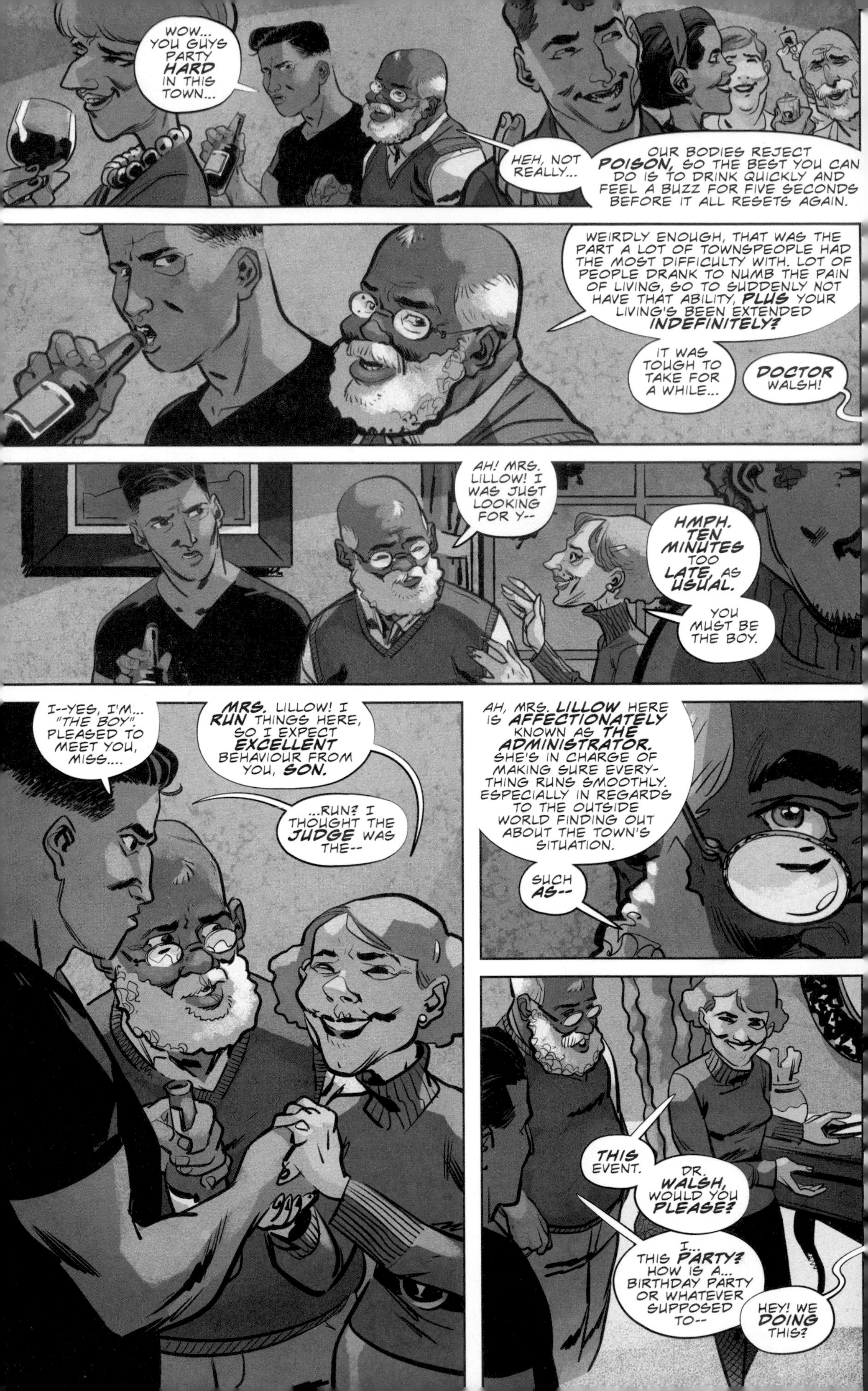

WOW... YOU GUYS PARTY HARD IN THIS TOWN...
HEH, NOT REALLY...
OUR BODIES REJECT POISON, SO THE BEST YOU CAN DO IS TO DRINK QUICKLY AND FEEL A BUZZ FOR FIVE SECONDS BEFORE IT ALL RESETS AGAIN.
WEIRDLY ENOUGH, THAT WAS THE PART A LOT OF TOWNSPEOPLE HAD THE MOST DIFFICULTY WITH. LOT OF PEOPLE DRANK TO NUMB THE PAIN OF LIVING, SO TO SUDDENLY NOT HAVE THAT ABILITY, PLUS YOUR LIVING'S BEEN EXTENDED INDEFINITELY?
IT WAS TOUGH TO TAKE FOR A WHILE...
DOCTOR WALSH!
AH! MRS. LILLOW! I WAS JUST LOOKING FOR Y--
HMPH. TEN MINUTES TOO LATE, AS USUAL.
YOU MUST BE THE BOY.
I--YES, I'M... "THE BOY". PLEASED TO MEET YOU, MISS....
MRS. LILLOW! I RUN THINGS HERE, SO I EXPECT EXCELLENT BEHAVIOUR FROM YOU, SON.
...RUN? I THOUGHT THE JUDGE WAS THE--
AH, MRS. LILLOW HERE IS AFFECTIONATELY KNOWN AS THE ADMINISTRATOR. SHE'S IN CHARGE OF MAKING SURE EVERYTHING RUNS SMOOTHLY. ESPECIALLY IN REGARDS TO THE OUTSIDE WORLD FINDING OUT ABOUT THE TOWN'S SITUATION.
SUCH AS--
THIS EVENT.
DR. WALSH, WOULD YOU PLEASE?
I... THIS PARTY? HOW IS A... BIRTHDAY PARTY OR WHATEVER SUPPOSED TO--
HEY! WE DOING THIS?

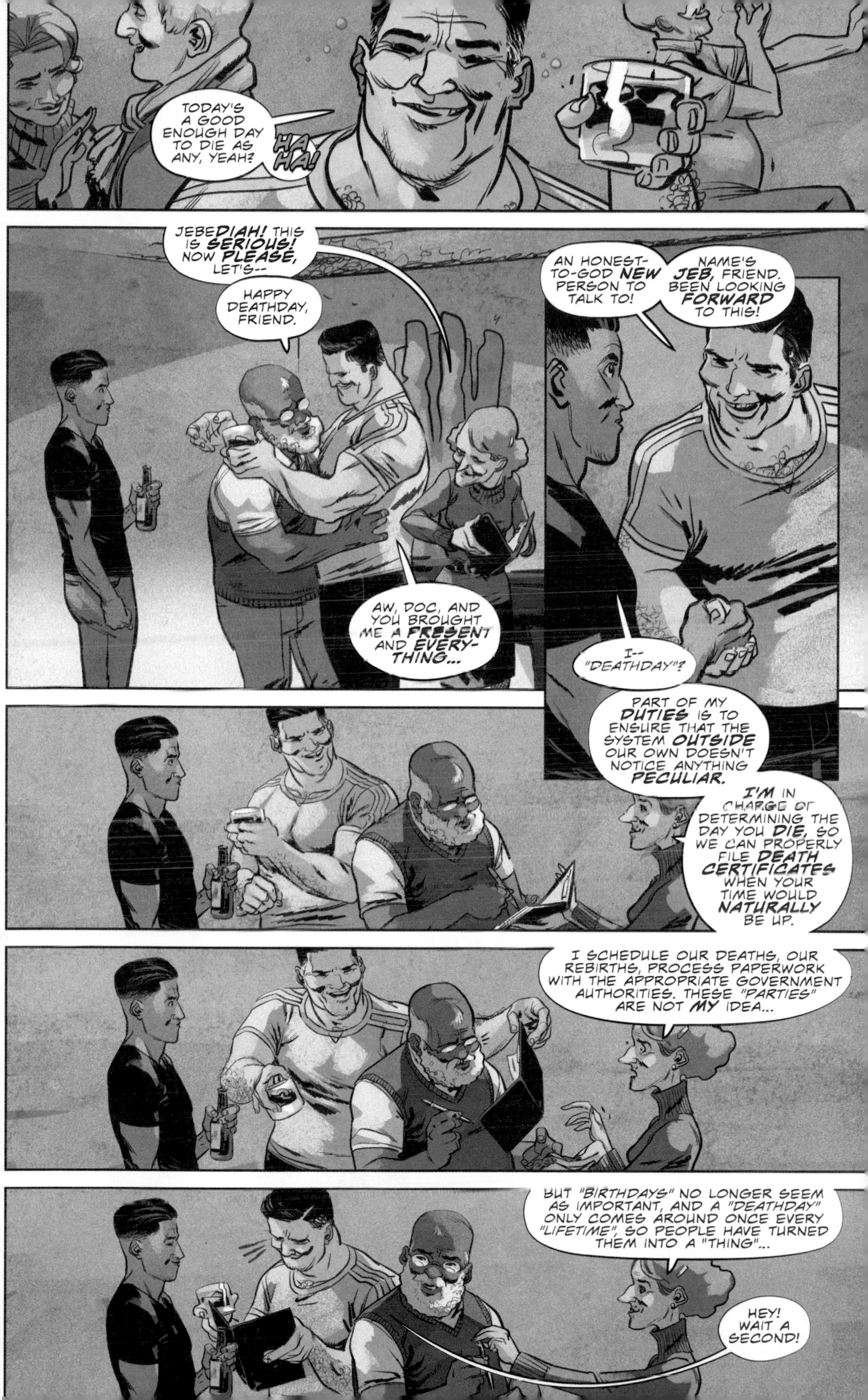
TODAY'S A GOOD ENOUGH DAY TO DIE AS ANY, YEAH?
HA HA!
JEBEDIAH! THIS IS SERIOUS! NOW PLEASE, LET'S--
HAPPY DEATHDAY, FRIEND.
AW, DOC, AND YOU BROUGHT ME A PRESENT AND EVERY-THING...
AN HONEST-TO-GOD NEW PERSON TO TALK TO!
NAME'S JEB, FRIEND. BEEN LOOKING FORWARD TO THIS!
I-- "DEATHDAY"?
PART OF MY DUTIES IS TO ENSURE THAT THE SYSTEM OUTSIDE OUR OWN DOESN'T NOTICE ANYTHING PECULIAR.
I'M IN CHARGE OF DETERMINING THE DAY YOU DIE, SO WE CAN PROPERLY FILE DEATH CERTIFICATES WHEN YOUR TIME WOULD NATURALLY BE UP.
I SCHEDULE OUR DEATHS, OUR REBIRTHS, PROCESS PAPERWORK WITH THE APPROPRIATE GOVERNMENT AUTHORITIES. THESE "PARTIES" ARE NOT MY IDEA...
BUT "BIRTHDAYS" NO LONGER SEEM AS IMPORTANT, AND A "DEATHDAY" ONLY COMES AROUND ONCE EVERY "LIFETIME", SO PEOPLE HAVE TURNED THEM INTO A "THING"...
HEY! WAIT A SECOND!

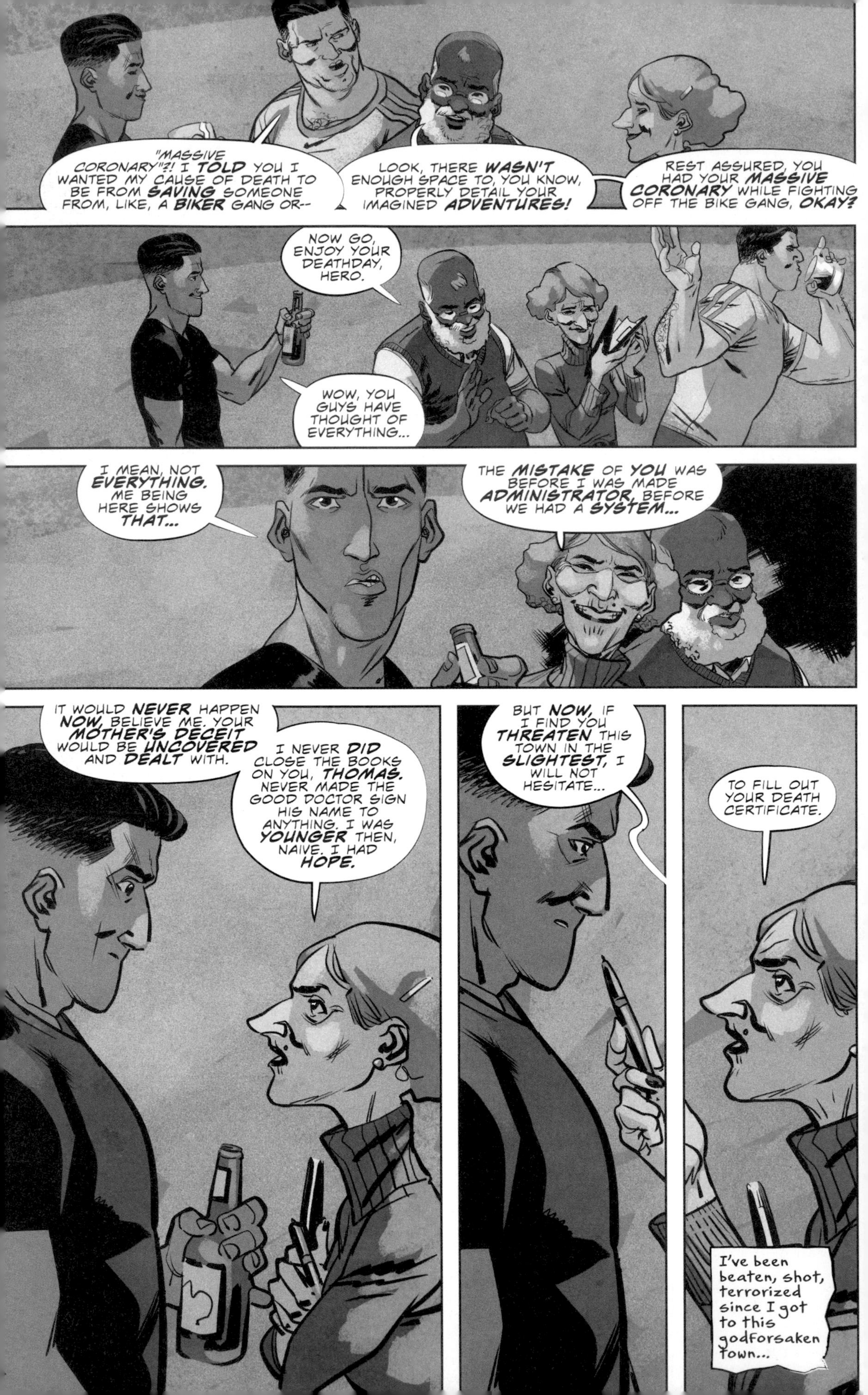
"MASSIVE CORONARY"?! I TOLD YOU I WANTED MY CAUSE OF DEATH TO BE FROM SAVING SOMEONE FROM, LIKE, A BIKER GANG OR--
LOOK, THERE WASN'T ENOUGH SPACE TO, YOU KNOW, PROPERLY DETAIL YOUR IMAGINED ADVENTURES!
REST ASSURED, YOU HAD YOUR MASSIVE CORONARY WHILE FIGHTING OFF THE BIKE GANG, OKAY?
NOW GO, ENJOY YOUR DEATHDAY, HERO.
WOW, YOU GUYS HAVE THOUGHT OF EVERYTHING...
I MEAN, NOT EVERYTHING. ME BEING HERE SHOWS THAT...
THE MISTAKE OF YOU WAS BEFORE I WAS MADE ADMINISTRATOR, BEFORE WE HAD A SYSTEM...
IT WOULD NEVER HAPPEN NOW, BELIEVE ME. YOUR MOTHER'S DECEIT WOULD BE UNCOVERED AND DEALT WITH.
I NEVER DID CLOSE THE BOOKS ON YOU, THOMAS. NEVER MADE THE GOOD DOCTOR SIGN HIS NAME TO ANYTHING. I WAS YOUNGER THEN, NAIVE. I HAD HOPE.
BUT NOW, IF I FIND YOU THREATEN THIS TOWN IN THE SLIGHTEST, I WILL NOT HESITATE...
TO FILL OUT YOUR DEATH CERTIFICATE.
I've been beaten, shot, terrorized since I got to this godforsaken town...

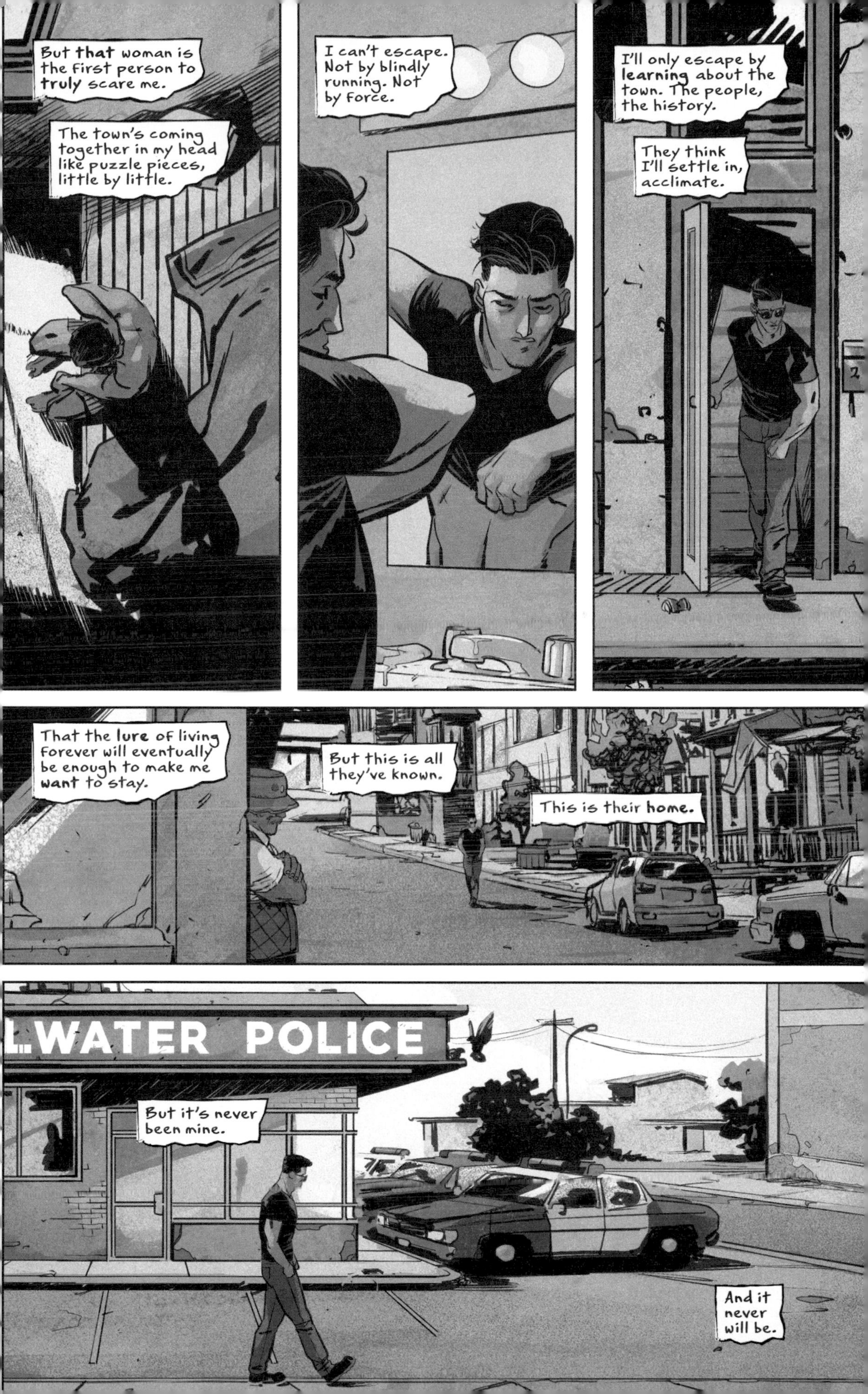
But that woman is the first person to truly scare me.
The town's coming together in my head like puzzle pieces, little by little.
I can't escape. Not by blindly running. Not by force.
I'll only escape by learning about the town. The people, the history.
They think I'll settle in, acclimate.
That the lure of living forever will eventually be enough to make me want to stay.
But this is all they've known.
This is their home.
LWATER POLICE
But it's never been mine.
And it never will be.

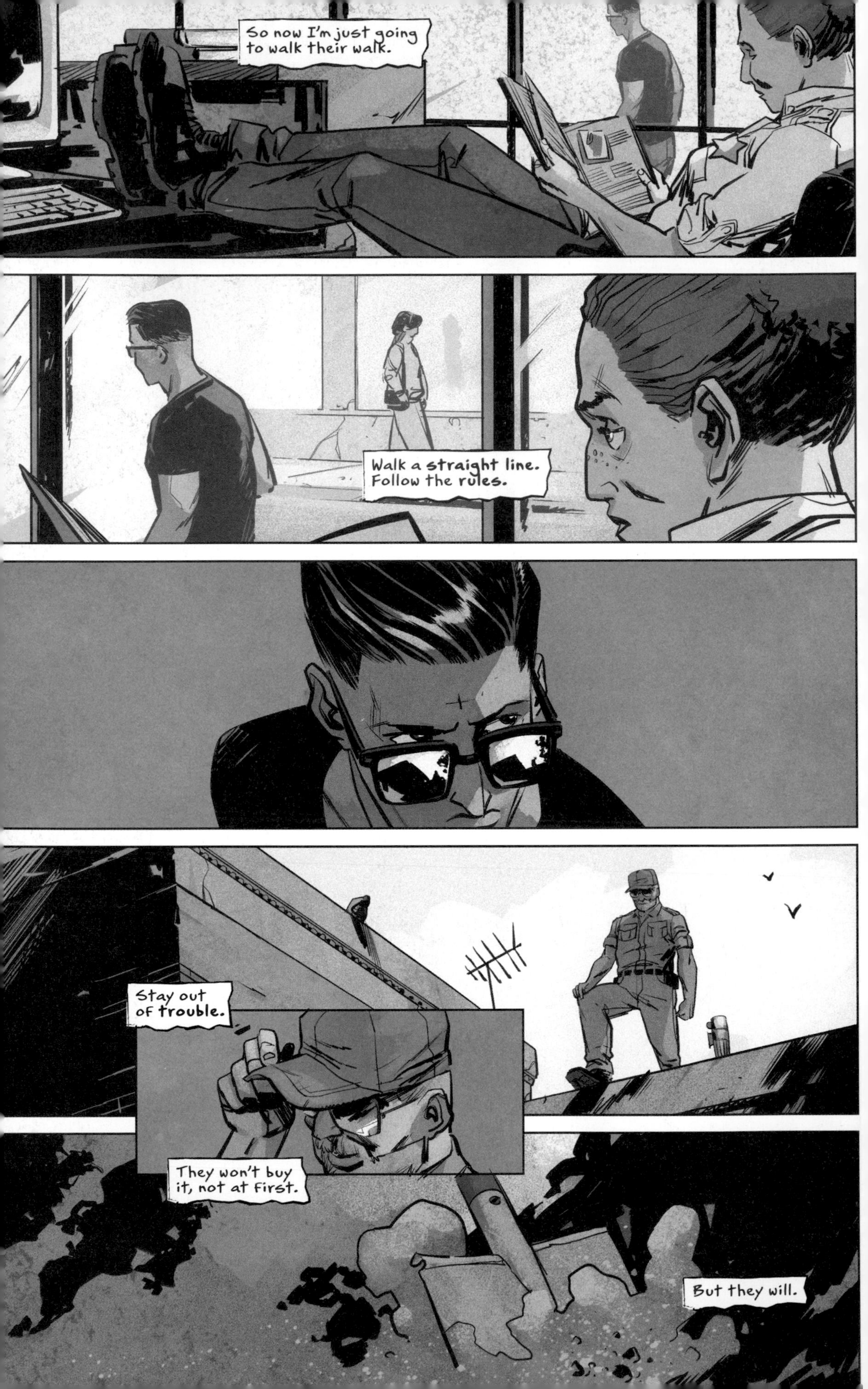
So now I'm just going to walk their walk.
Walk a straight line. Follow the rules.
Stay out of trouble.
They won't buy it, not at first.
But they will.

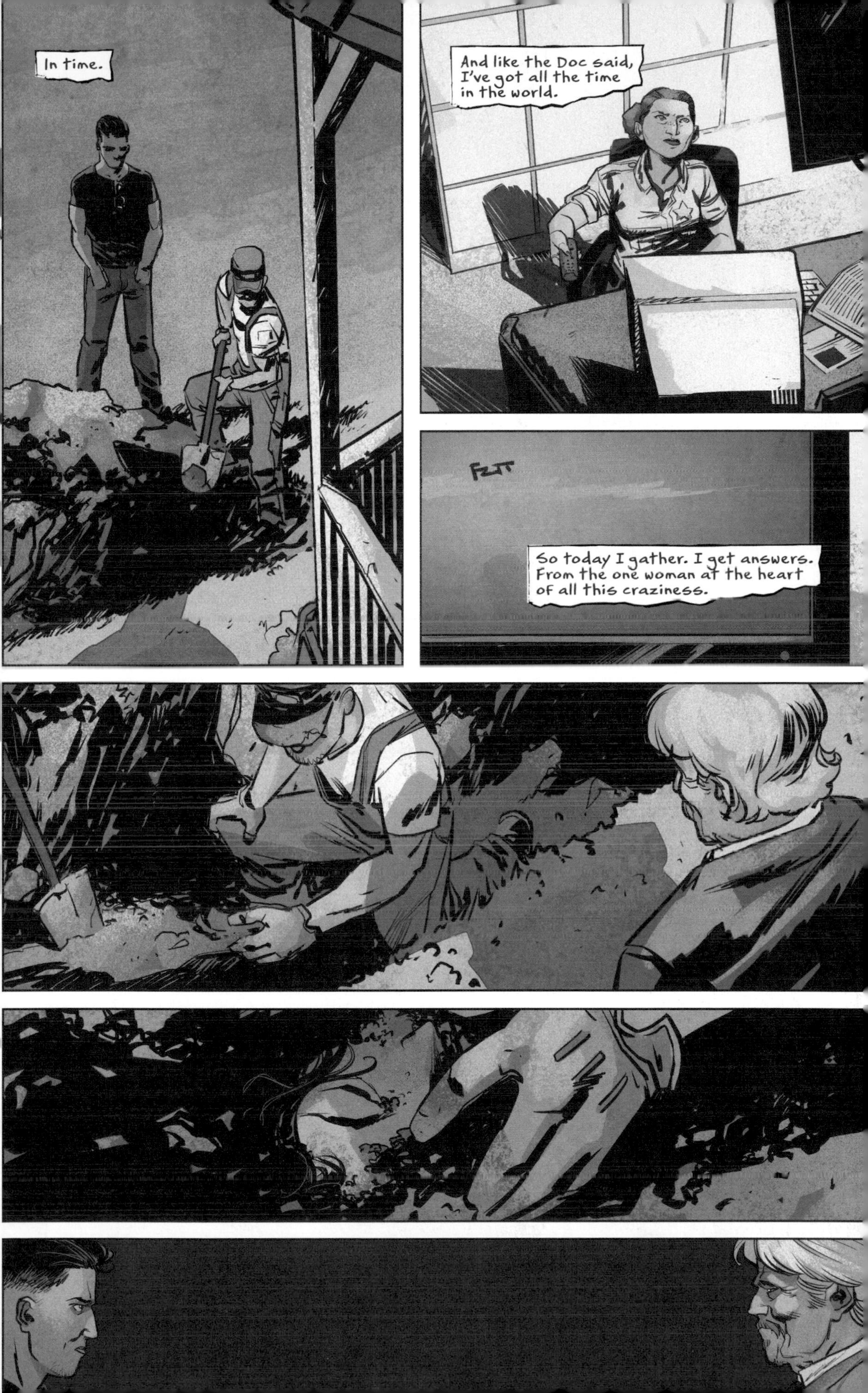
In time.
And like the Doc said, I've got all the time in the world.
FZZT
So today I gather. I get answers. From the one woman at the heart of all this craziness.

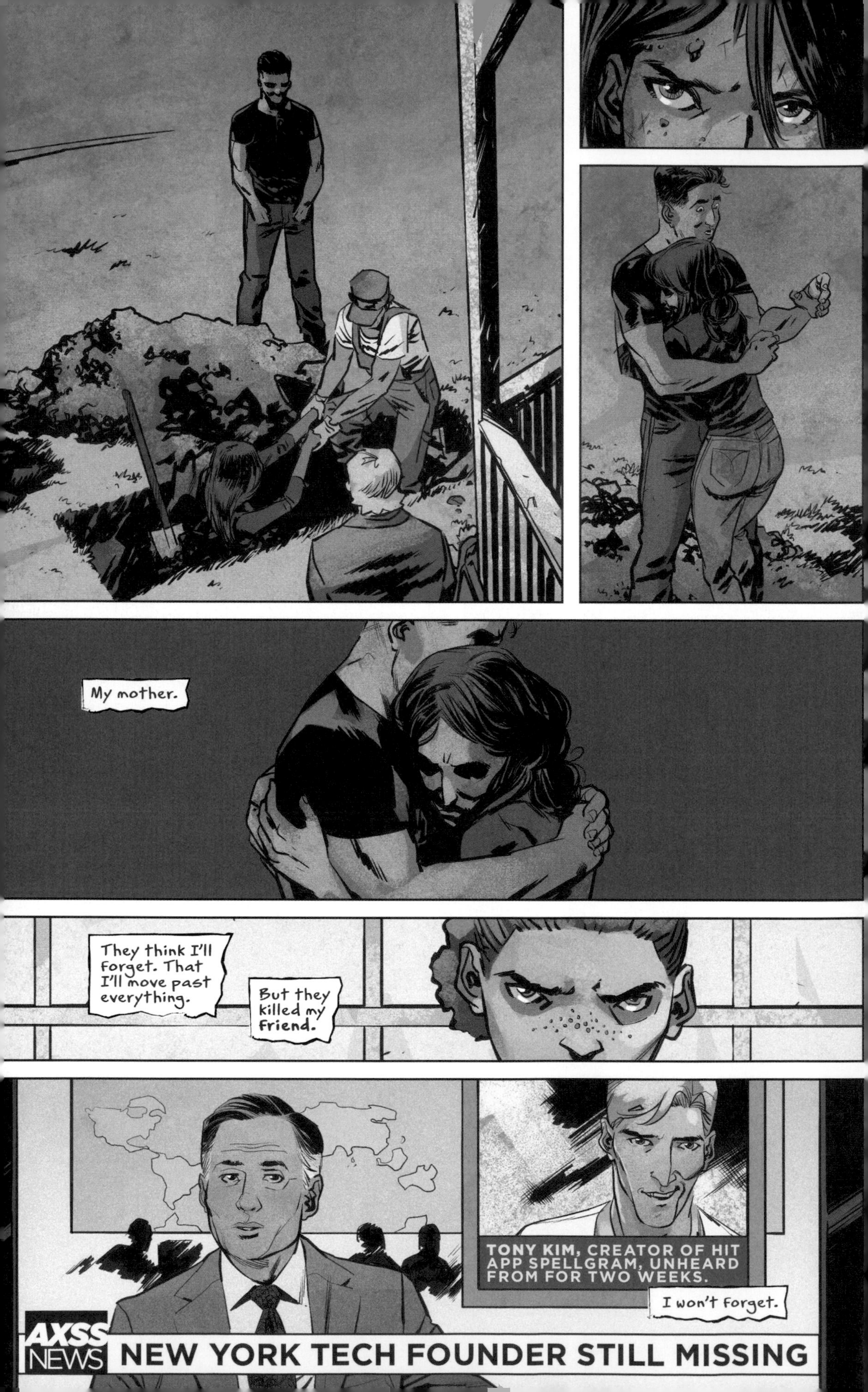
My mother.
They think I'll forget. That I'll move past everything.
But they killed my friend.
TONY KIM, CREATOR OF HIT APP SPELLGRAM, UNHEARD FROM FOR TWO WEEKS.
I won't forget.
AXSS NEWS
NEW YORK TECH FOUNDER STILL MISSING

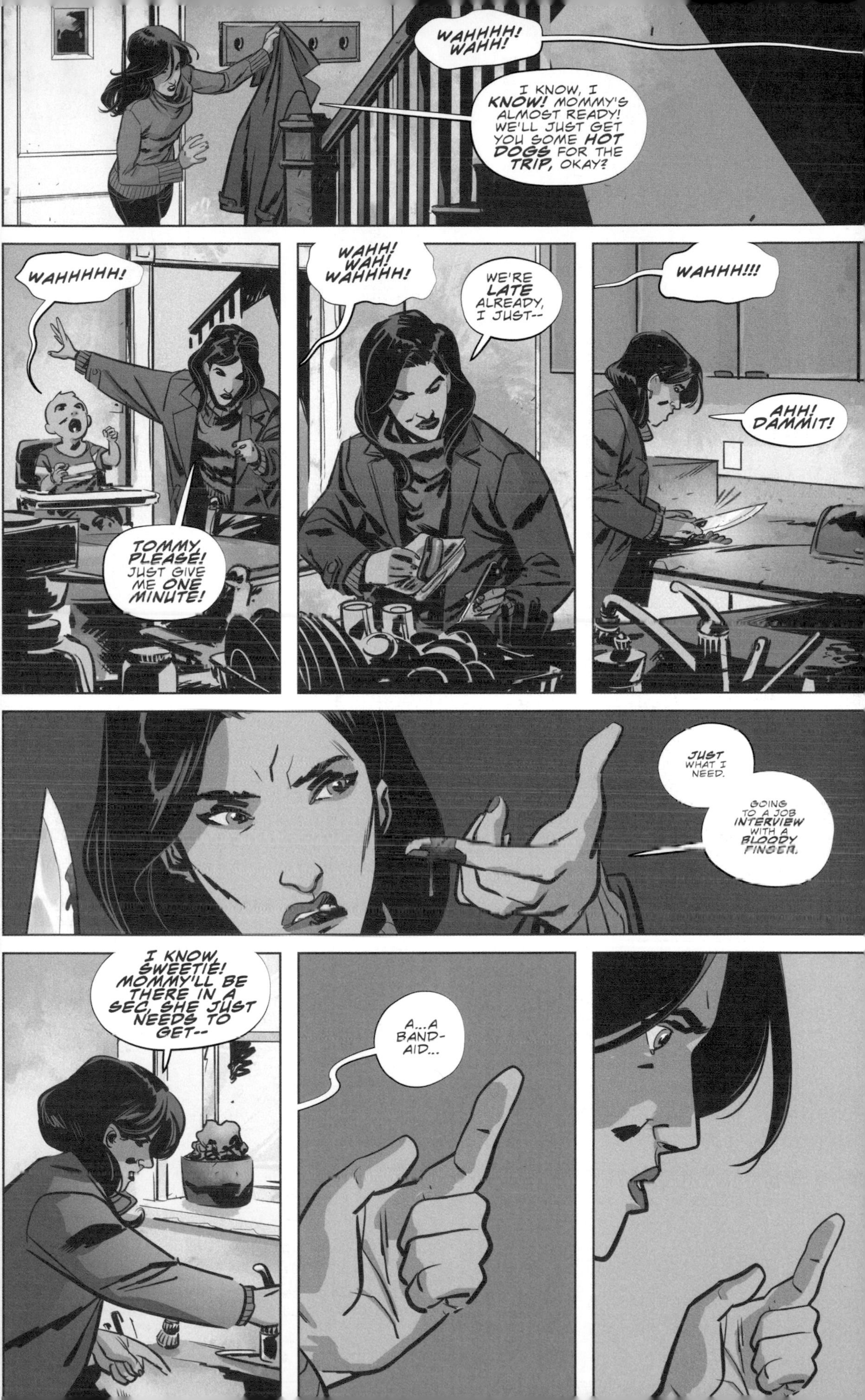
WAHHHH! WAHH!
I KNOW, I KNOW! MOMMY'S ALMOST READY! WE'LL JUST GET YOU SOME HOT DOGS FOR THE TRIP, OKAY?
WAHHHHH!
TOMMY, PLEASE! JUST GIVE ME ONE MINUTE!
WAHH! WAH! WAHHHH!
WE'RE LATE ALREADY, I JUST--
WAHHH!!!
AHH! DAMMIT!
JUST WHAT I NEED.
GOING TO A JOB INTERVIEW WITH A BLOODY FINGER.
I KNOW, SWEETIE! MOMMY'LL BE THERE IN A SEC, SHE JUST NEEDS TO GET--
A...A BAND-AID...

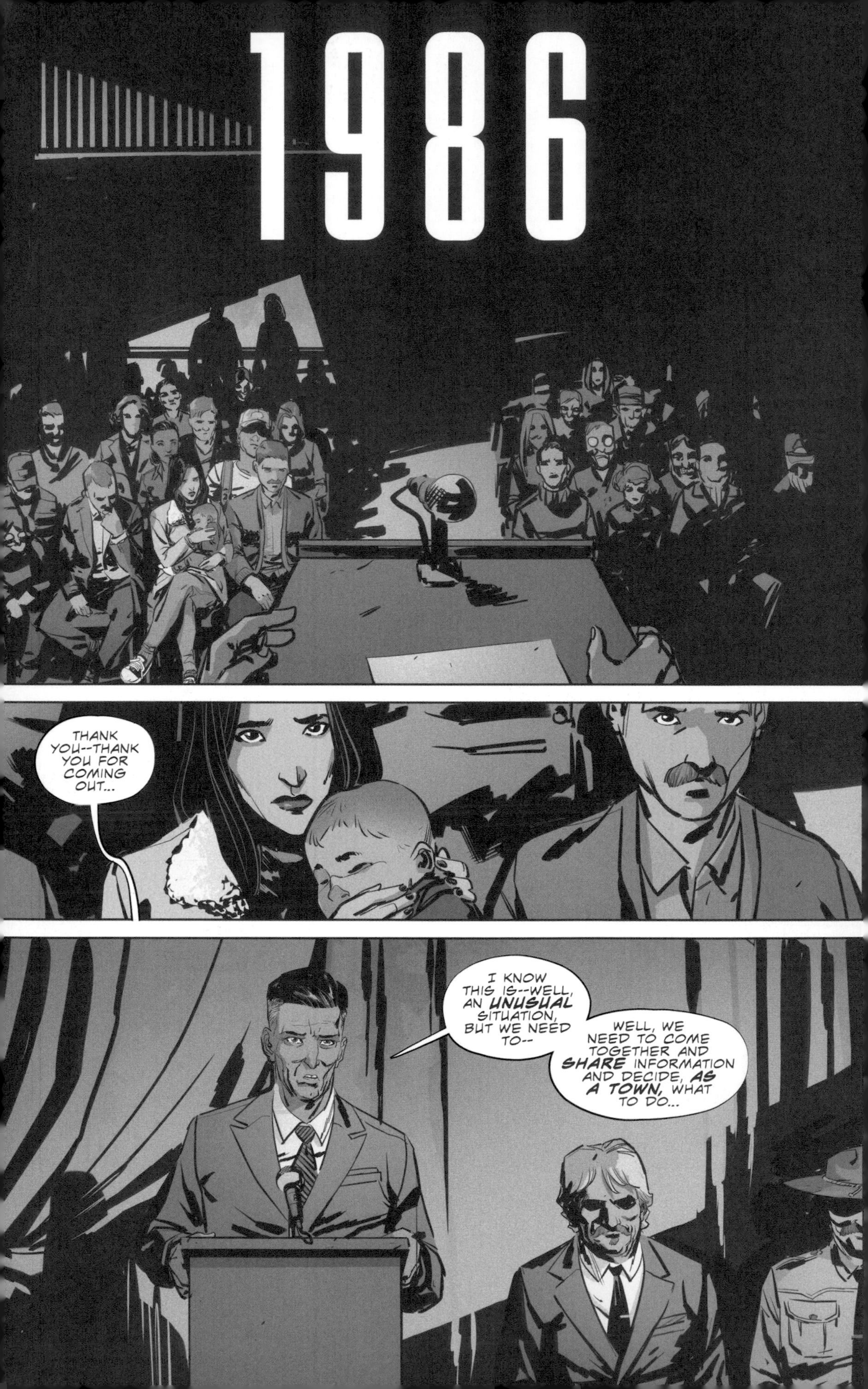
1986
THANK YOU--THANK YOU FOR COMING OUT...
I KNOW THIS IS--WELL, AN UNUSUAL SITUATION, BUT WE NEED TO--
WELL, WE NEED TO COME TOGETHER AND SHARE INFORMATION AND DECIDE, AS A TOWN, WHAT TO DO...

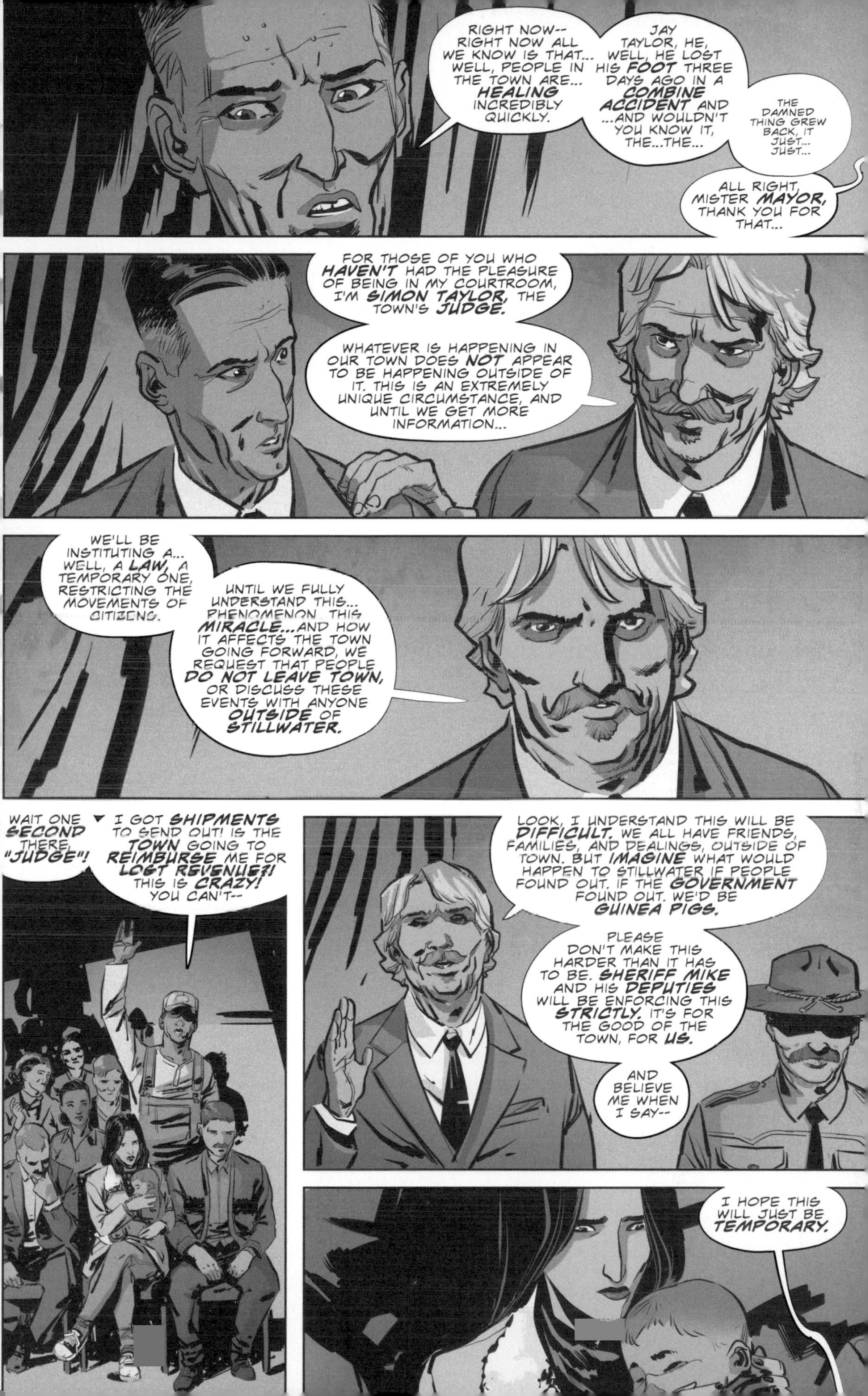

RIGHT NOW-- RIGHT NOW ALL WE KNOW IS THAT... WELL, PEOPLE IN THE TOWN ARE... HEALING INCREDIBLY QUICKLY.
JAY TAYLOR, HE, WELL, HE LOST HIS FOOT THREE DAYS AGO IN A COMBINE ACCIDENT AND ...AND WOULDN'T YOU KNOW IT, THE...THE...
THE DAMNED THING GREW BACK, IT JUST... JUST...
ALL RIGHT, MISTER MAYOR, THANK YOU FOR THAT...
FOR THOSE OF YOU WHO HAVEN'T HAD THE PLEASURE OF BEING IN MY COURTROOM, I'M SIMON TAYLOR, THE TOWN'S JUDGE.
WHATEVER IS HAPPENING IN OUR TOWN DOES NOT APPEAR TO BE HAPPENING OUTSIDE OF IT. THIS IS AN EXTREMELY UNIQUE CIRCUMSTANCE, AND UNTIL WE GET MORE INFORMATION...
WE'LL BE INSTITUTING A... WELL, A LAW, A TEMPORARY ONE, RESTRICTING THE MOVEMENTS OF CITIZENS.
UNTIL WE FULLY UNDERSTAND THIS... PHENOMENON, THIS MIRACLE...AND HOW IT AFFECTS THE TOWN GOING FORWARD, WE REQUEST THAT PEOPLE DO NOT LEAVE TOWN, OR DISCUSS THESE EVENTS WITH ANYONE OUTSIDE OF STILLWATER.
WAIT ONE SECOND THERE, "JUDGE"!
I GOT SHIPMENTS TO SEND OUT! IS THE TOWN GOING TO REIMBURSE ME FOR LOST REVENUE?! THIS IS CRAZY! YOU CAN'T--
LOOK, I UNDERSTAND THIS WILL BE DIFFICULT. WE ALL HAVE FRIENDS, FAMILIES, AND DEALINGS, OUTSIDE OF TOWN. BUT IMAGINE WHAT WOULD HAPPEN TO STILLWATER IF PEOPLE FOUND OUT. IF THE GOVERNMENT FOUND OUT. WE'D BE GUINEA PIGS.
PLEASE DON'T MAKE THIS HARDER THAN IT HAS TO BE. SHERIFF MIKE AND HIS DEPUTIES WILL BE ENFORCING THIS STRICTLY. IT'S FOR THE GOOD OF THE TOWN, FOR US.
AND BELIEVE ME WHEN I SAY--
I HOPE THIS WILL JUST BE TEMPORARY.

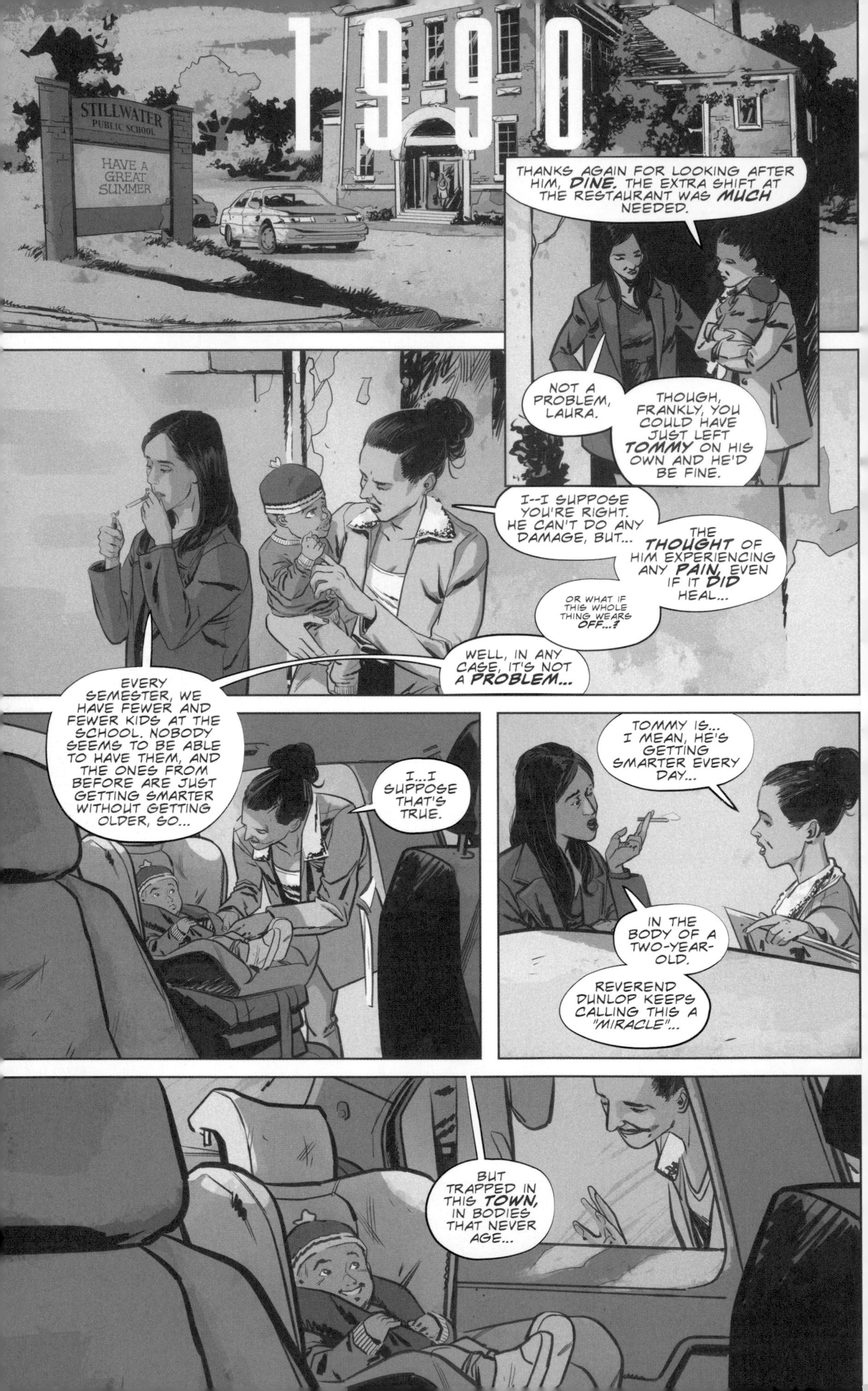
1990
STILLWATER PUBLIC SCHOOL
HAVE A GREAT SUMMER
THANKS AGAIN FOR LOOKING AFTER HIM, DINE. THE EXTRA SHIFT AT THE RESTAURANT WAS MUCH NEEDED.
NOT A PROBLEM, LAURA.
THOUGH, FRANKLY, YOU COULD HAVE JUST LEFT TOMMY ON HIS OWN AND HE'D BE FINE.
I--I SUPPOSE YOU'RE RIGHT. HE CAN'T DO ANY DAMAGE, BUT...
THE THOUGHT OF HIM EXPERIENCING ANY PAIN, EVEN IF IT DID HEAL...
OR WHAT IF THIS WHOLE THING WEARS OFF...?
WELL, IN ANY CASE, IT'S NOT A PROBLEM...
EVERY SEMESTER, WE HAVE FEWER AND FEWER KIDS AT THE SCHOOL. NOBODY SEEMS TO BE ABLE TO HAVE THEM, AND THE ONES FROM BEFORE ARE JUST GETTING SMARTER WITHOUT GETTING OLDER, SO...
I...I SUPPOSE THAT'S TRUE.
TOMMY IS... I MEAN, HE'S GETTING SMARTER EVERY DAY...
IN THE BODY OF A TWO-YEAR-OLD.
REVEREND DUNLOP KEEPS CALLING THIS A "MIRACLE"...
BUT TRAPPED IN THIS TOWN, IN BODIES THAT NEVER AGE...

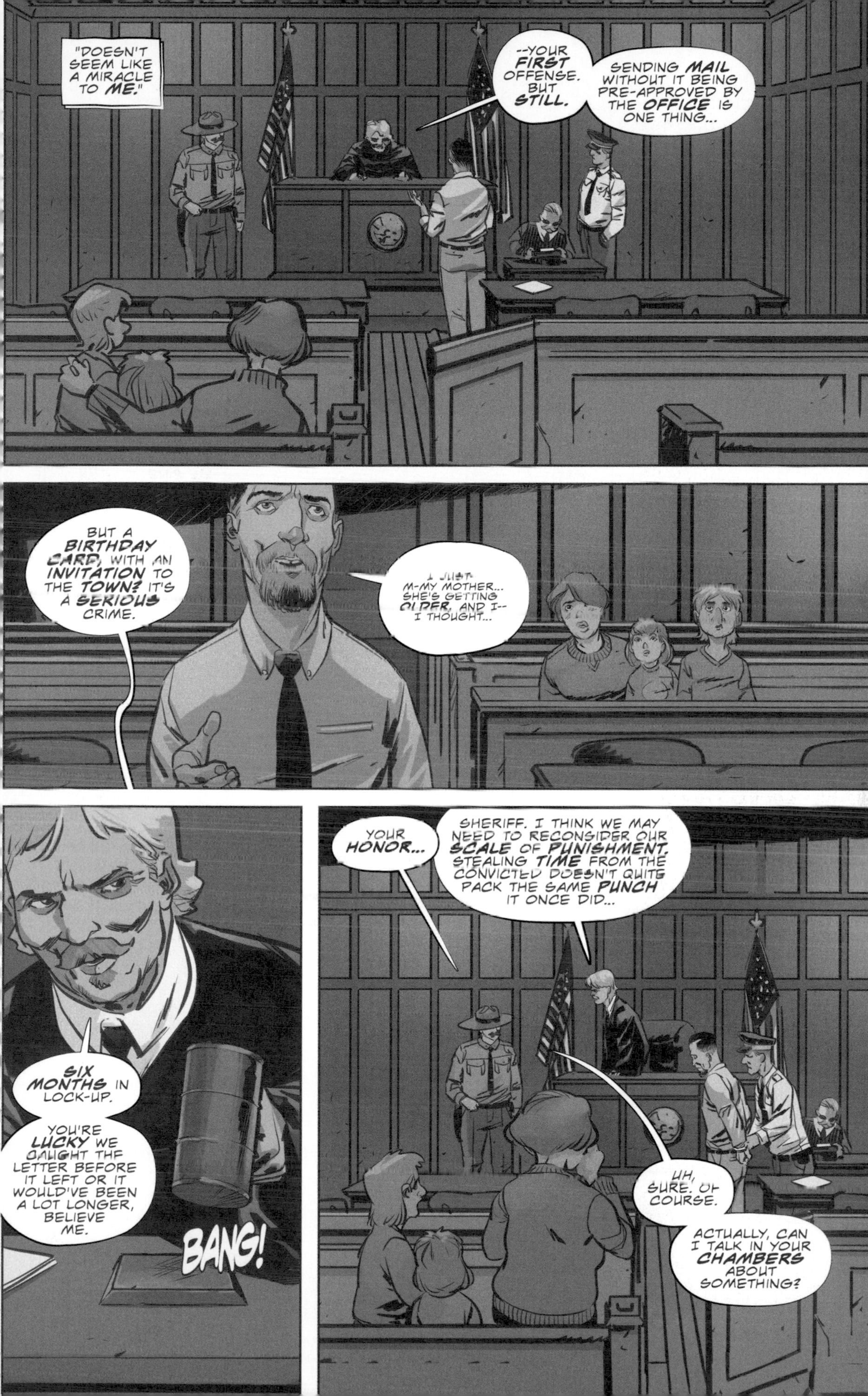
"DOESN'T SEEM LIKE A MIRACLE TO ME."
--YOUR FIRST OFFENSE. BUT STILL.
SENDING MAIL WITHOUT IT BEING PRE-APPROVED BY THE OFFICE IS ONE THING...
BUT A BIRTHDAY CARD, WITH AN INVITATION TO THE TOWN? IT'S A SERIOUS CRIME.
M-MY MOTHER... SHE'S GETTING OLDER, AND I-- I THOUGHT...
SIX MONTHS IN LOCK-UP.
YOU'RE LUCKY WE CAUGHT THE LETTER BEFORE IT LEFT OR IT WOULD'VE BEEN A LOT LONGER, BELIEVE ME.
BANG!
YOUR HONOR...
SHERIFF. I THINK WE MAY NEED TO RECONSIDER OUR SCALE OF PUNISHMENT. STEALING TIME FROM THE CONVICTED DOESN'T QUITE PACK THE SAME PUNCH IT ONCE DID...
UH, SURE. OF COURSE.
ACTUALLY, CAN I TALK IN YOUR CHAMBERS ABOUT SOMETHING?

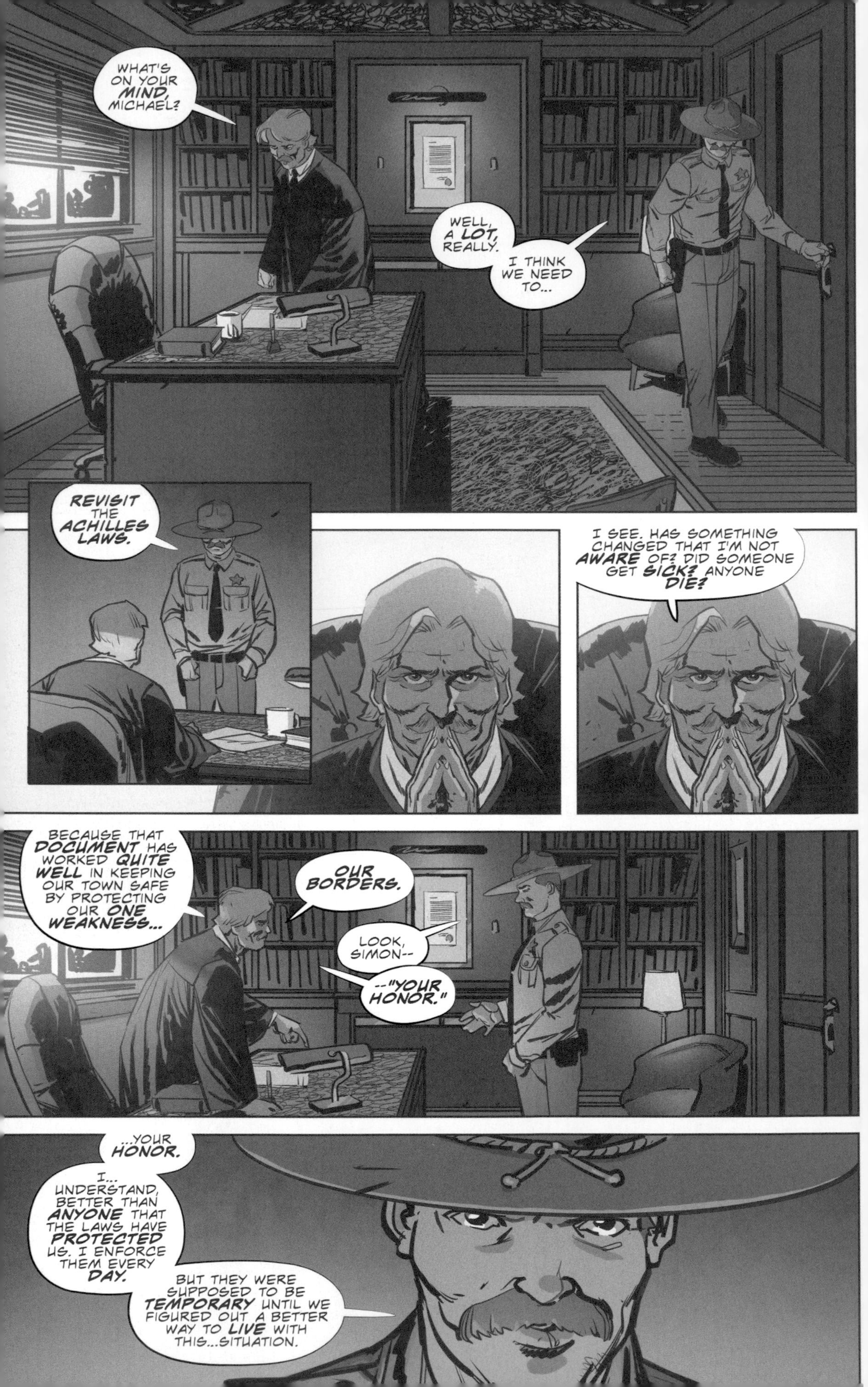
WHAT'S ON YOUR MIND, MICHAEL?
WELL, A LOT, REALLY.
I THINK WE NEED TO...
REVISIT THE ACHILLES LAWS.
I SEE. HAS SOMETHING CHANGED THAT I'M NOT AWARE OF? DID SOMEONE GET SICK? ANYONE DIE?
BECAUSE THAT DOCUMENT HAS WORKED QUITE WELL IN KEEPING OUR TOWN SAFE BY PROTECTING OUR ONE WEAKNESS...
OUR BORDERS.
LOOK, SIMON--
--"YOUR HONOR."
...YOUR HONOR.
I... UNDERSTAND, BETTER THAN ANYONE THAT THE LAWS HAVE PROTECTED US. I ENFORCE THEM EVERY DAY.
BUT THEY WERE SUPPOSED TO BE TEMPORARY UNTIL WE FIGURED OUT A BETTER WAY TO LIVE WITH THIS...SITUATION.

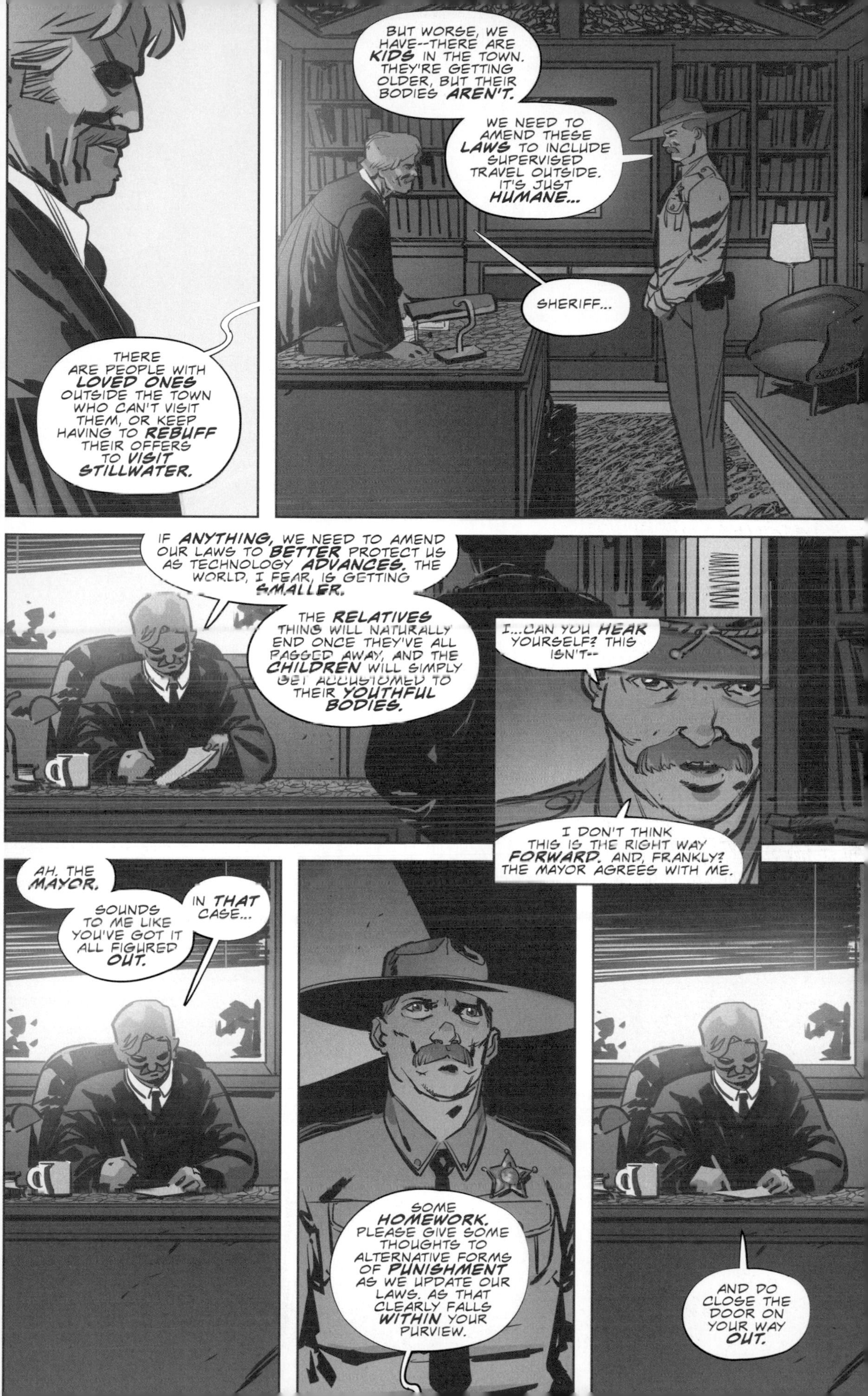
BUT WORSE, WE HAVE--THERE ARE KIDS IN THE TOWN. THEY'RE GETTING OLDER, BUT THEIR BODIES AREN'T.
WE NEED TO AMEND THESE LAWS TO INCLUDE SUPERVISED TRAVEL OUTSIDE. IT'S JUST HUMANE...
THERE ARE PEOPLE WITH LOVED ONES OUTSIDE THE TOWN WHO CAN'T VISIT THEM, OR KEEP HAVING TO REBUFF THEIR OFFERS TO VISIT STILLWATER.
SHERIFF...
IF ANYTHING, WE NEED TO AMEND OUR LAWS TO BETTER PROTECT US AS TECHNOLOGY ADVANCES. THE WORLD, I FEAR, IS GETTING SMALLER.
THE RELATIVES THING WILL NATURALLY END ONCE THEY'VE ALL PASSED AWAY, AND THE CHILDREN WILL SIMPLY GET ACCUSTOMED TO THEIR YOUTHFUL BODIES.
I...CAN YOU HEAR YOURSELF? THIS ISN'T--
I DON'T THINK THIS IS THE RIGHT WAY FORWARD. AND, FRANKLY? THE MAYOR AGREES WITH ME.
AH. THE MAYOR.
SOUNDS TO ME LIKE YOU'VE GOT IT ALL FIGURED OUT.
IN THAT CASE...
SOME HOMEWORK. PLEASE GIVE SOME THOUGHTS TO ALTERNATIVE FORMS OF PUNISHMENT AS WE UPDATE OUR LAWS. AS THAT CLEARLY FALLS WITHIN YOUR PURVIEW.
AND DO CLOSE THE DOOR ON YOUR WAY OUT.

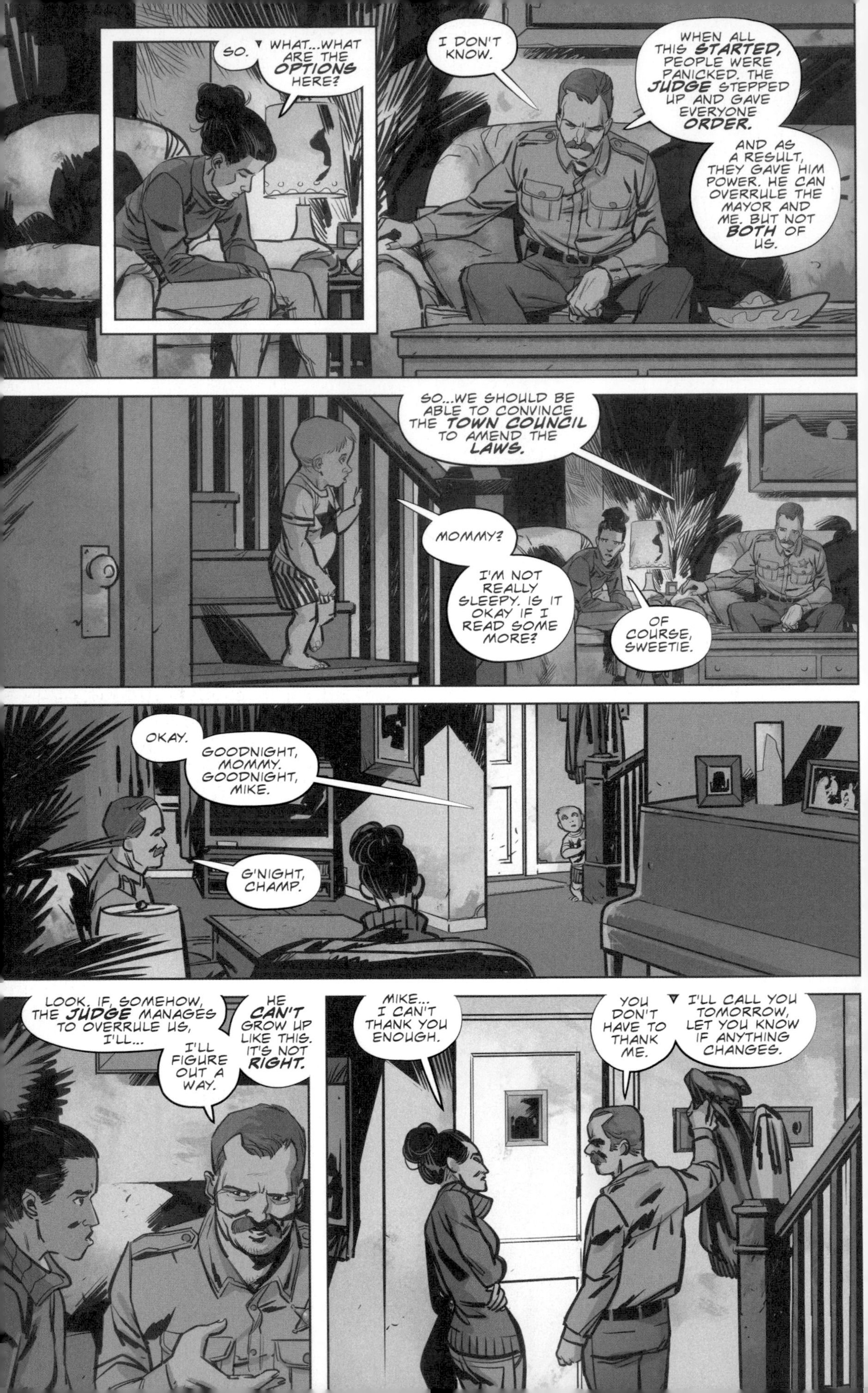
SO.
WHAT...WHAT ARE THE OPTIONS HERE?
I DON'T KNOW.
WHEN ALL THIS STARTED, PEOPLE WERE PANICKED. THE JUDGE STEPPED UP AND GAVE EVERYONE ORDER.
AND AS A RESULT, THEY GAVE HIM POWER. HE CAN OVERRULE THE MAYOR AND ME. BUT NOT BOTH OF US.
SO...WE SHOULD BE ABLE TO CONVINCE THE TOWN COUNCIL TO AMEND THE LAWS.
MOMMY?
I'M NOT REALLY SLEEPY. IS IT OKAY IF I READ SOME MORE?
OF COURSE, SWEETIE.
OKAY.
GOODNIGHT, MOMMY. GOODNIGHT, MIKE.
G'NIGHT, CHAMP.
LOOK. IF, SOMEHOW, THE JUDGE MANAGES TO OVERRULE US, I'LL...
I'LL FIGURE OUT A WAY.
HE CAN'T GROW UP LIKE THIS. IT'S NOT RIGHT.
MIKE... I CAN'T THANK YOU ENOUGH.
YOU DON'T HAVE TO THANK ME.
I'LL CALL YOU TOMORROW, LET YOU KNOW IF ANYTHING CHANGES.

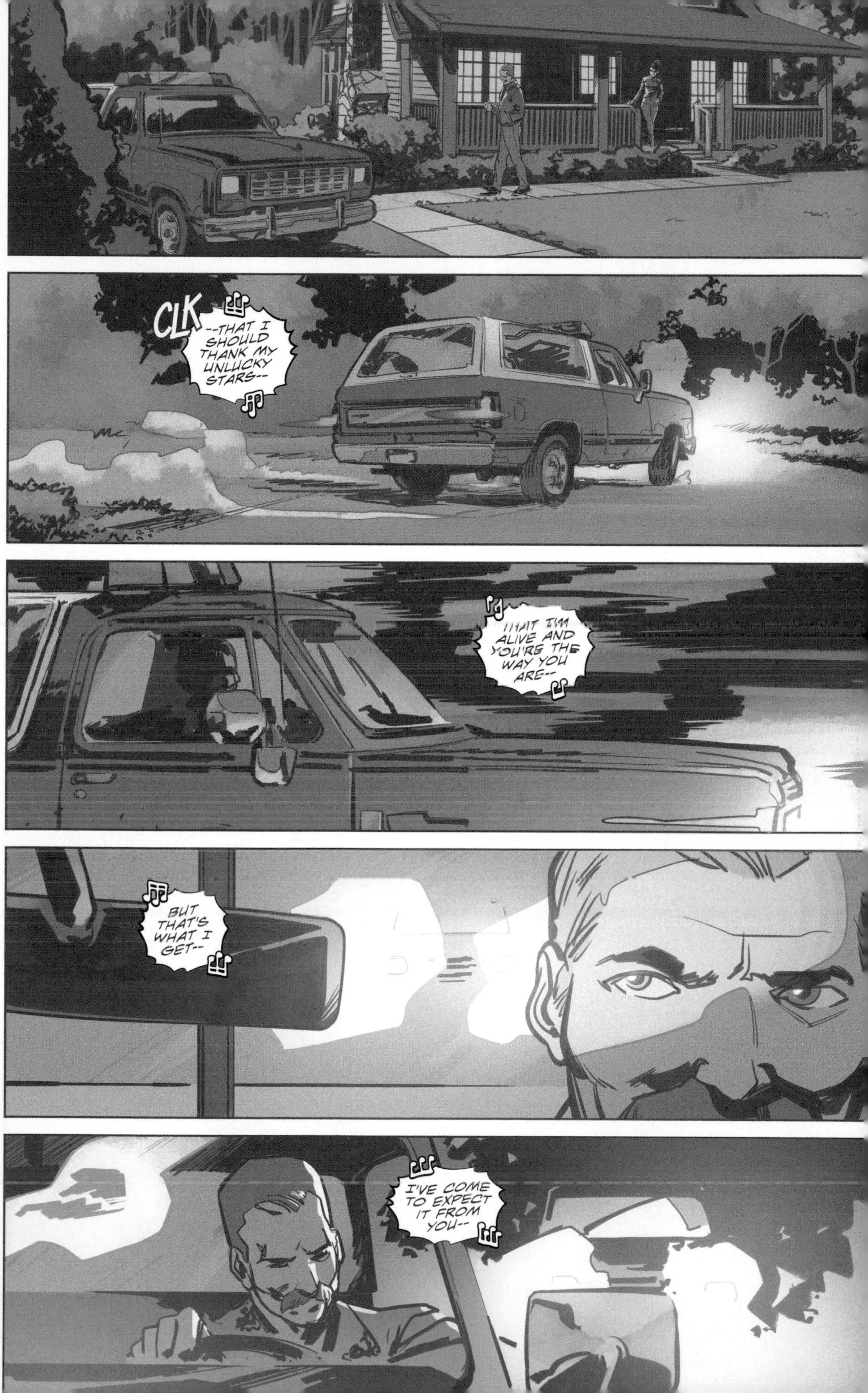
CLK
--THAT I SHOULD THANK MY UNLUCKY STARS--
THAT I'M ALIVE AND YOU'RE THE WAY YOU ARE--
BUT THAT'S WHAT I GET--
I'VE COME TO EXPECT IT FROM YOU--

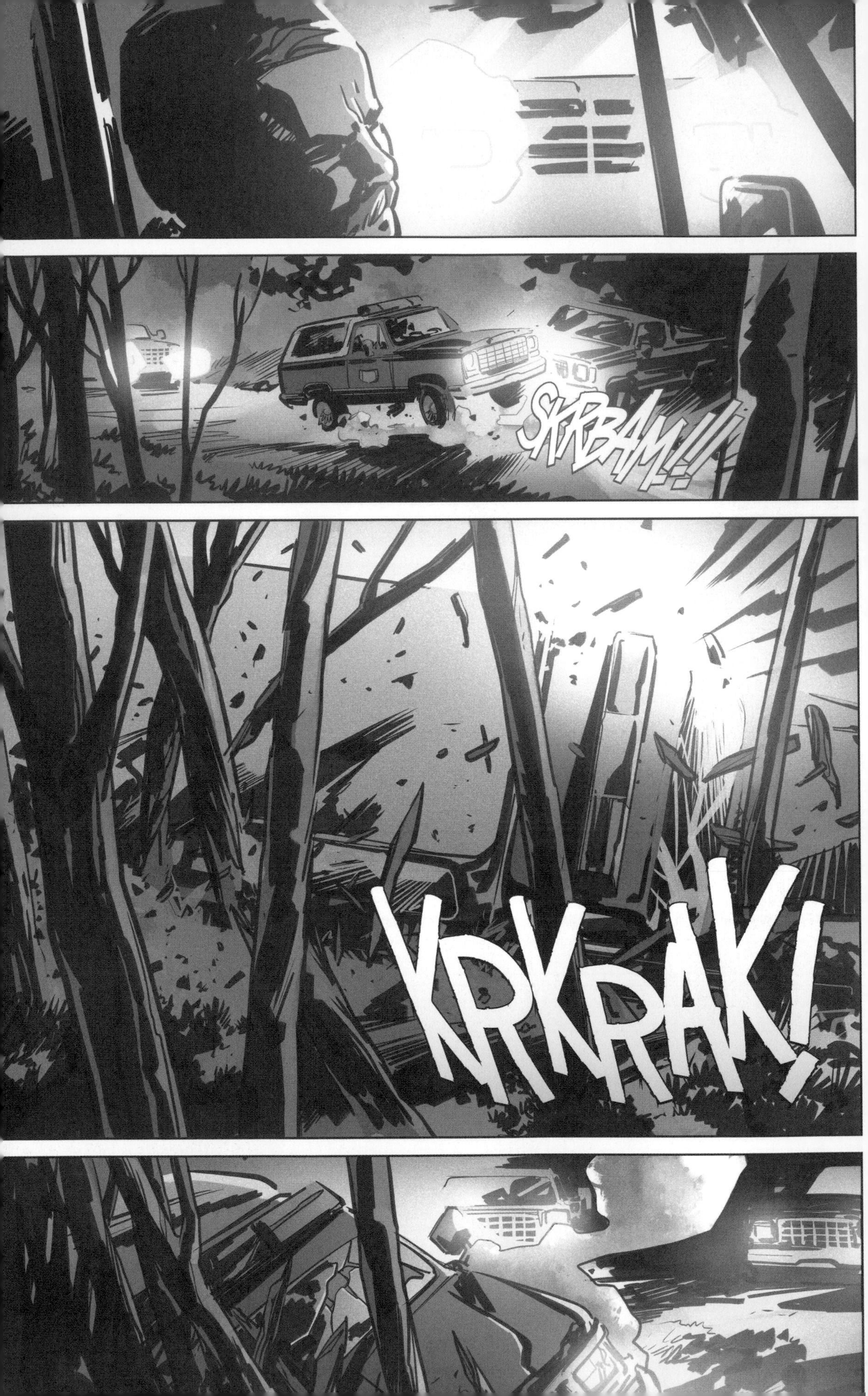
SKRBAM!!
KRKRAK!

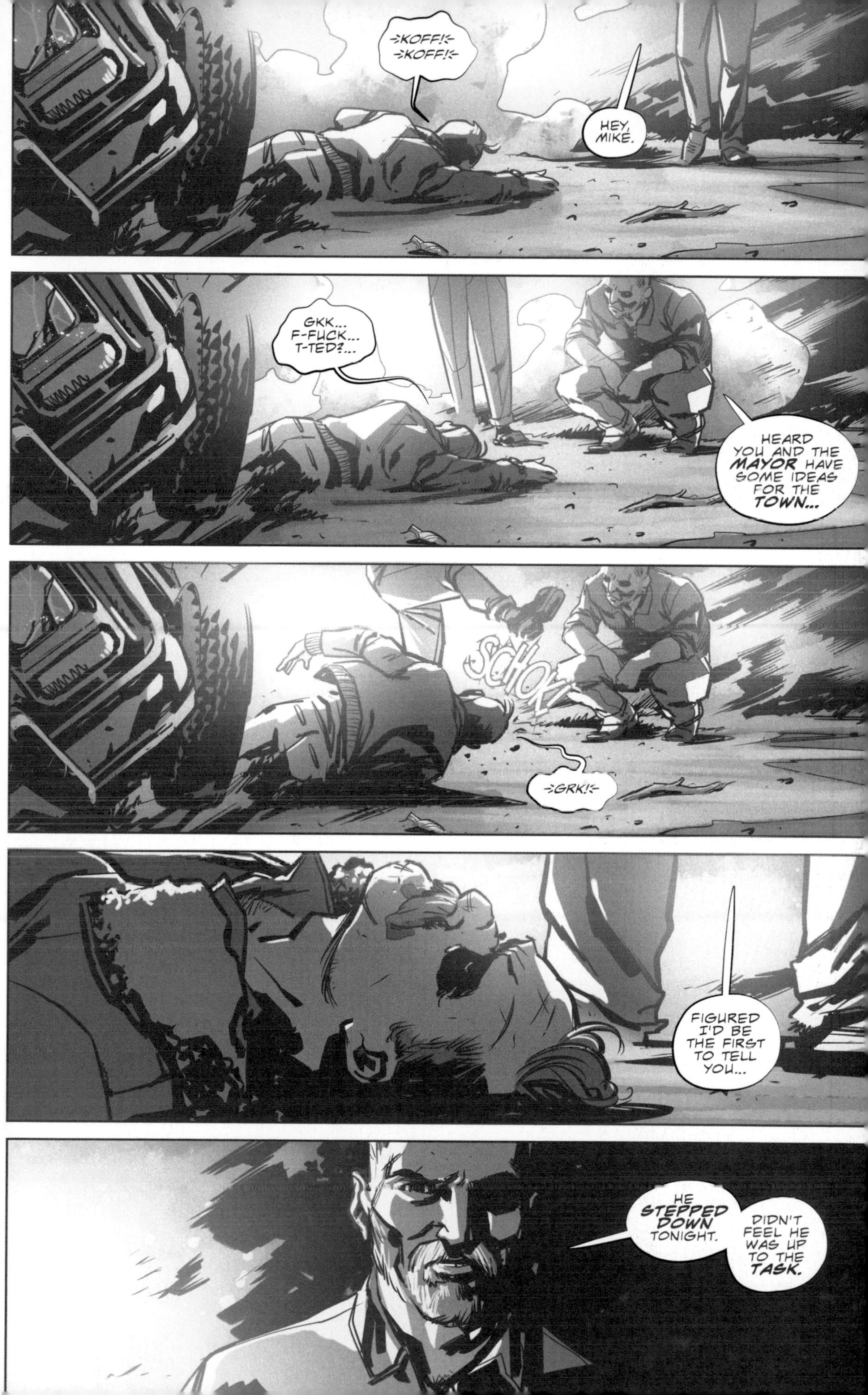

-KOFF!- -KOFF!-
HEY, MIKE.
GKK... F-FUCK... T-TED?...
HEARD YOU AND THE MAYOR HAVE SOME IDEAS FOR THE TOWN...
SCHOK!
-GRK!-
FIGURED I'D BE THE FIRST TO TELL YOU...
HE STEPPED DOWN TONIGHT.
DIDN'T FEEL HE WAS UP TO THE TASK.

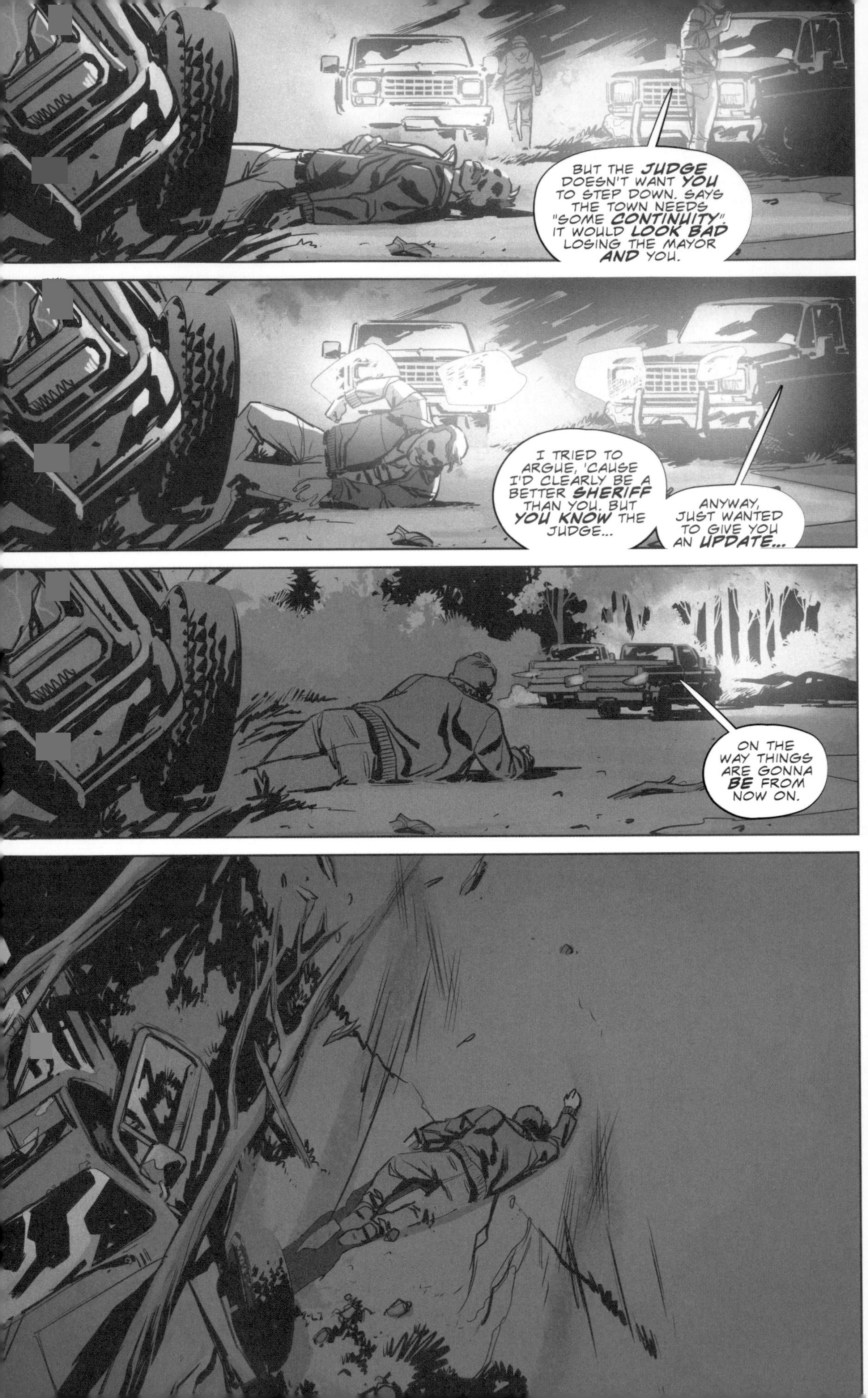
BUT THE JUDGE DOESN'T WANT YOU TO STEP DOWN. SAYS THE TOWN NEEDS "SOME CONTINUITY". IT WOULD LOOK BAD LOSING THE MAYOR AND YOU.
I TRIED TO ARGUE, 'CAUSE I'D CLEARLY BE A BETTER SHERIFF THAN YOU. BUT YOU KNOW THE JUDGE...
ANYWAY, JUST WANTED TO GIVE YOU AN UPDATE...
ON THE WAY THINGS ARE GONNA BE FROM NOW ON.

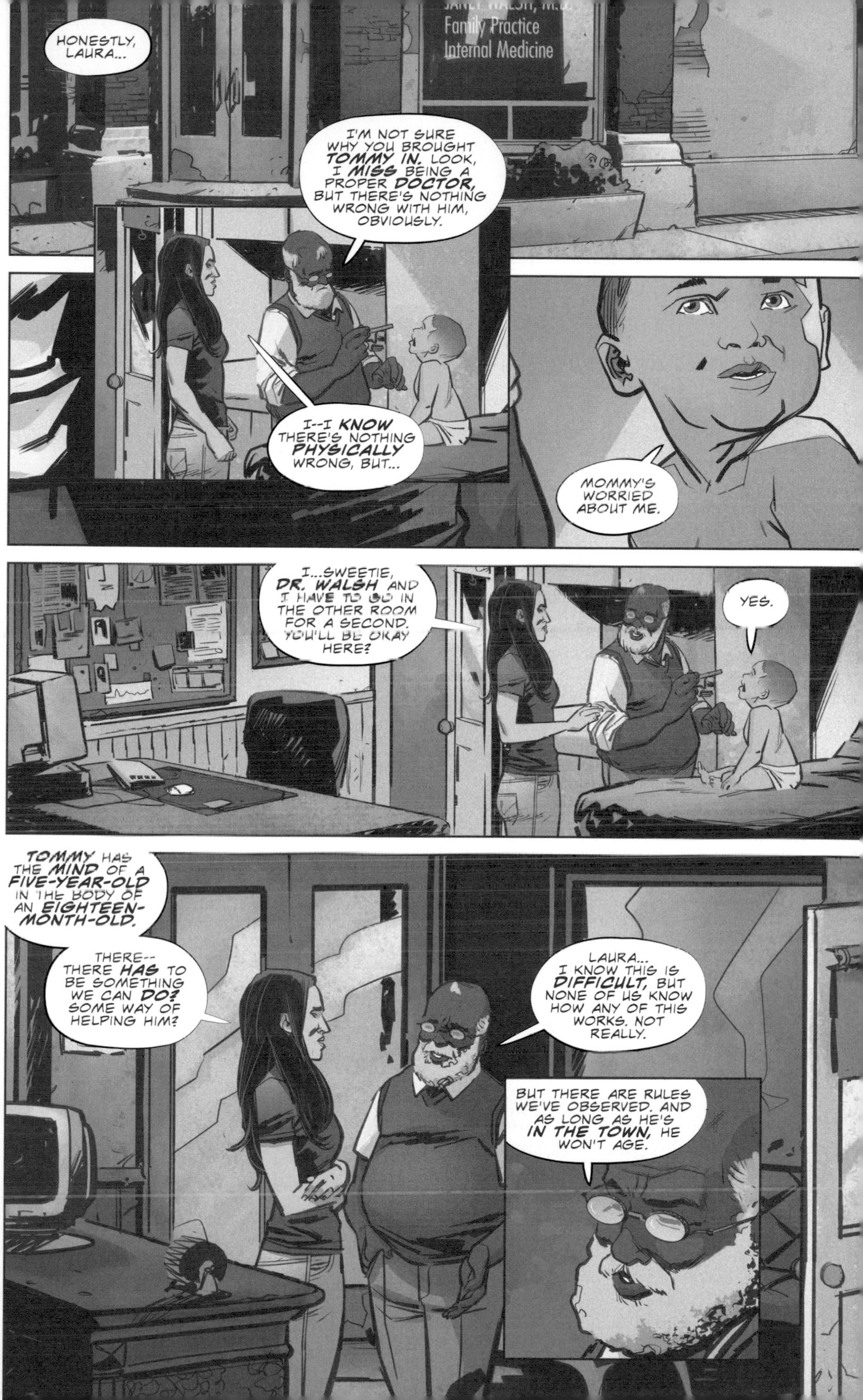
JANET WALSH, M.D.
Family Practice
Internal Medicine
HONESTLY, LAURA...
I'M NOT SURE WHY YOU BROUGHT TOMMY IN. LOOK, I MISS BEING A PROPER DOCTOR, BUT THERE'S NOTHING WRONG WITH HIM, OBVIOUSLY.
I--I KNOW THERE'S NOTHING PHYSICALLY WRONG, BUT...
MOMMY'S WORRIED ABOUT ME.
I...SWEETIE, DR. WALSH AND I HAVE TO GO IN THE OTHER ROOM FOR A SECOND. YOU'LL BE OKAY HERE?
YES.
TOMMY HAS THE MIND OF A FIVE-YEAR-OLD IN THE BODY OF AN EIGHTEEN-MONTH-OLD.
THERE--THERE HAS TO BE SOMETHING WE CAN DO? SOME WAY OF HELPING HIM?
LAURA... I KNOW THIS IS DIFFICULT, BUT NONE OF US KNOW HOW ANY OF THIS WORKS. NOT REALLY.
BUT THERE ARE RULES WE'VE OBSERVED. AND AS LONG AS HE'S IN THE TOWN, HE WON'T AGE.

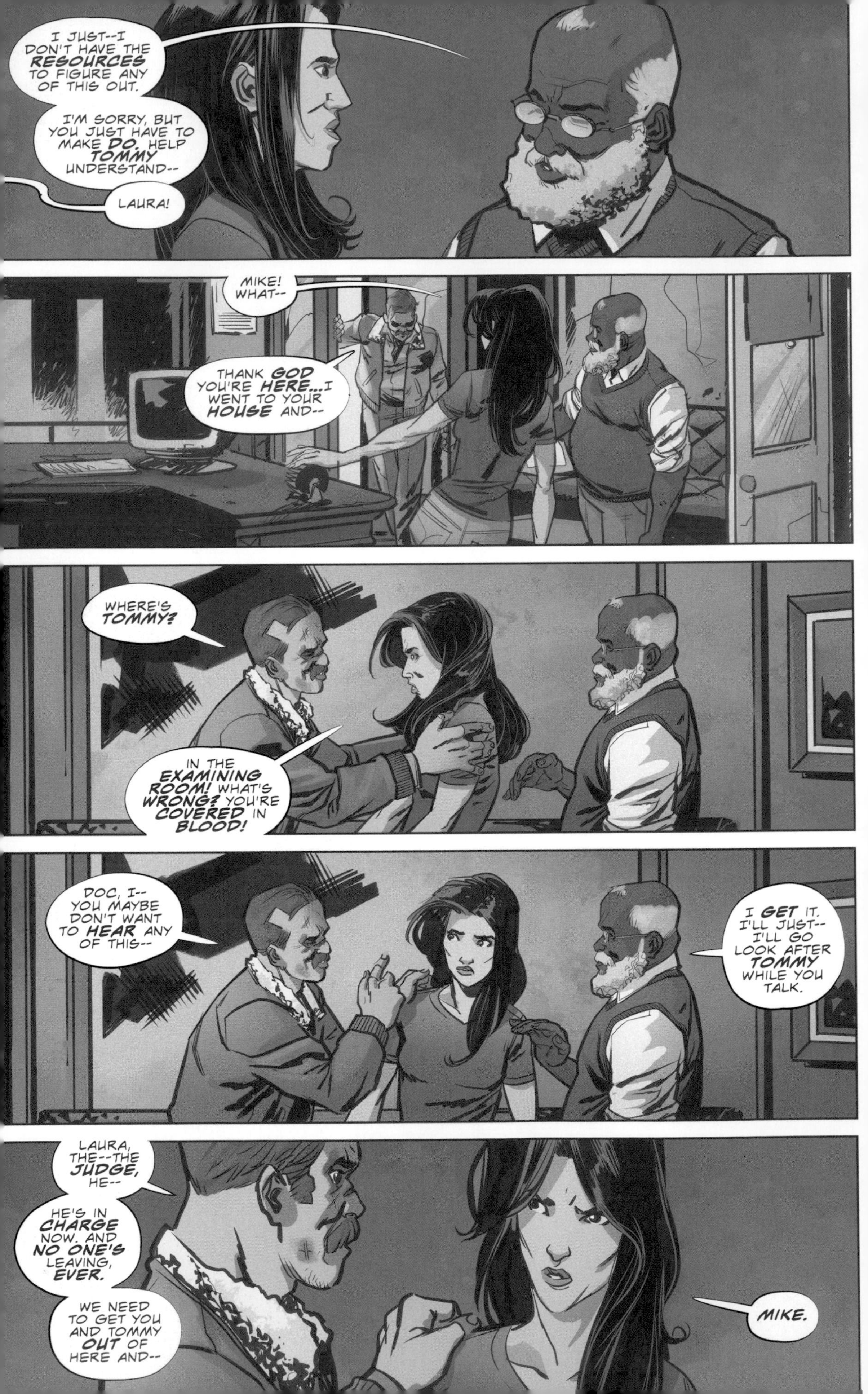
I JUST--I DON'T HAVE THE RESOURCES TO FIGURE ANY OF THIS OUT.
I'M SORRY, BUT YOU JUST HAVE TO MAKE DO. HELP TOMMY UNDERSTAND--
LAURA!
MIKE! WHAT--
THANK GOD YOU'RE HERE...I WENT TO YOUR HOUSE AND--
WHERE'S TOMMY?
IN THE EXAMINING ROOM! WHAT'S WRONG? YOU'RE COVERED IN BLOOD!
DOC, I-- YOU MAYBE DON'T WANT TO HEAR ANY OF THIS--
I GET IT. I'LL JUST-- I'LL GO LOOK AFTER TOMMY WHILE YOU TALK.
LAURA, THE--THE JUDGE, HE--
HE'S IN CHARGE NOW. AND NO ONE'S LEAVING, EVER.
WE NEED TO GET YOU AND TOMMY OUT OF HERE AND--
MIKE.

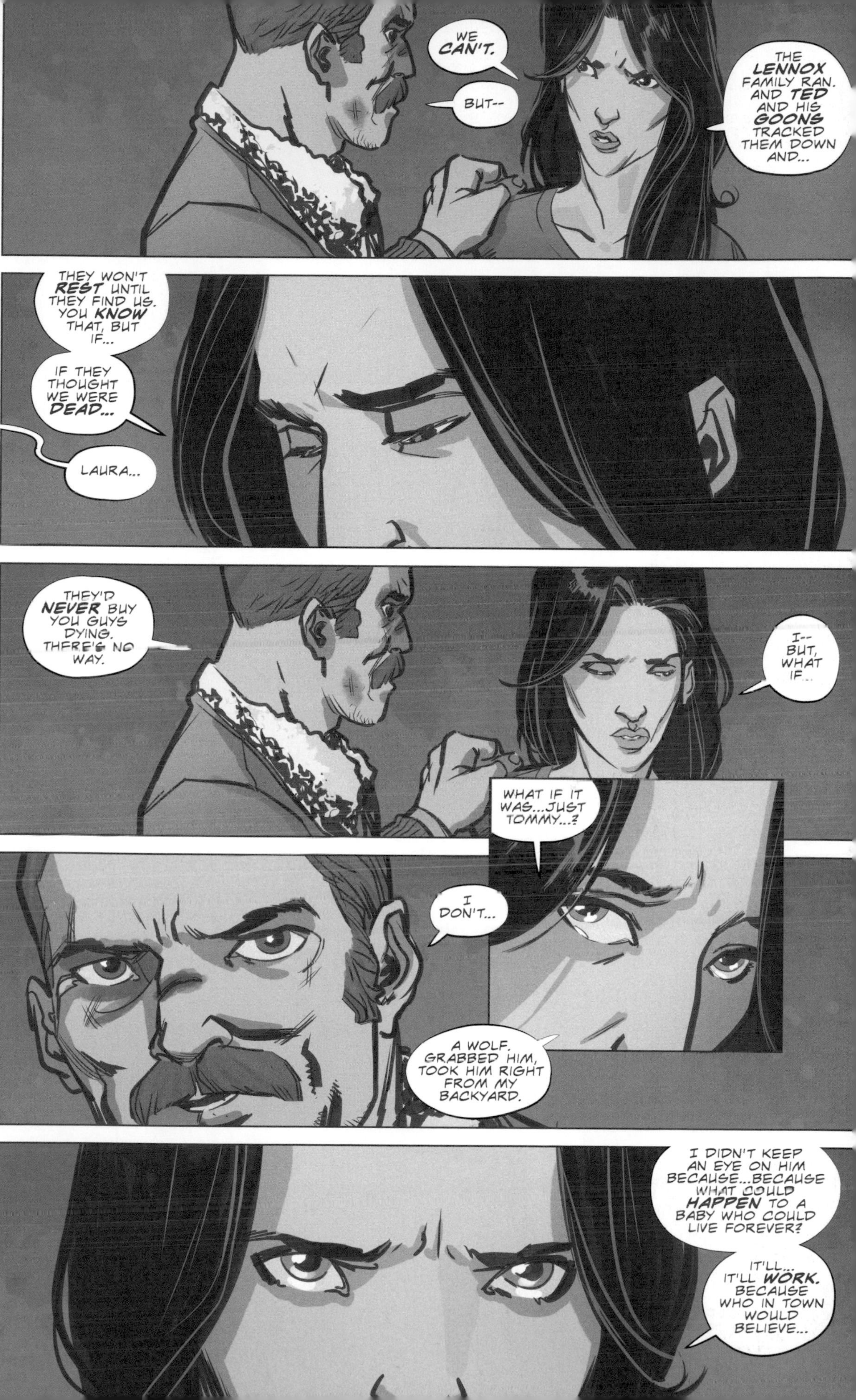
WE CAN'T.
BUT--
THE LENNOX FAMILY RAN. AND TED AND HIS GOONS TRACKED THEM DOWN AND...
THEY WON'T REST UNTIL THEY FIND US. YOU KNOW THAT, BUT IF...
IF THEY THOUGHT WE WERE DEAD...
LAURA...
THEY'D NEVER BUY YOU GUYS DYING. THERE'S NO WAY.
I-- BUT, WHAT IF...
WHAT IF IT WAS...JUST TOMMY...?
I DON'T...
A WOLF. GRABBED HIM, TOOK HIM RIGHT FROM MY BACKYARD.
I DIDN'T KEEP AN EYE ON HIM BECAUSE...BECAUSE WHAT COULD HAPPEN TO A BABY WHO COULD LIVE FOREVER?
IT'LL... IT'LL WORK. BECAUSE WHO IN TOWN WOULD BELIEVE...

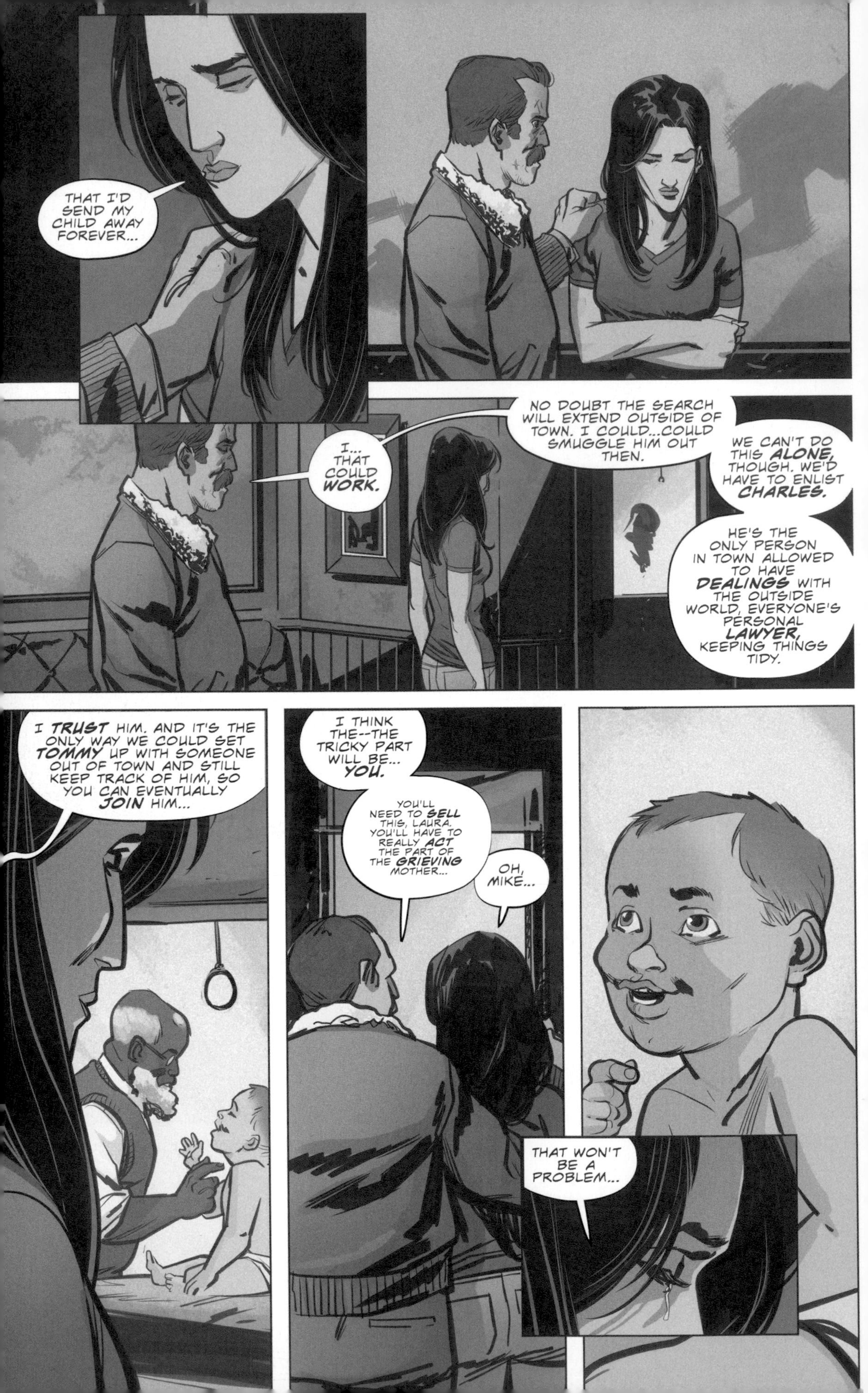
THAT I'D SEND MY CHILD AWAY FOREVER...
I... THAT COULD WORK.
NO DOUBT THE SEARCH WILL EXTEND OUTSIDE OF TOWN. I COULD...COULD SMUGGLE HIM OUT THEN.
WE CAN'T DO THIS ALONE, THOUGH. WE'D HAVE TO ENLIST CHARLES.
HE'S THE ONLY PERSON IN TOWN ALLOWED TO HAVE DEALINGS WITH THE OUTSIDE WORLD, EVERYONE'S PERSONAL LAWYER, KEEPING THINGS TIDY.
I TRUST HIM. AND IT'S THE ONLY WAY WE COULD SET TOMMY UP WITH SOMEONE OUT OF TOWN AND STILL KEEP TRACK OF HIM, SO YOU CAN EVENTUALLY JOIN HIM...
I THINK THE--THE TRICKY PART WILL BE... YOU.
YOU'LL NEED TO SELL THIS, LAURA. YOU'LL HAVE TO REALLY ACT THE PART OF THE GRIEVING MOTHER...
OH, MIKE...
THAT WON'T BE A PROBLEM...

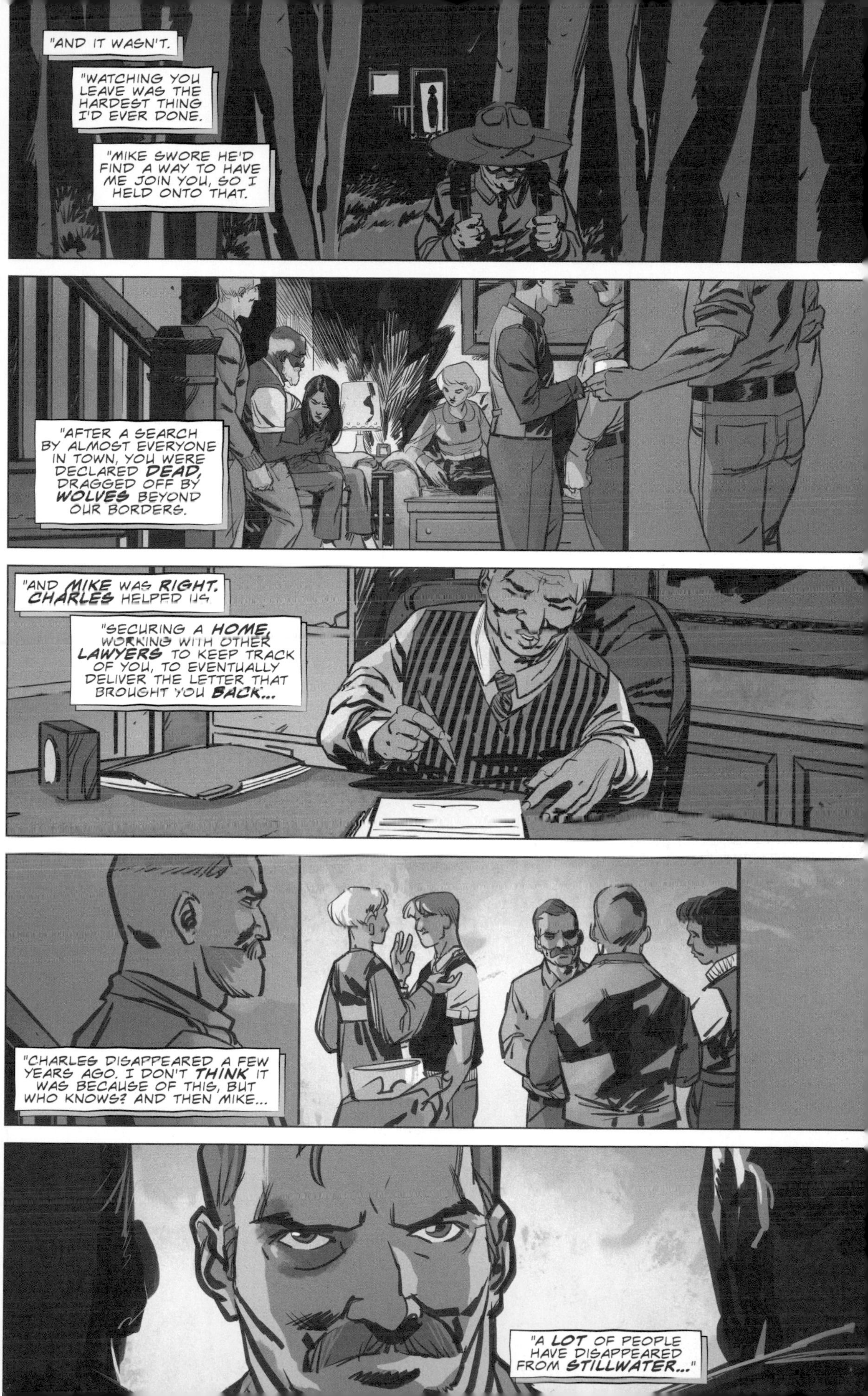
"AND IT WASN'T.
"WATCHING YOU LEAVE WAS THE HARDEST THING I'D EVER DONE.
"MIKE SWORE HE'D FIND A WAY TO HAVE ME JOIN YOU, SO I HELD ONTO THAT.
"AFTER A SEARCH BY ALMOST EVERYONE IN TOWN, YOU WERE DECLARED DEAD, DRAGGED OFF BY WOLVES BEYOND OUR BORDERS.
"AND MIKE WAS RIGHT. CHARLES HELPED US
"SECURING A HOME, WORKING WITH OTHER LAWYERS TO KEEP TRACK OF YOU, TO EVENTUALLY DELIVER THE LETTER THAT BROUGHT YOU BACK...
"CHARLES DISAPPEARED A FEW YEARS AGO. I DON'T THINK IT WAS BECAUSE OF THIS, BUT WHO KNOWS? AND THEN MIKE...
"A LOT OF PEOPLE HAVE DISAPPEARED FROM STILLWATER..."

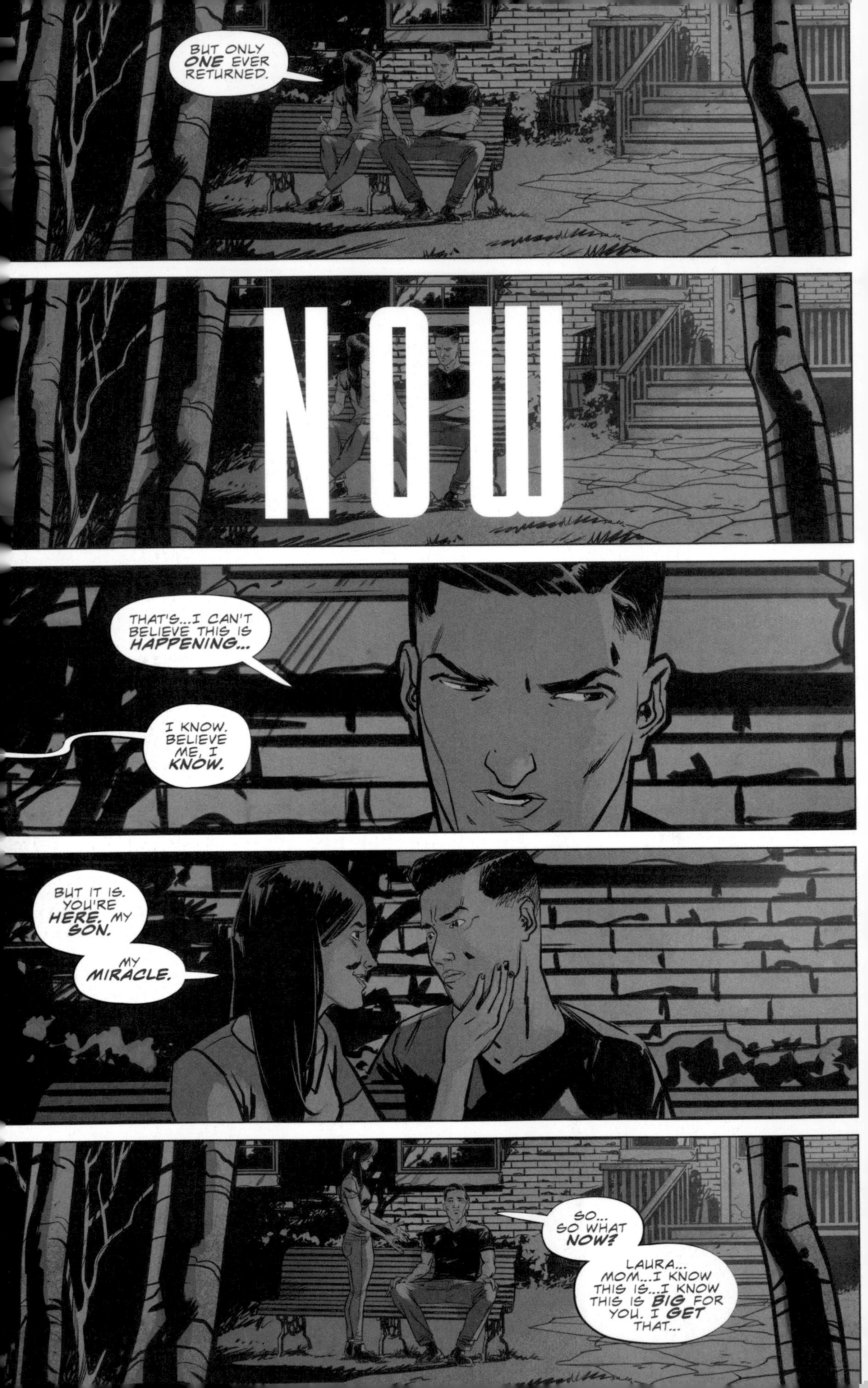
BUT ONLY ONE EVER RETURNED.
NOW
THAT'S...I CAN'T BELIEVE THIS IS HAPPENING...
I KNOW. BELIEVE ME, I KNOW.
BUT IT IS. YOU'RE HERE. MY SON.
MY MIRACLE.
SO... SO WHAT NOW?
LAURA... MOM...I KNOW THIS IS...I KNOW THIS IS BIG FOR YOU. I GET THAT...

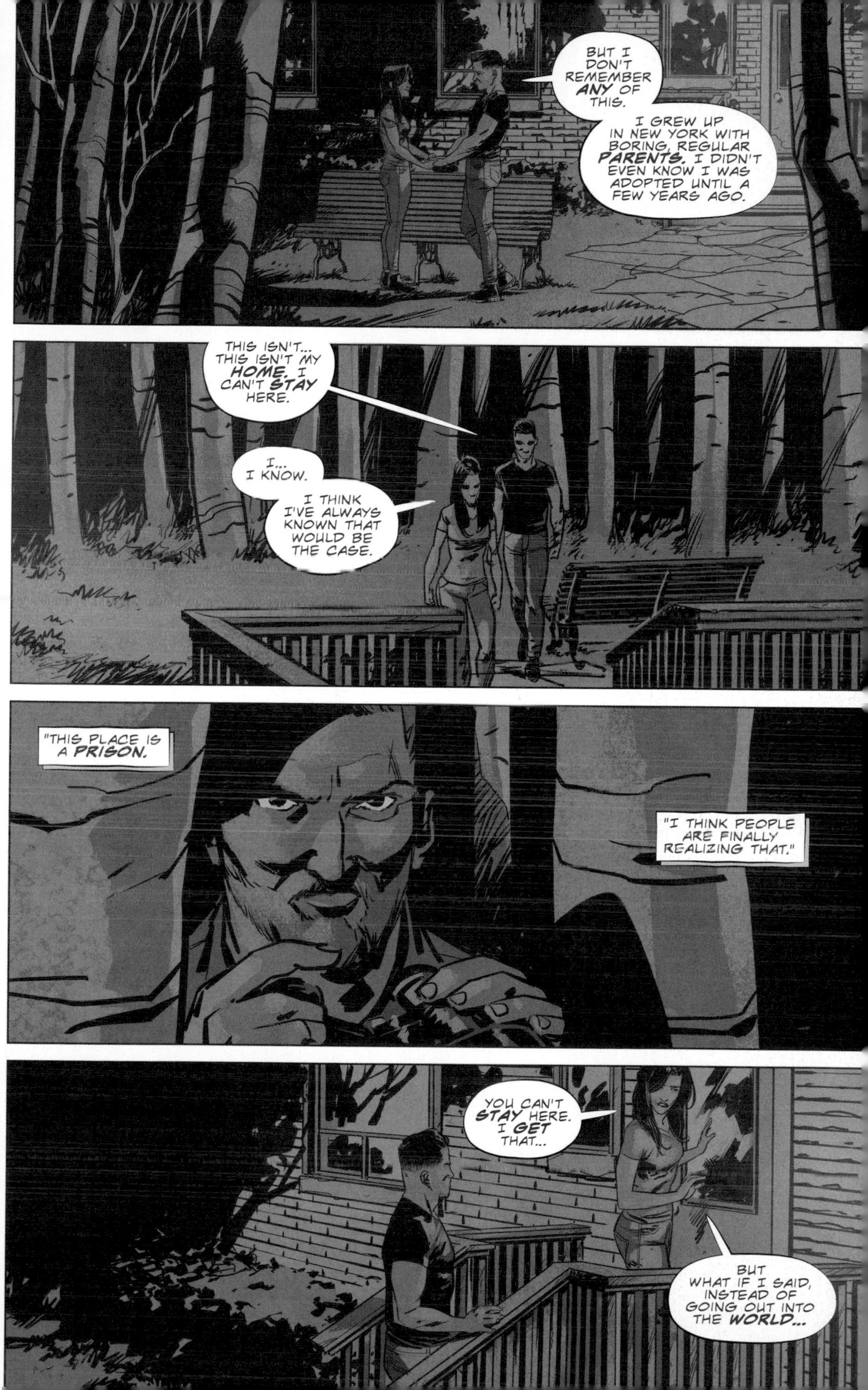
BUT I DON'T REMEMBER ANY OF THIS.
I GREW UP IN NEW YORK WITH BORING, REGULAR PARENTS. I DIDN'T EVEN KNOW I WAS ADOPTED UNTIL A FEW YEARS AGO.
THIS ISN'T... THIS ISN'T MY HOME. I CAN'T STAY HERE.
I... I KNOW.
I THINK I'VE ALWAYS KNOWN THAT WOULD BE THE CASE.
"THIS PLACE IS A PRISON.
"I THINK PEOPLE ARE FINALLY REALIZING THAT."
YOU CAN'T STAY HERE. I GET THAT...
BUT WHAT IF I SAID, INSTEAD OF GOING OUT INTO THE WORLD...

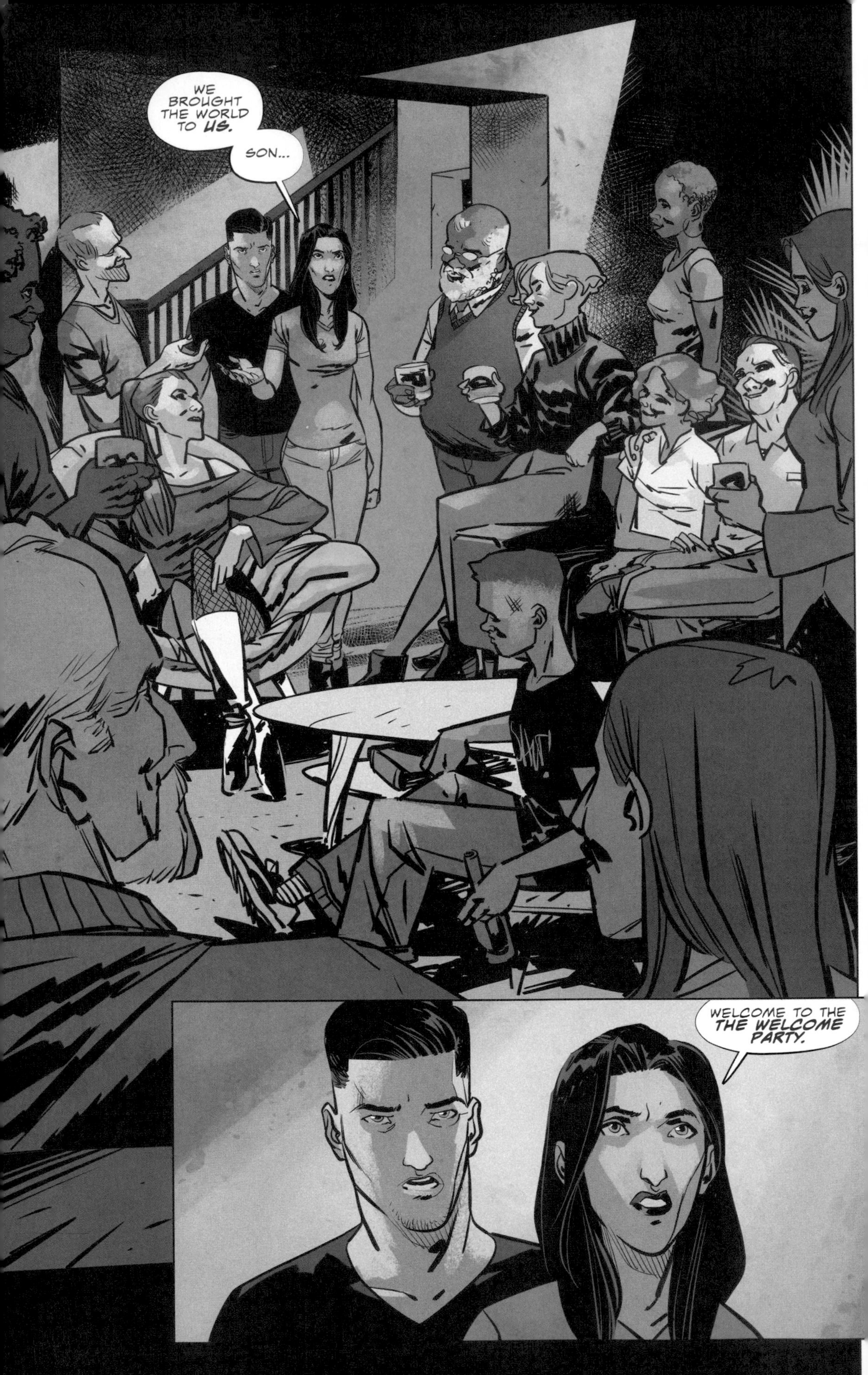
WE BROUGHT THE WORLD TO US.
SON...
WELCOME TO THE THE WELCOME PARTY.

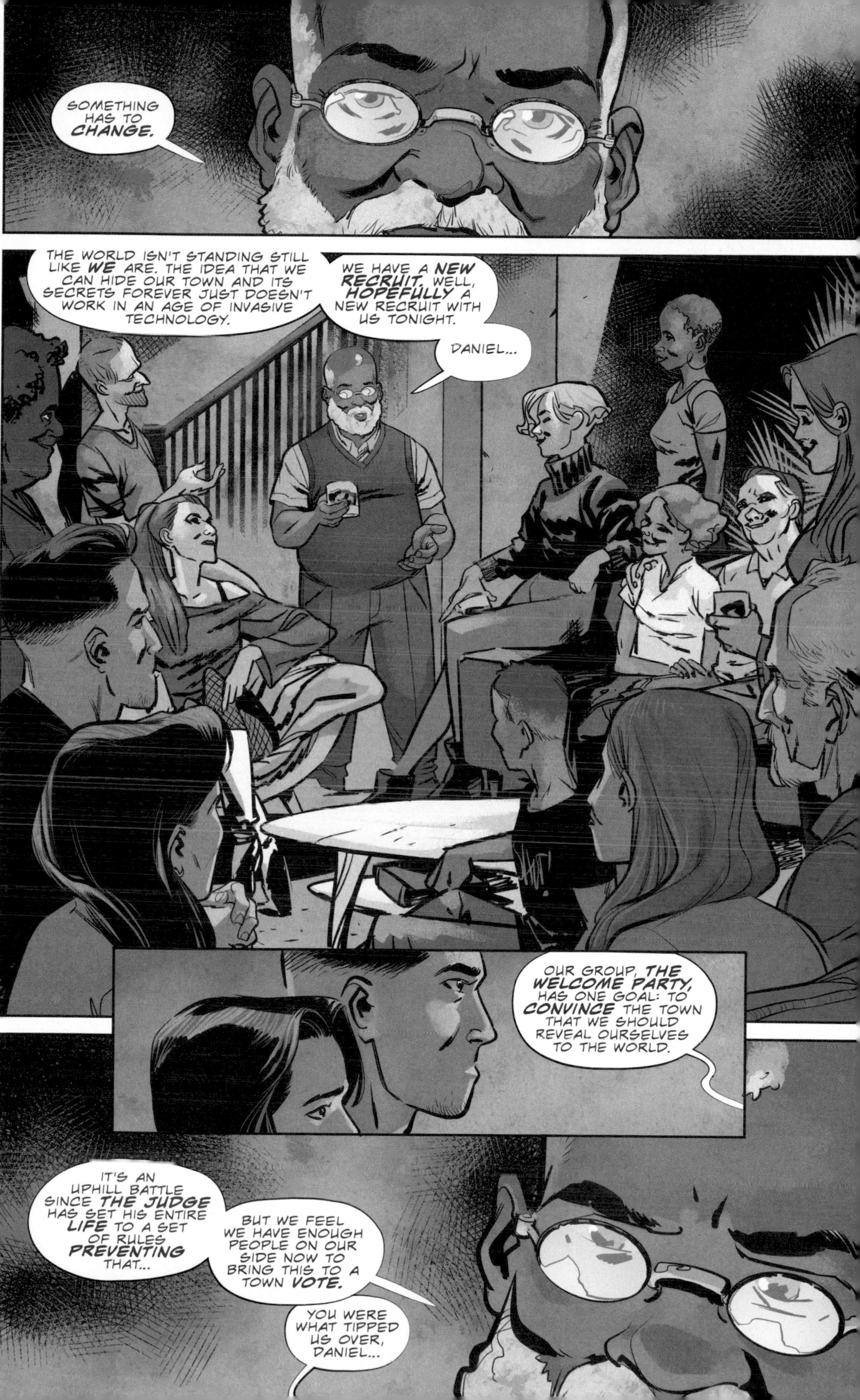
SOMETHING HAS TO **CHANGE.**
THE WORLD ISN'T STANDING STILL LIKE **WE** ARE. THE IDEA THAT WE CAN HIDE OUR TOWN AND ITS SECRETS FOREVER JUST DOESN'T WORK IN AN AGE OF INVASIVE TECHNOLOGY.
WE HAVE A **NEW RECRUIT.** WELL, **HOPEFULLY** A NEW RECRUIT WITH US TONIGHT.
DANIEL...
OUR GROUP, **THE WELCOME PARTY,** HAS ONE GOAL: TO **CONVINCE** THE TOWN THAT WE SHOULD REVEAL OURSELVES TO THE WORLD.
IT'S AN UPHILL BATTLE SINCE **THE JUDGE** HAS SET HIS ENTIRE **LIFE** TO A SET OF RULES **PREVENTING** THAT...
BUT WE FEEL WE HAVE ENOUGH PEOPLE ON OUR SIDE NOW TO BRING THIS TO A TOWN **VOTE.**
YOU WERE WHAT TIPPED US OVER, DANIEL...

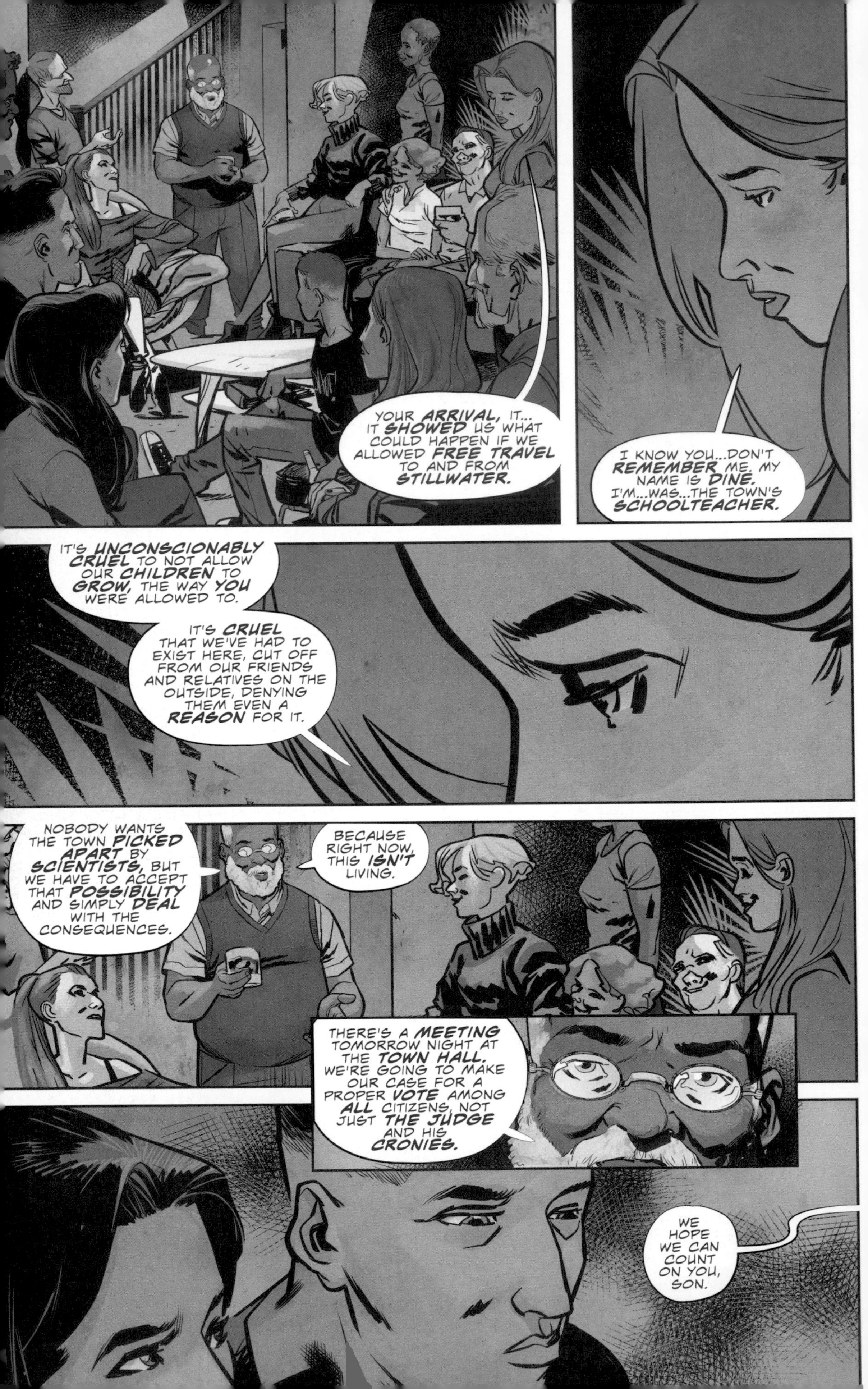
YOUR ARRIVAL, IT... IT SHOWED US WHAT COULD HAPPEN IF WE ALLOWED FREE TRAVEL TO AND FROM STILLWATER.
I KNOW YOU...DON'T REMEMBER ME. MY NAME IS DINE. I'M...WAS...THE TOWN'S SCHOOLTEACHER.
IT'S UNCONSCIONABLY CRUEL TO NOT ALLOW OUR CHILDREN TO GROW, THE WAY YOU WERE ALLOWED TO.
IT'S CRUEL THAT WE'VE HAD TO EXIST HERE, CUT OFF FROM OUR FRIENDS AND RELATIVES ON THE OUTSIDE, DENYING THEM EVEN A REASON FOR IT.
NOBODY WANTS THE TOWN PICKED APART BY SCIENTISTS, BUT WE HAVE TO ACCEPT THAT POSSIBILITY AND SIMPLY DEAL WITH THE CONSEQUENCES.
BECAUSE RIGHT NOW, THIS ISN'T LIVING.
THERE'S A MEETING TOMORROW NIGHT AT THE TOWN HALL. WE'RE GOING TO MAKE OUR CASE FOR A PROPER VOTE AMONG ALL CITIZENS, NOT JUST THE JUDGE AND HIS CRONIES.
WE HOPE WE CAN COUNT ON YOU, SON.

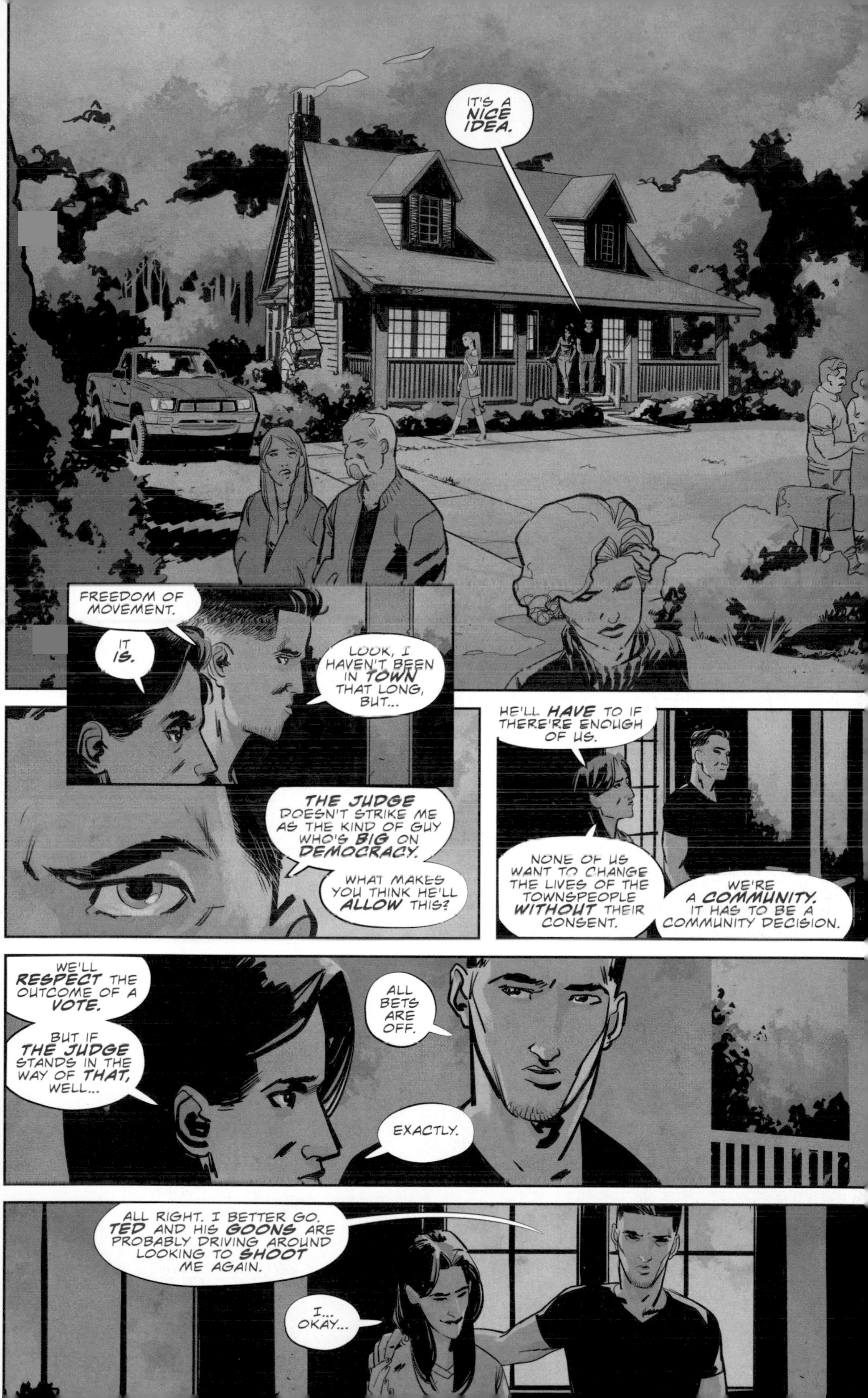
IT'S A NICE IDEA.
FREEDOM OF MOVEMENT.
IT IS.
LOOK, I HAVEN'T BEEN IN TOWN THAT LONG, BUT...
THE JUDGE DOESN'T STRIKE ME AS THE KIND OF GUY WHO'S BIG ON DEMOCRACY.
WHAT MAKES YOU THINK HE'LL ALLOW THIS?
HE'LL HAVE TO IF THERE'RE ENOUGH OF US.
NONE OF US WANT TO CHANGE THE LIVES OF THE TOWNSPEOPLE WITHOUT THEIR CONSENT.
WE'RE A COMMUNITY. IT HAS TO BE A COMMUNITY DECISION.
WE'LL RESPECT THE OUTCOME OF A VOTE.
BUT IF THE JUDGE STANDS IN THE WAY OF THAT, WELL...
ALL BETS ARE OFF.
EXACTLY.
ALL RIGHT. I BETTER GO. TED AND HIS GOONS ARE PROBABLY DRIVING AROUND LOOKING TO SHOOT ME AGAIN.
I... OKAY...

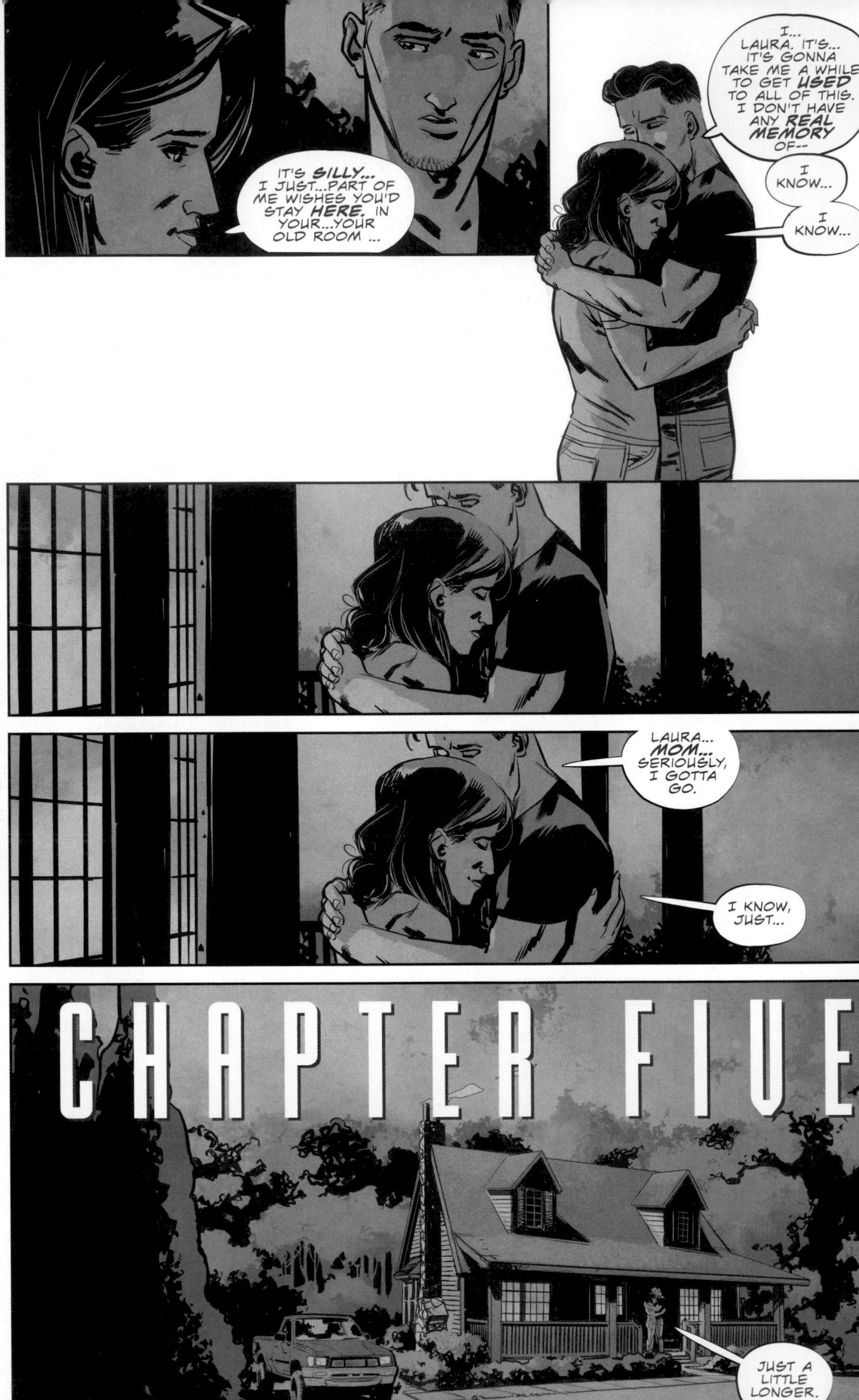
IT'S SILLY... I JUST...PART OF ME WISHES YOU'D STAY HERE. IN YOUR...YOUR OLD ROOM ...
I... LAURA. IT'S... IT'S GONNA TAKE ME A WHILE TO GET USED TO ALL OF THIS. I DON'T HAVE ANY REAL MEMORY OF--
I KNOW...
I KNOW...
LAURA... MOM... SERIOUSLY, I GOTTA GO.
I KNOW, JUST...
CHAPTER FIVE
JUST A LITTLE LONGER.

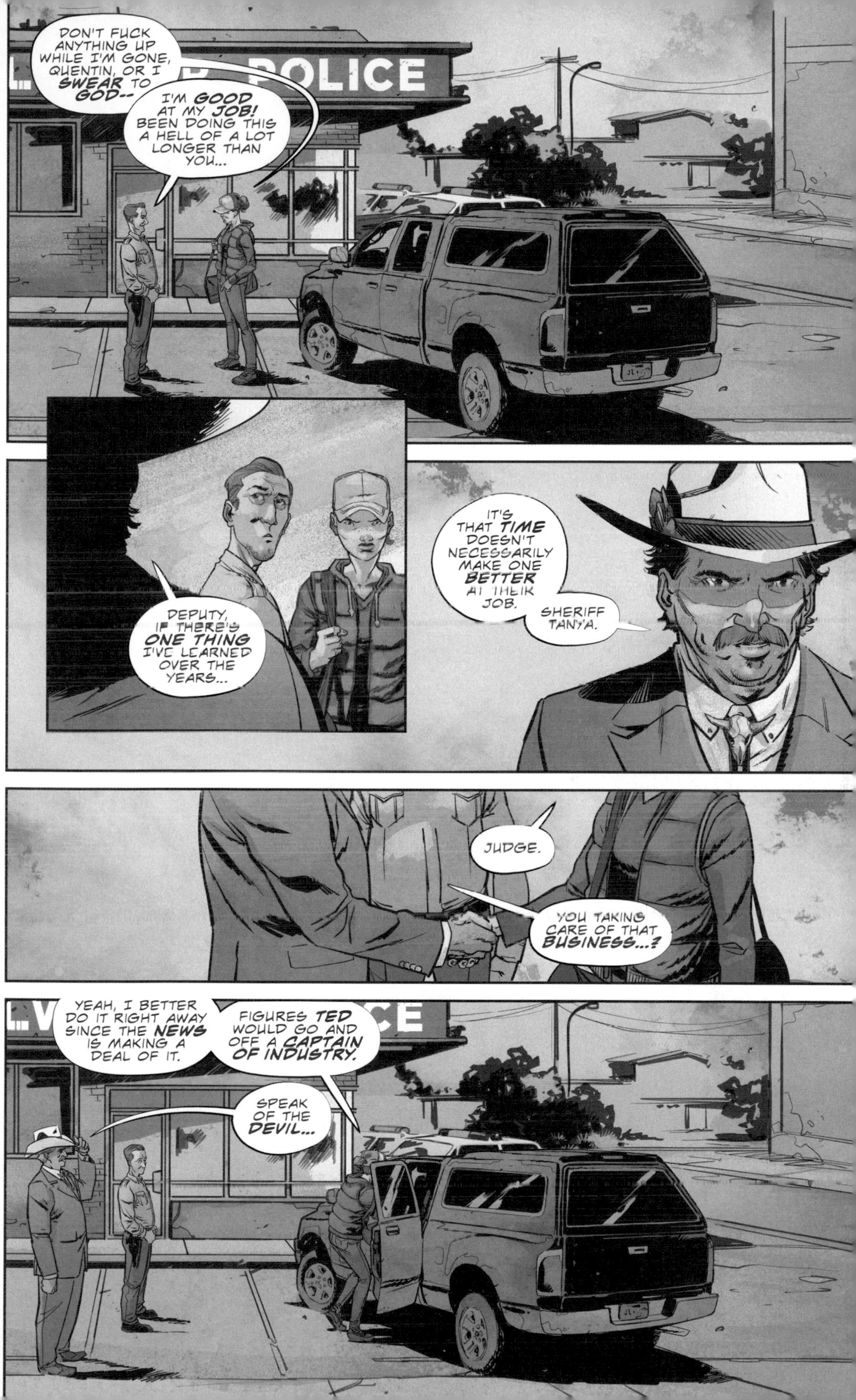
POLICE
DON'T FUCK ANYTHING UP WHILE I'M GONE, QUENTIN, OR I SWEAR TO GOD--
I'M GOOD AT MY JOB! BEEN DOING THIS A HELL OF A LOT LONGER THAN YOU...
DEPUTY, IF THERE'S ONE THING I'VE LEARNED OVER THE YEARS...
IT'S THAT TIME DOESN'T NECESSARILY MAKE ONE BETTER AT THEIR JOB.
SHERIFF TANYA.
JUDGE.
YOU TAKING CARE OF THAT BUSINESS...?
YEAH, I BETTER DO IT RIGHT AWAY SINCE THE NEWS IS MAKING A DEAL OF IT.
FIGURES TED WOULD GO AND OFF A CAPTAIN OF INDUSTRY.
SPEAK OF THE DEVIL...

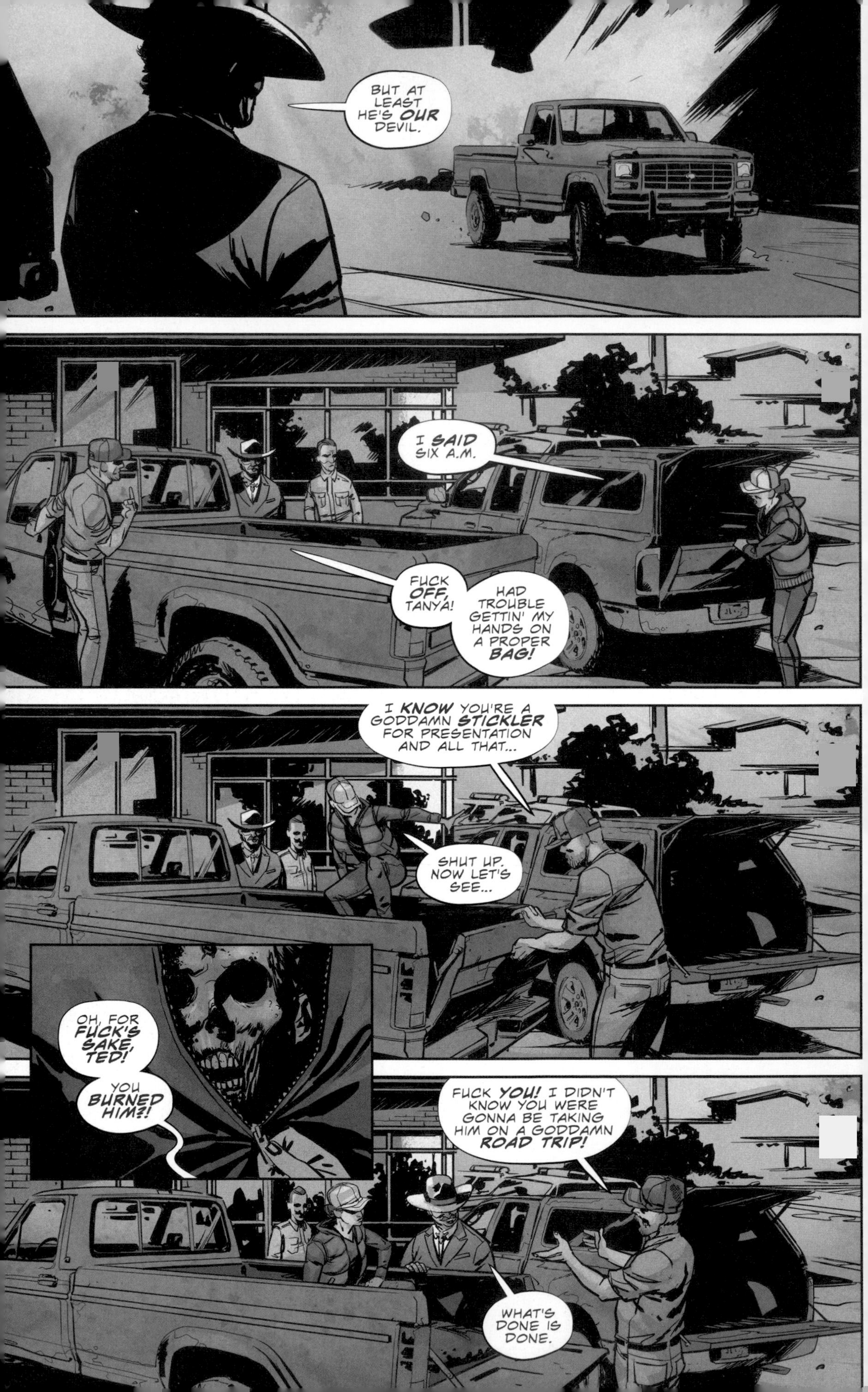
BUT AT LEAST HE'S OUR DEVIL.
I SAID SIX A.M.
FUCK OFF, TANYA!
HAD TROUBLE GETTIN' MY HANDS ON A PROPER BAG!
I KNOW YOU'RE A GODDAMN STICKLER FOR PRESENTATION AND ALL THAT...
SHUT UP. NOW LET'S SEE...
OH, FOR FUCK'S SAKE, TED!
YOU BURNED HIM?!
FUCK YOU! I DIDN'T KNOW YOU WERE GONNA BE TAKING HIM ON A GODDAMN ROAD TRIP!
WHAT'S DONE IS DONE.

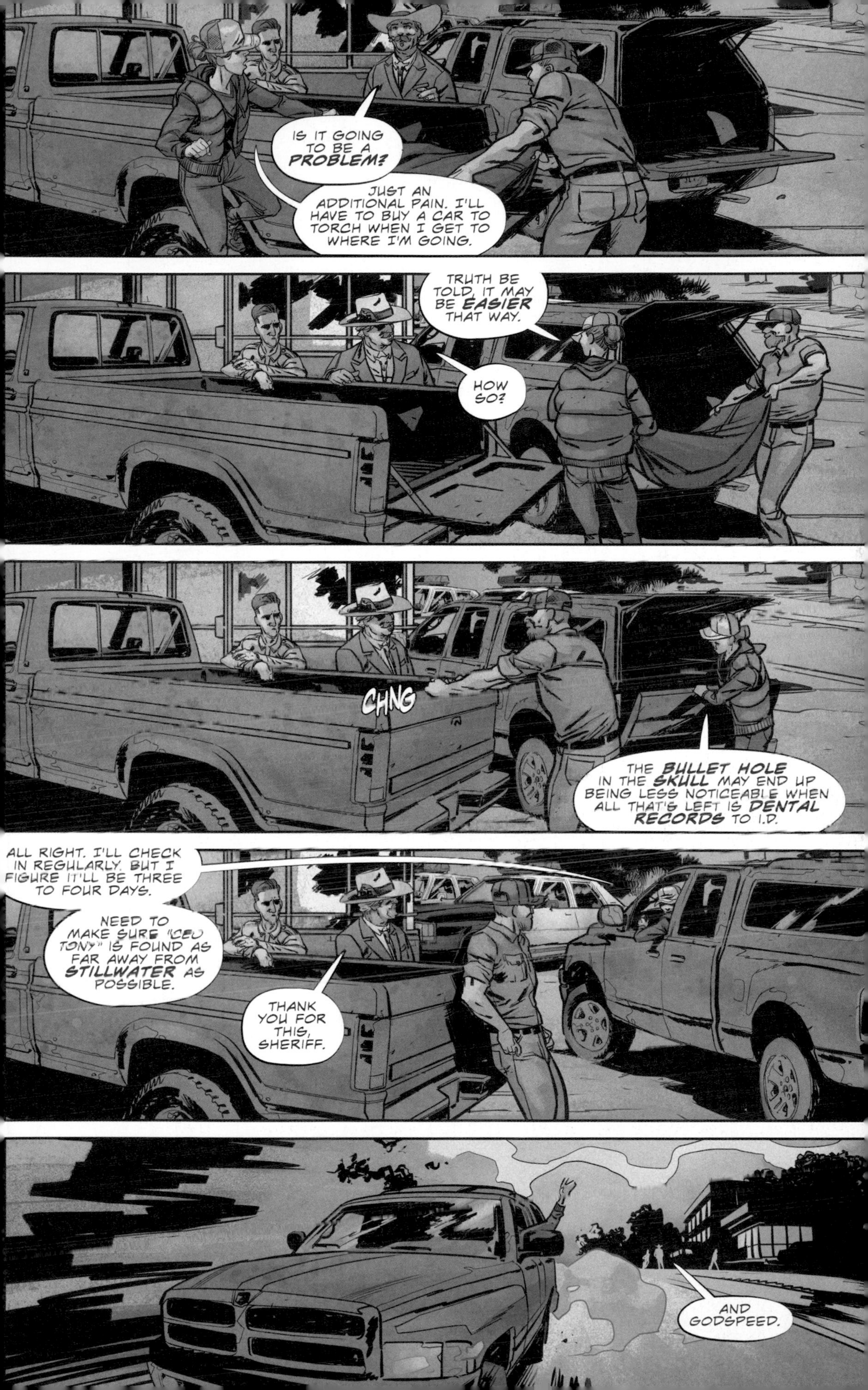
IS IT GOING TO BE A PROBLEM?
JUST AN ADDITIONAL PAIN. I'LL HAVE TO BUY A CAR TO TORCH WHEN I GET TO WHERE I'M GOING.
TRUTH BE TOLD, IT MAY BE EASIER THAT WAY.
HOW SO?
CHNG
THE BULLET HOLE IN THE SKULL MAY END UP BEING LESS NOTICEABLE WHEN ALL THAT'S LEFT IS DENTAL RECORDS TO I.D.
ALL RIGHT. I'LL CHECK IN REGULARLY. BUT I FIGURE IT'LL BE THREE TO FOUR DAYS.
NEED TO MAKE SURE "CEO TONY" IS FOUND AS FAR AWAY FROM STILLWATER AS POSSIBLE.
THANK YOU FOR THIS, SHERIFF.
AND GODSPEED.

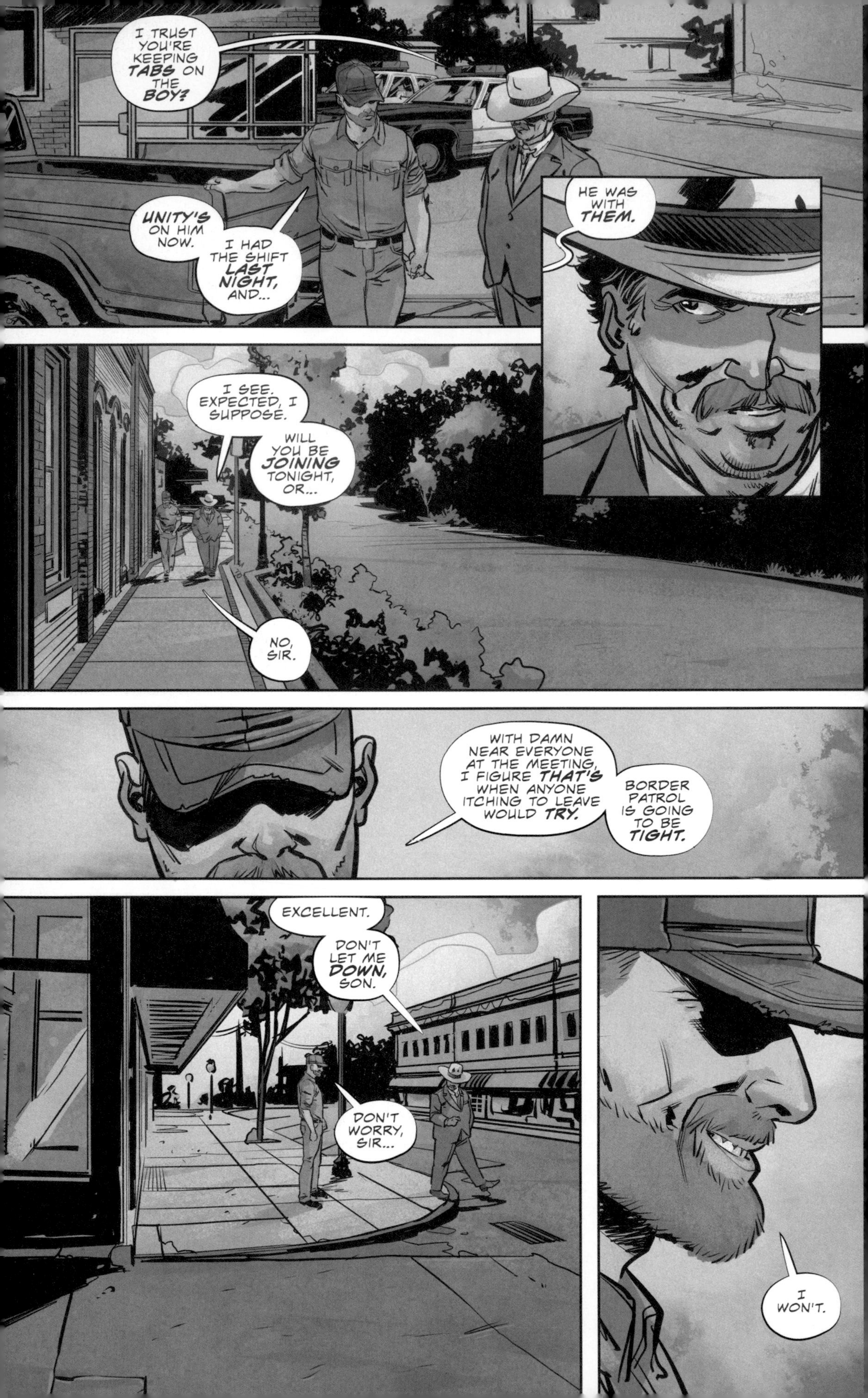
I TRUST YOU'RE KEEPING TABS ON THE BOY?
UNITY'S ON HIM NOW.
I HAD THE SHIFT LAST NIGHT, AND...
HE WAS WITH THEM.
I SEE. EXPECTED, I SUPPOSE.
WILL YOU BE JOINING TONIGHT, OR...
NO, SIR.
WITH DAMN NEAR EVERYONE AT THE MEETING, I FIGURE THAT'S WHEN ANYONE ITCHING TO LEAVE WOULD TRY.
BORDER PATROL IS GOING TO BE TIGHT.
EXCELLENT.
DON'T LET ME DOWN, SON.
DON'T WORRY, SIR...
I WON'T.

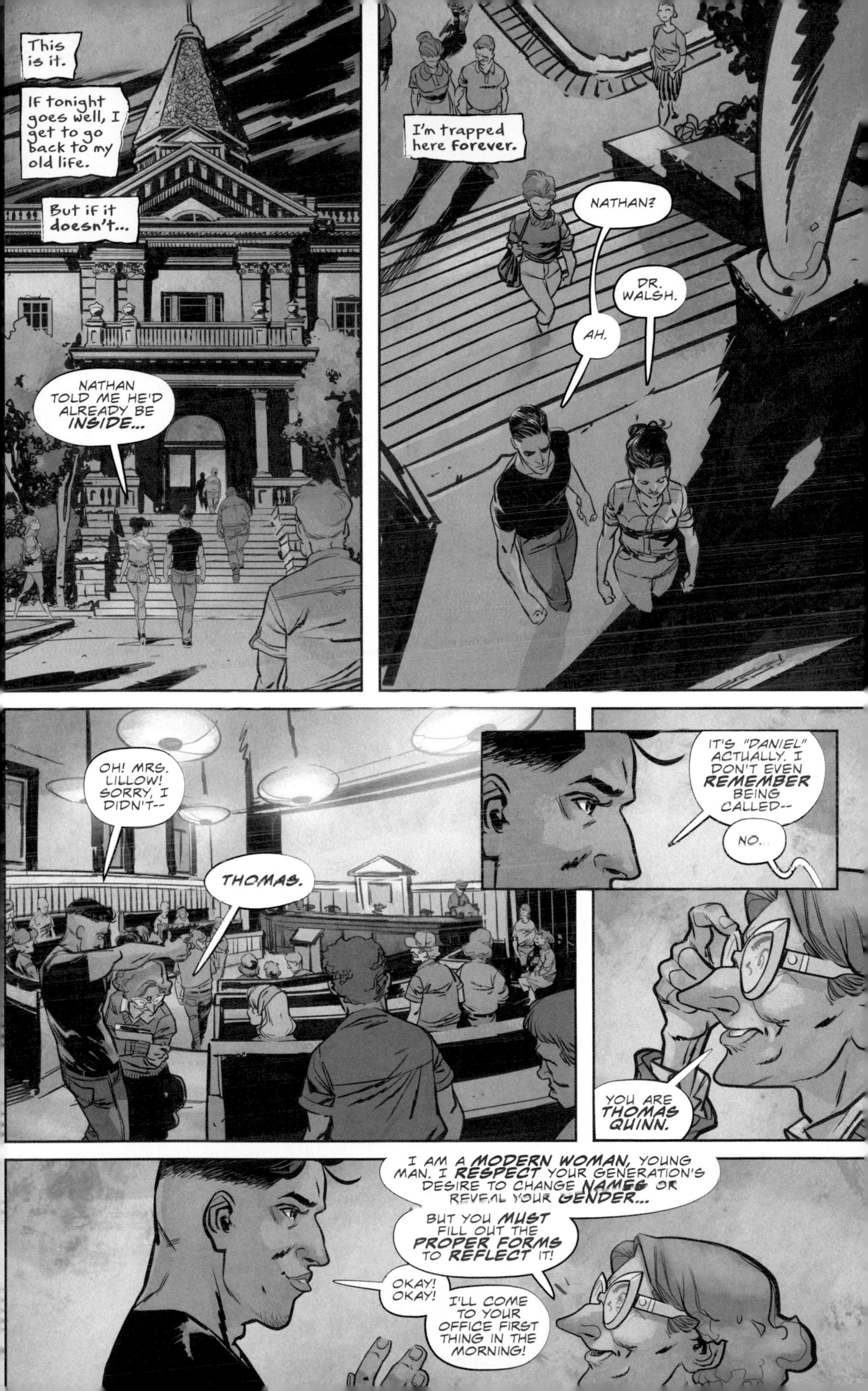
This is it.
If tonight goes well, I get to go back to my old life.
But if it doesn't...
NATHAN TOLD ME HE'D ALREADY BE INSIDE...
I'm trapped here forever.
NATHAN?
DR. WALSH.
AH.
OH! MRS. LILLOW! SORRY, I DIDN'T--
THOMAS.
IT'S "DANIEL" ACTUALLY. I DON'T EVEN REMEMBER BEING CALLED--
NO...
YOU ARE THOMAS QUINN.
I AM A MODERN WOMAN, YOUNG MAN. I RESPECT YOUR GENERATION'S DESIRE TO CHANGE NAMES OR REVEAL YOUR GENDER...
BUT YOU MUST FILL OUT THE PROPER FORMS TO REFLECT IT!
OKAY! OKAY!
I'LL COME TO YOUR OFFICE FIRST THING IN THE MORNING!

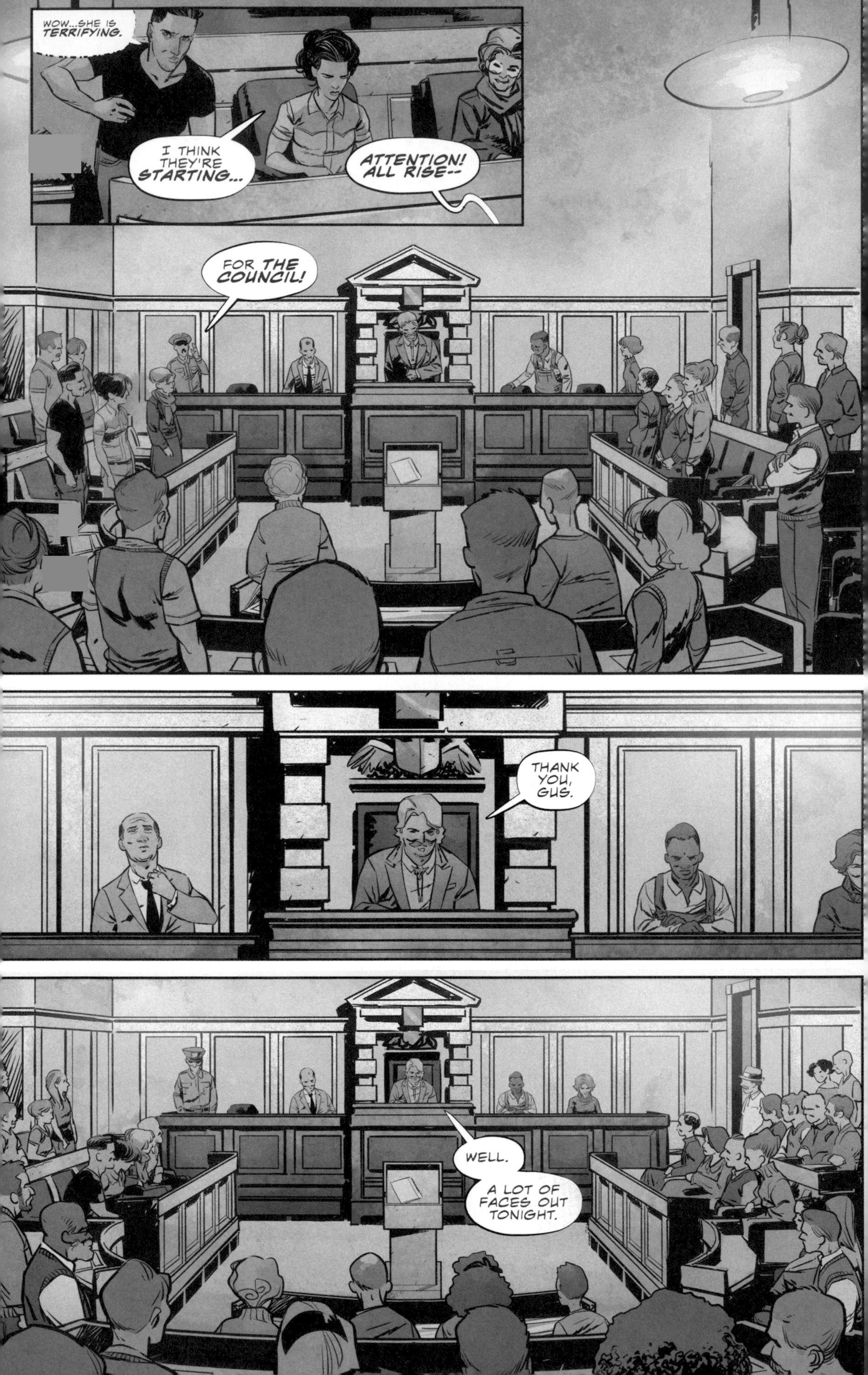
WOW...SHE IS TERRIFYING.
I THINK THEY'RE STARTING...
ATTENTION! ALL RISE--
FOR THE COUNCIL!
THANK YOU, GUS.
WELL.
A LOT OF FACES OUT TONIGHT.

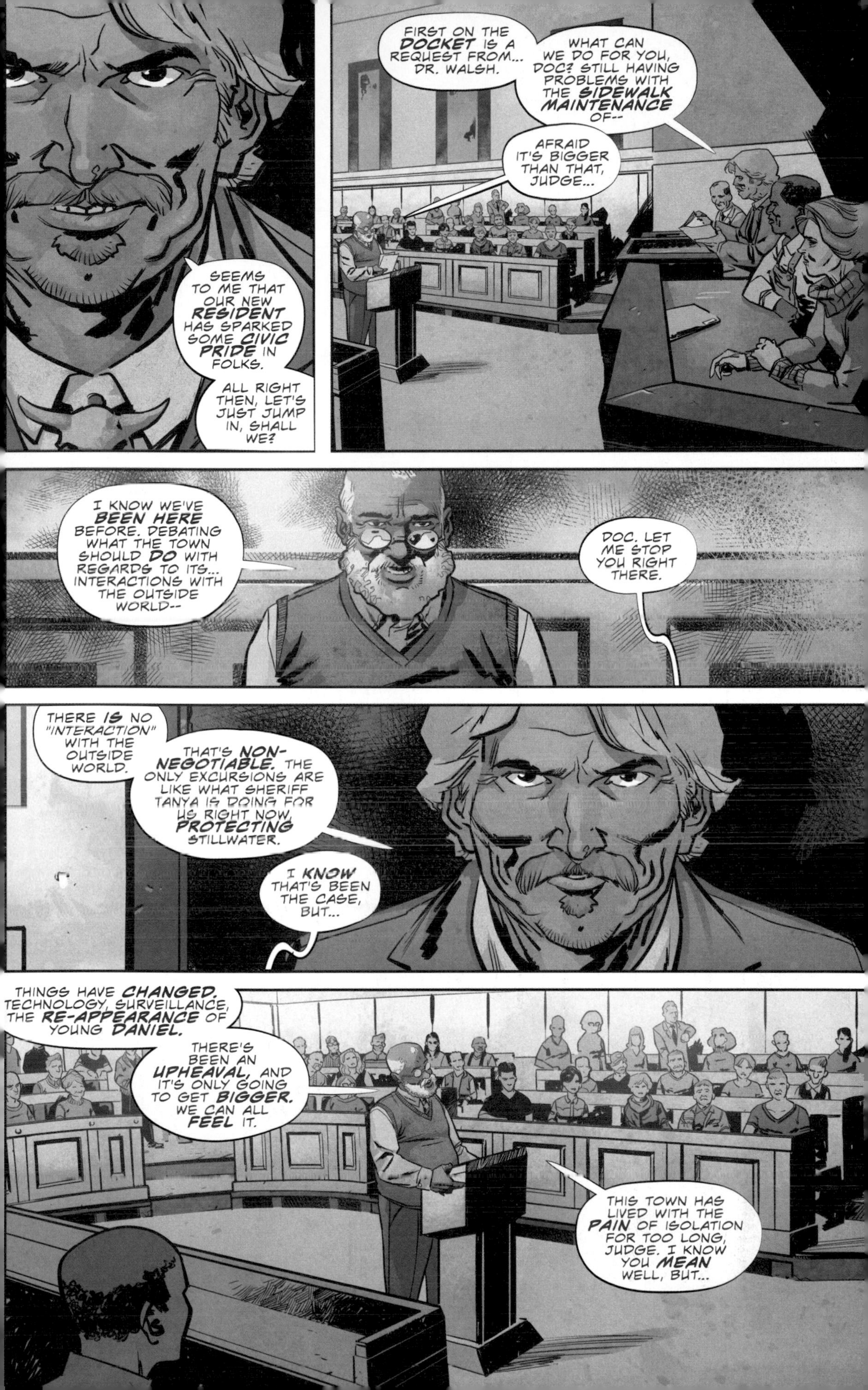
SEEMS TO ME THAT OUR NEW RESIDENT HAS SPARKED SOME CIVIC PRIDE IN FOLKS.
ALL RIGHT THEN, LET'S JUST JUMP IN, SHALL WE?
FIRST ON THE DOCKET IS A REQUEST FROM... DR. WALSH.
WHAT CAN WE DO FOR YOU, DOC? STILL HAVING PROBLEMS WITH THE SIDEWALK MAINTENANCE OF--
AFRAID IT'S BIGGER THAN THAT, JUDGE...
I KNOW WE'VE BEEN HERE BEFORE. DEBATING WHAT THE TOWN SHOULD DO WITH REGARDS TO ITS... INTERACTIONS WITH THE OUTSIDE WORLD--
DOC. LET ME STOP YOU RIGHT THERE.
THERE IS NO "INTERACTION" WITH THE OUTSIDE WORLD.
THAT'S NON-NEGOTIABLE. THE ONLY EXCURSIONS ARE LIKE WHAT SHERIFF TANYA IS DOING FOR US RIGHT NOW, PROTECTING STILLWATER.
I KNOW THAT'S BEEN THE CASE, BUT...
THINGS HAVE CHANGED. TECHNOLOGY, SURVEILLANCE, THE RE-APPEARANCE OF YOUNG DANIEL.
THERE'S BEEN AN UPHEAVAL, AND IT'S ONLY GOING TO GET BIGGER. WE CAN ALL FEEL IT.
THIS TOWN HAS LIVED WITH THE PAIN OF ISOLATION FOR TOO LONG, JUDGE. I KNOW YOU MEAN WELL, BUT...

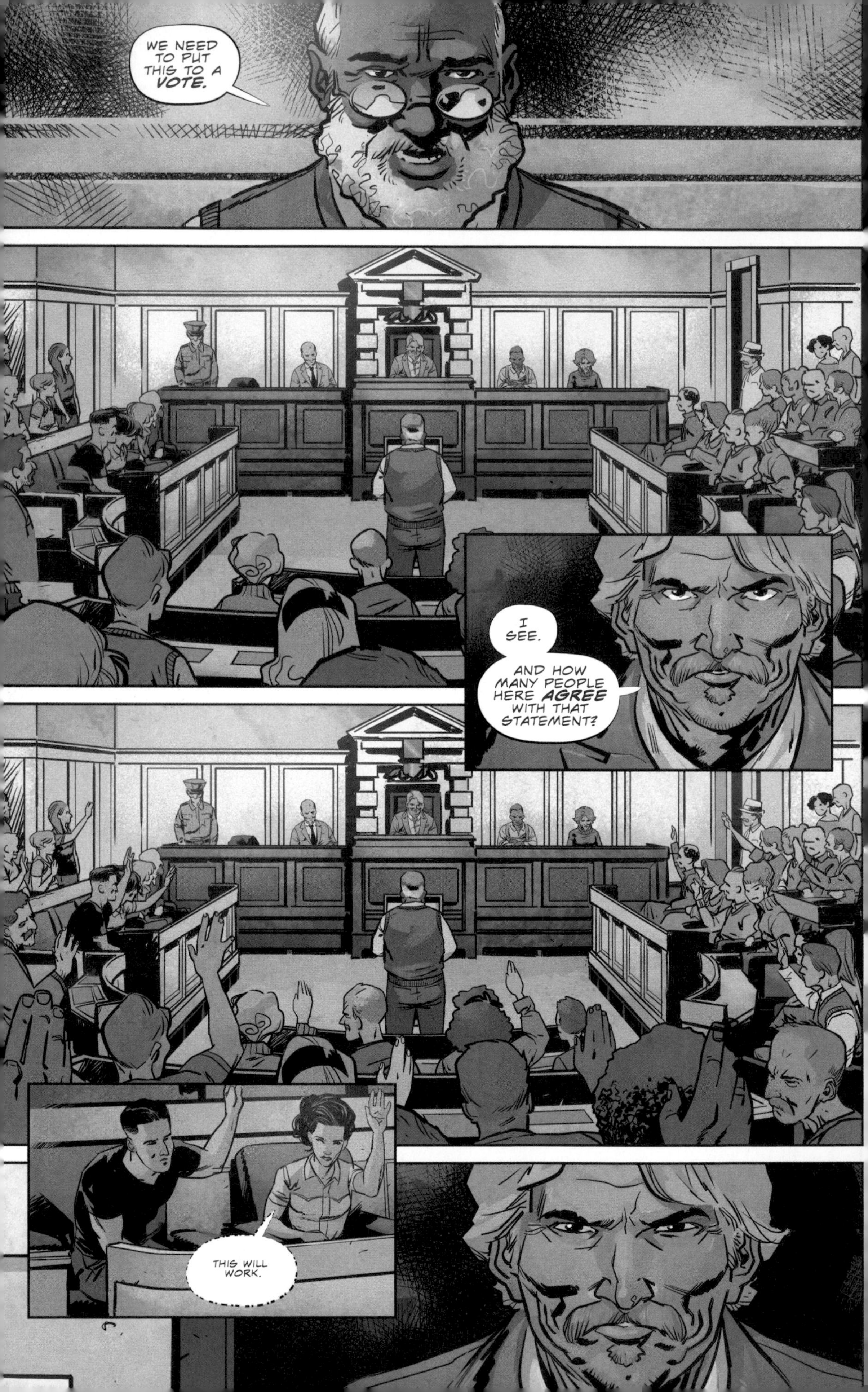
WE NEED TO PUT THIS TO A VOTE.
I SEE.
AND HOW MANY PEOPLE HERE AGREE WITH THAT STATEMENT?
THIS WILL WORK.

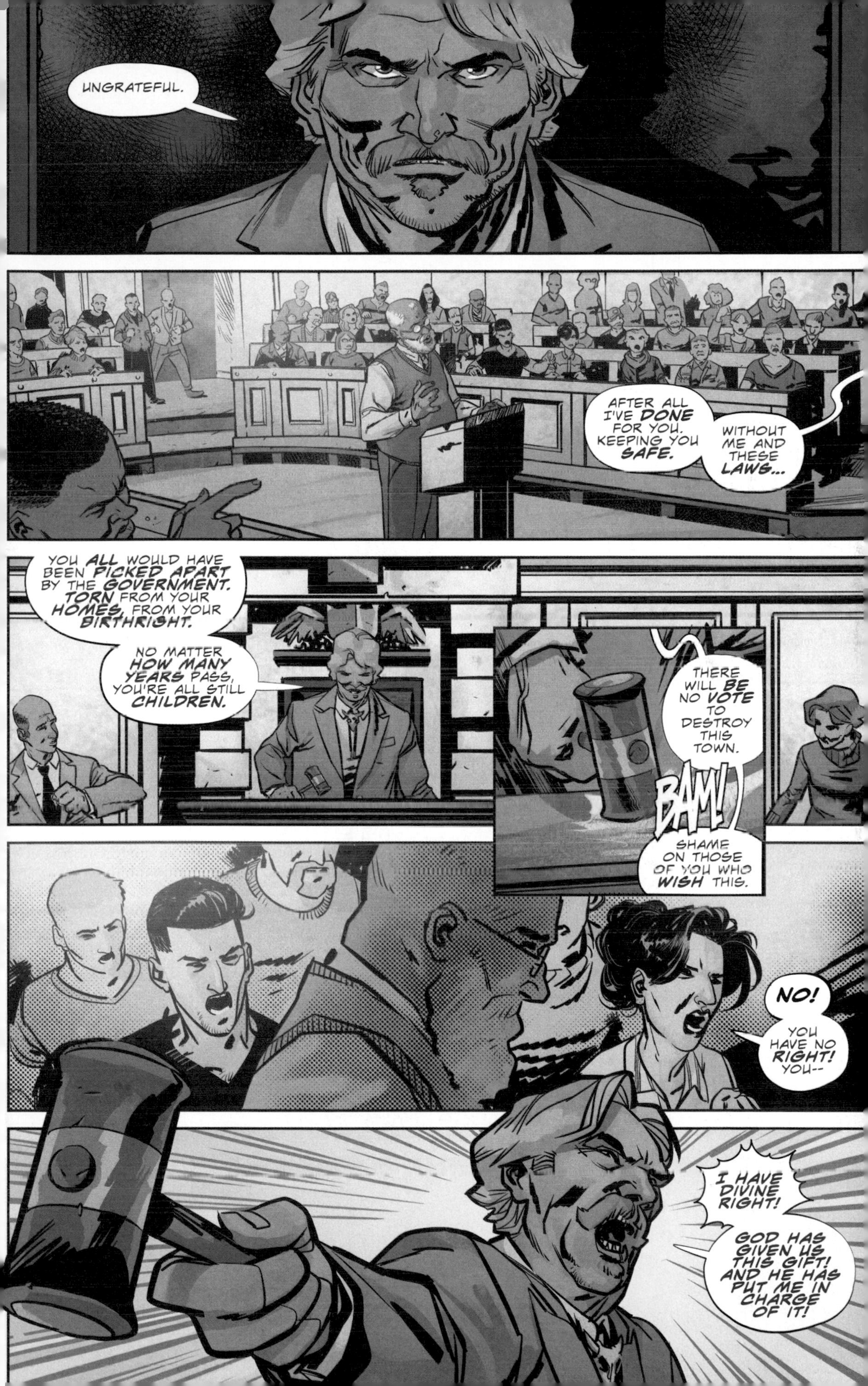
UNGRATEFUL.
AFTER ALL I'VE DONE FOR YOU. KEEPING YOU SAFE.
WITHOUT ME AND THESE LAWS...
YOU ALL WOULD HAVE BEEN PICKED APART BY THE GOVERNMENT. TORN FROM YOUR HOMES, FROM YOUR BIRTHRIGHT.
NO MATTER HOW MANY YEARS PASS, YOU'RE ALL STILL CHILDREN.
THERE WILL BE NO VOTE TO DESTROY THIS TOWN.
BAM!
SHAME ON THOSE OF YOU WHO WISH THIS.
NO!
YOU HAVE NO RIGHT! YOU--
I HAVE DIVINE RIGHT!
GOD HAS GIVEN US THIS GIFT! AND HE HAS PUT ME IN CHARGE OF IT!

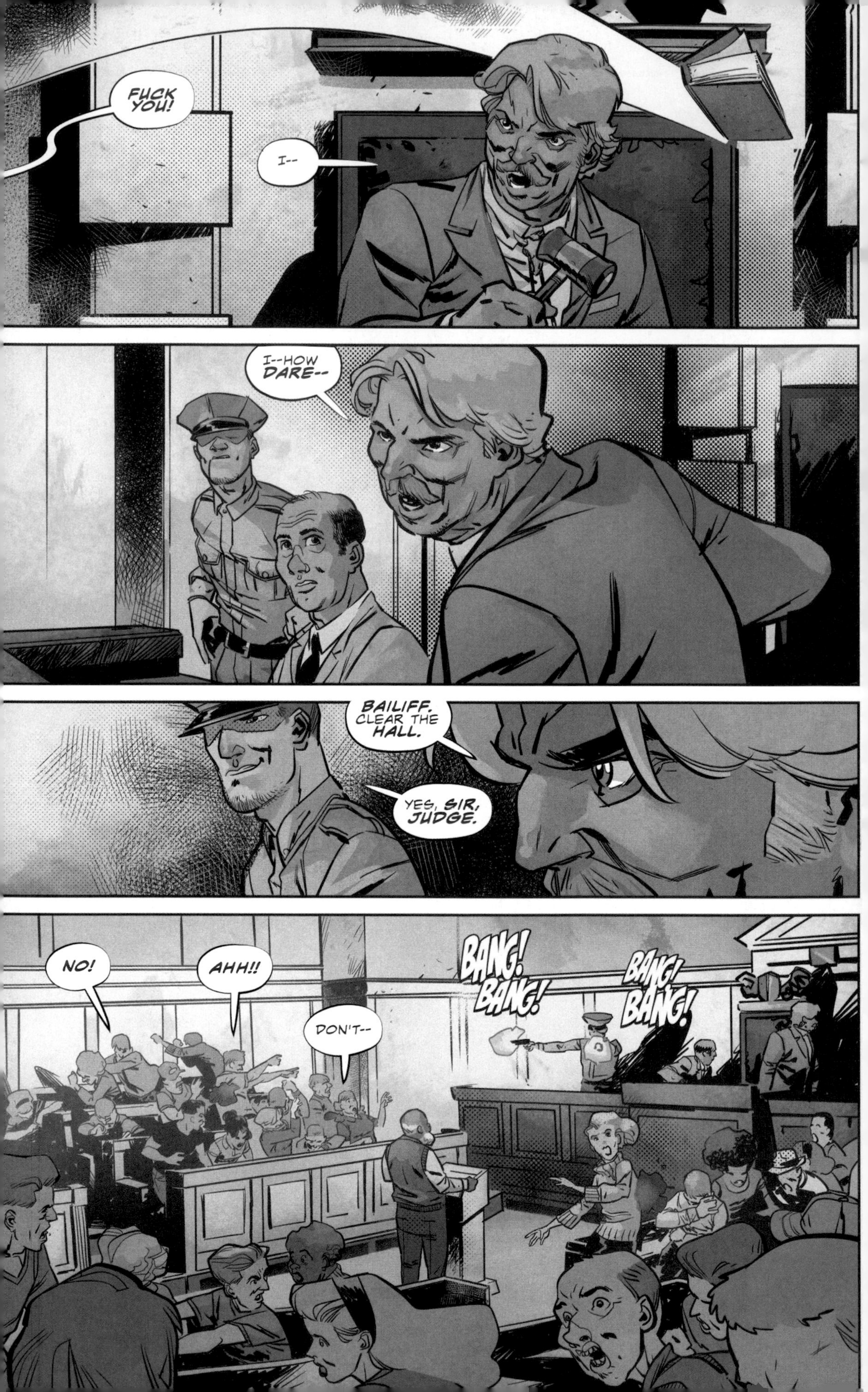
FUCK YOU!
I--
I--HOW DARE--
BAILIFF. CLEAR THE HALL.
YES, SIR, JUDGE.
NO!
AHH!!
DON'T--
BANG! BANG!
BANG! BANG!

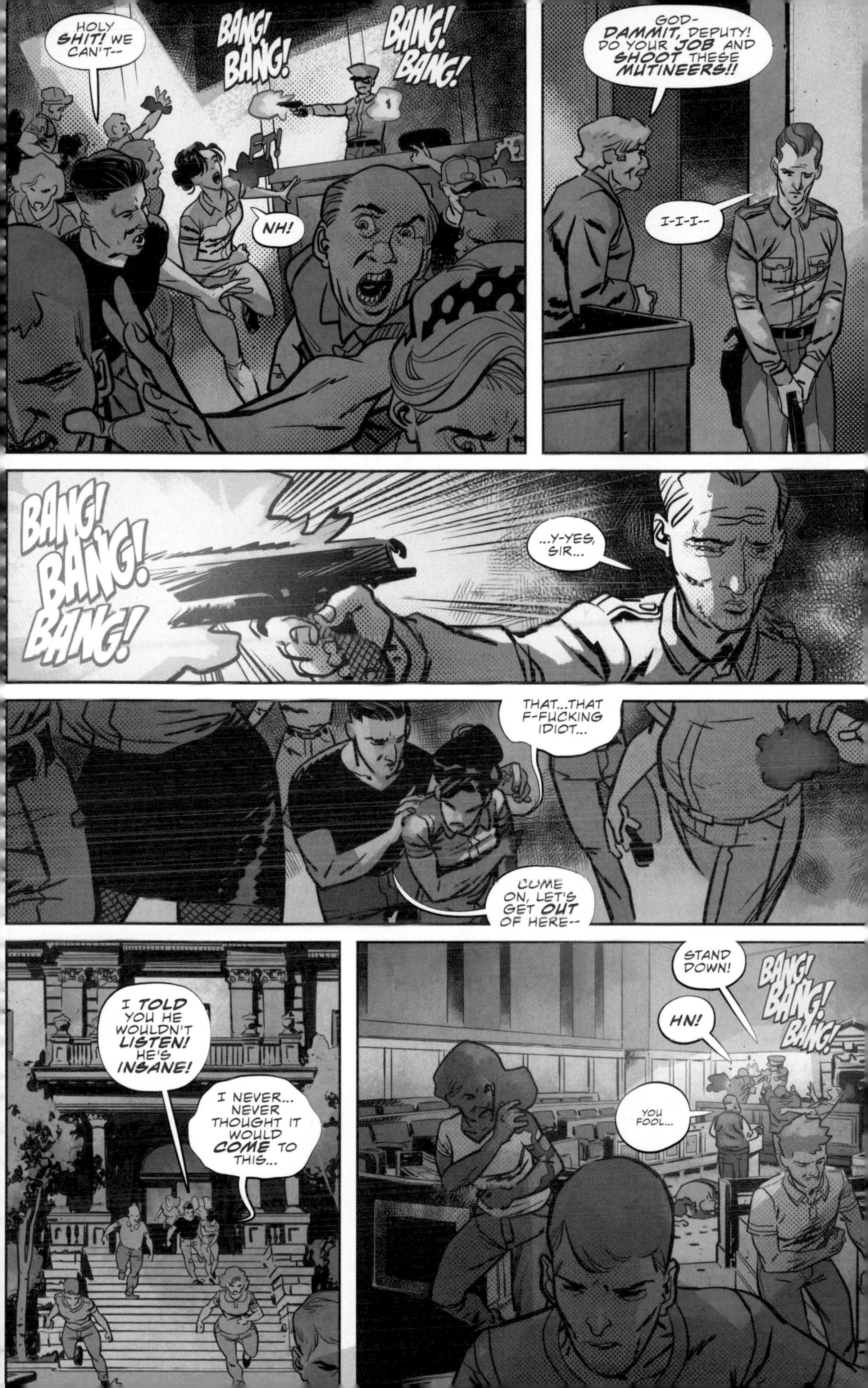
HOLY SHIT! WE CAN'T--
BANG! BANG!
BANG! BANG!
NH!
GOD-DAMMIT, DEPUTY! DO YOUR JOB AND SHOOT THESE MUTINEERS!!
I-I-I--
BANG! BANG! BANG!
...Y-YES, SIR...
THAT...THAT F-FUCKING IDIOT...
COME ON, LET'S GET OUT OF HERE--
I TOLD YOU HE WOULDN'T LISTEN! HE'S INSANE!
I NEVER... NEVER THOUGHT IT WOULD COME TO THIS...
STAND DOWN!
BANG! BANG! BANG!
HN!
YOU FOOL...

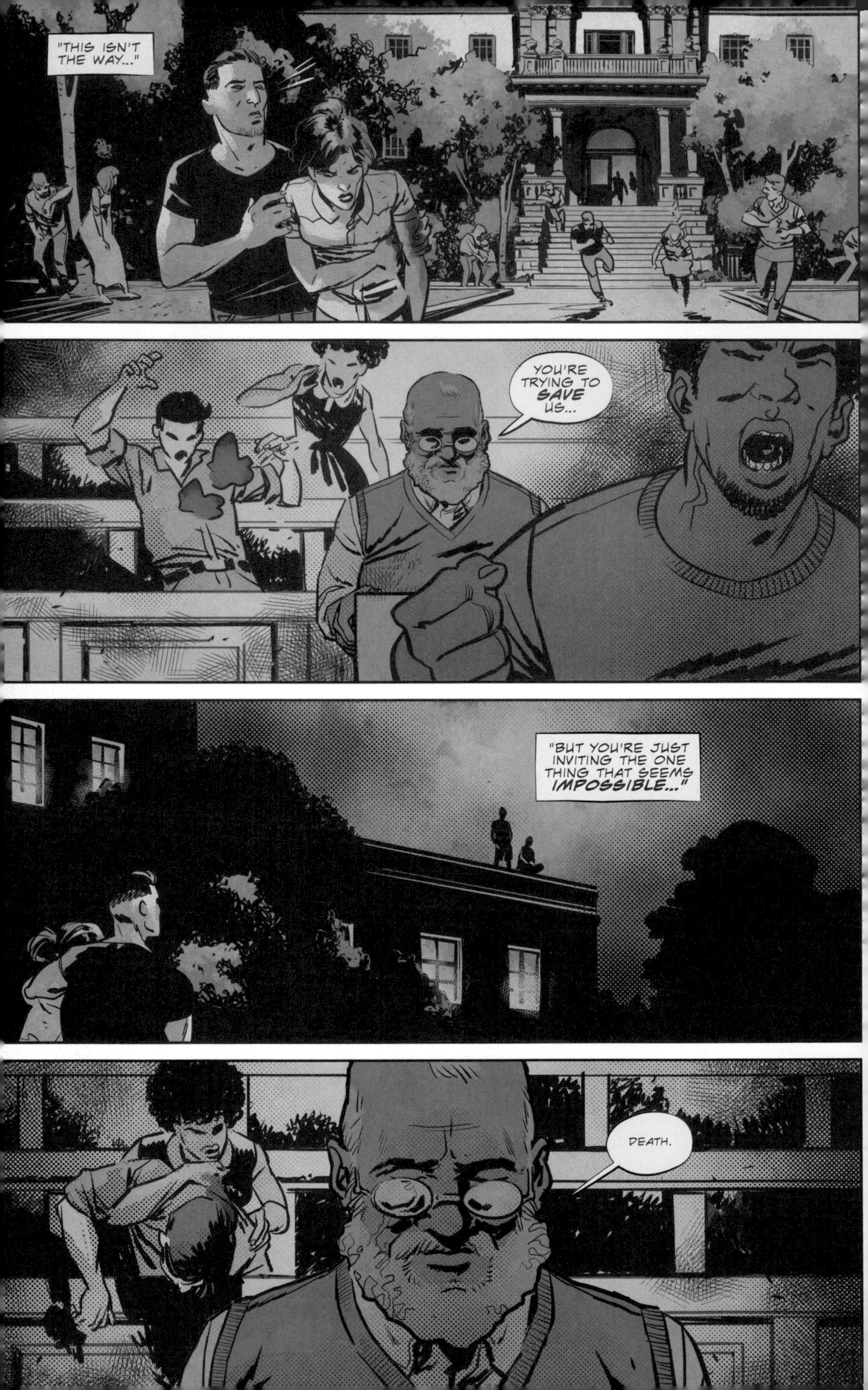
"THIS ISN'T THE WAY..."
YOU'RE TRYING TO SAVE US...
"BUT YOU'RE JUST INVITING THE ONE THING THAT SEEMS IMPOSSIBLE..."
DEATH.

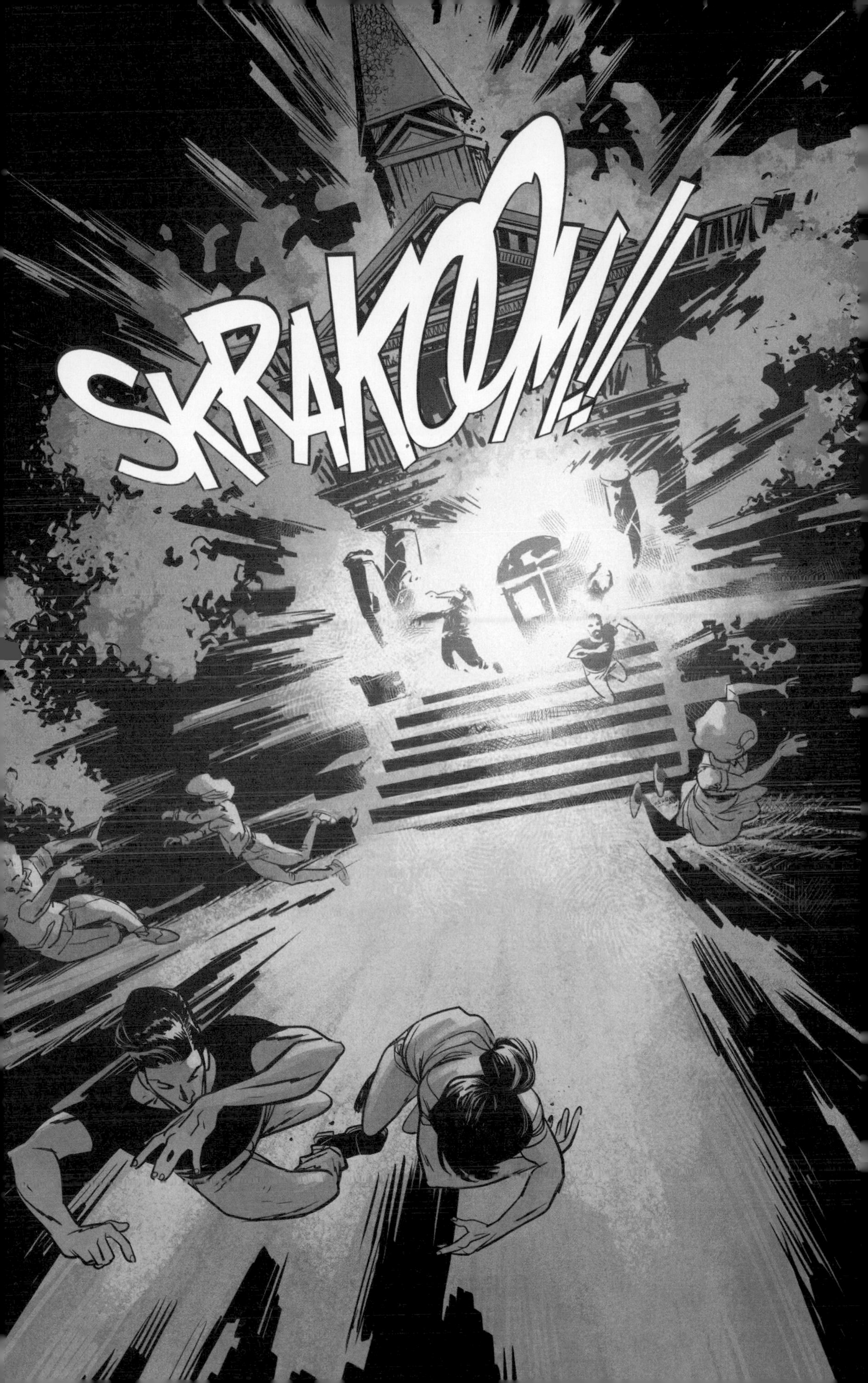
SKRAKOOM!!

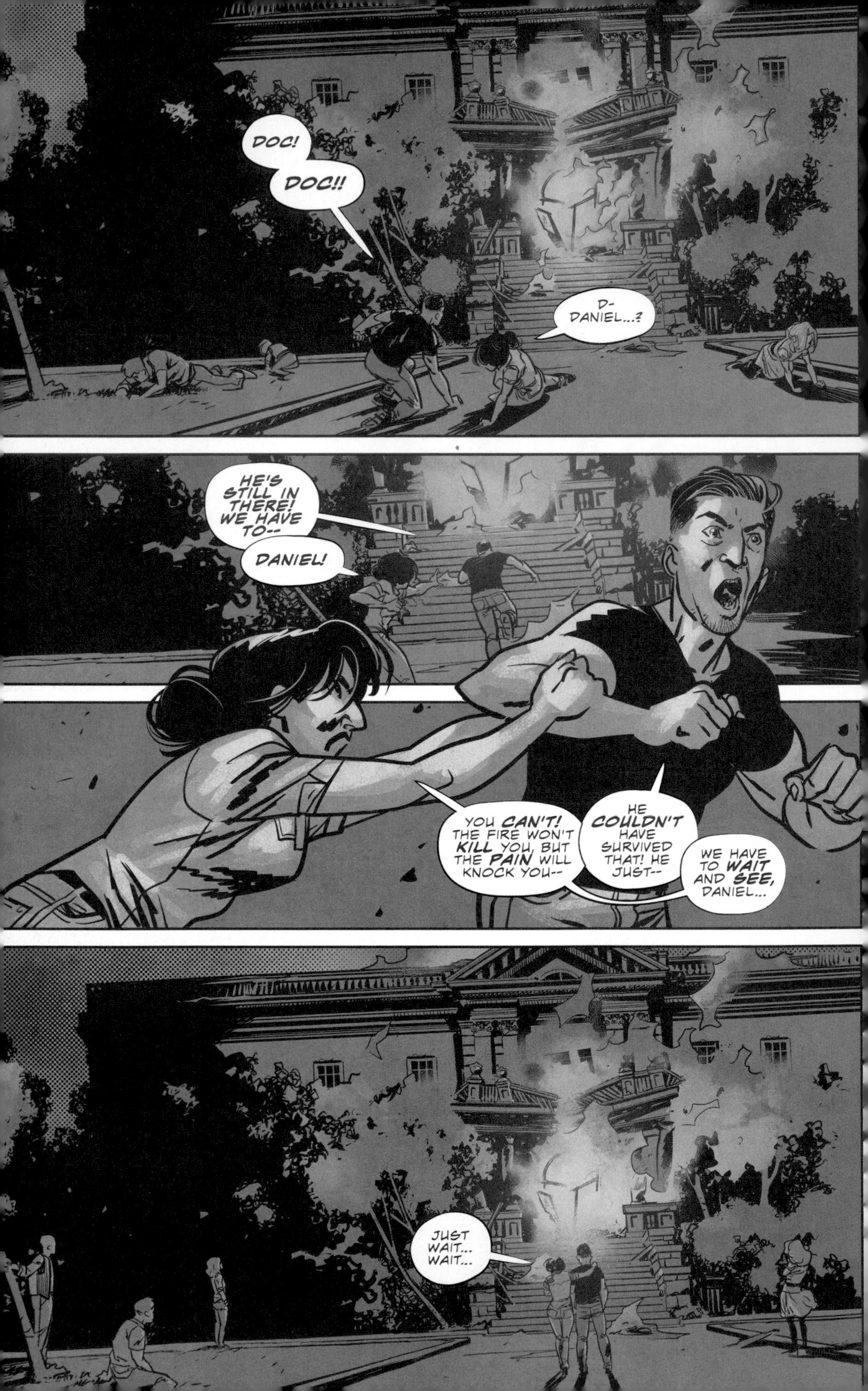
DOC!
DOC!!
D- DANIEL...?
HE'S STILL IN THERE! WE HAVE TO--
DANIEL!
YOU CAN'T! THE FIRE WON'T KILL YOU, BUT THE PAIN WILL KNOCK YOU--
HE COULDN'T HAVE SURVIVED THAT! HE JUST--
WE HAVE TO WAIT AND SEE, DANIEL...
JUST WAIT... WAIT...

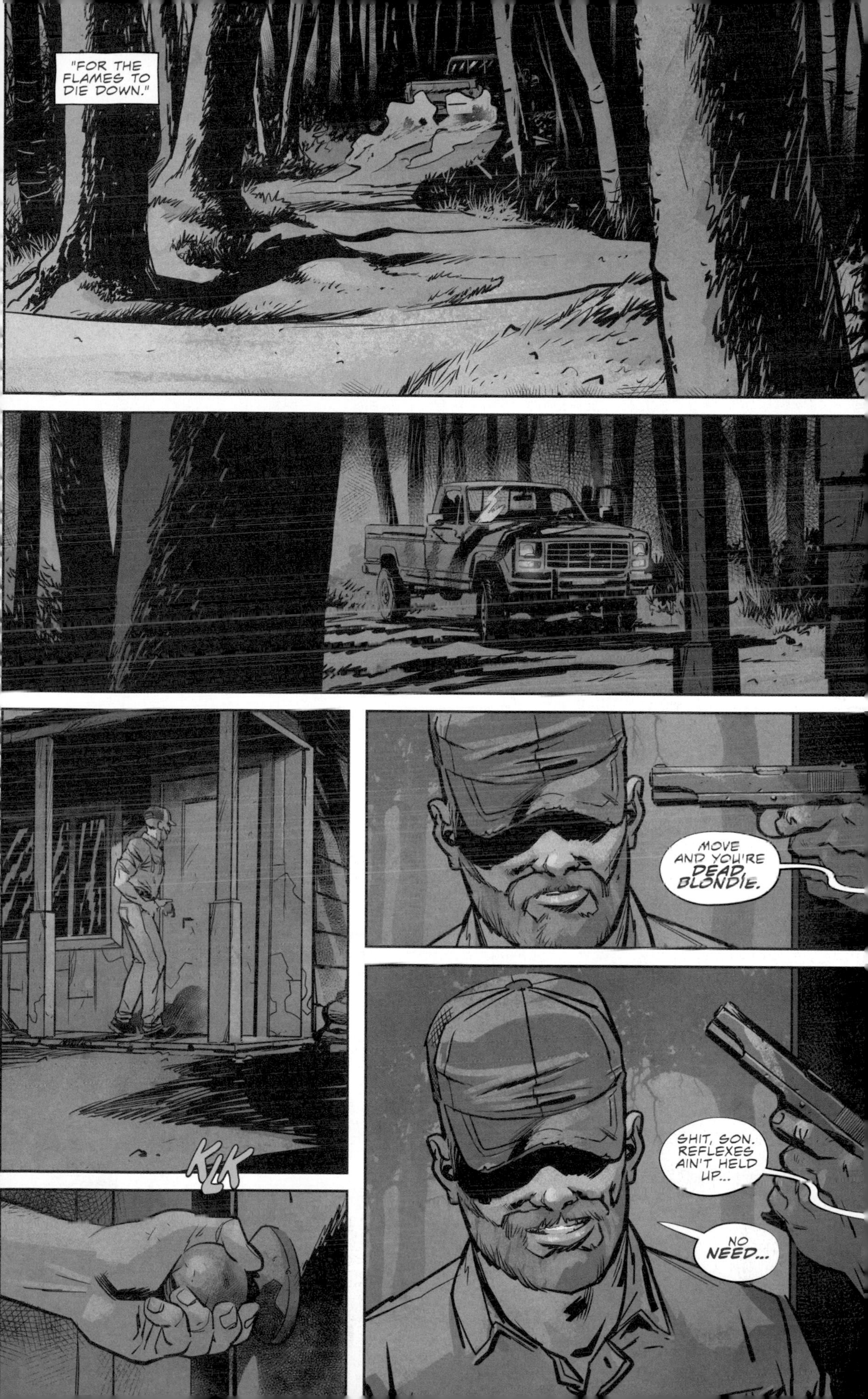
"FOR THE FLAMES TO DIE DOWN."
KLK
MOVE AND YOU'RE DEAD, BLONDIE.
SHIT, SON. REFLEXES AIN'T HELD UP...
NO NEED...

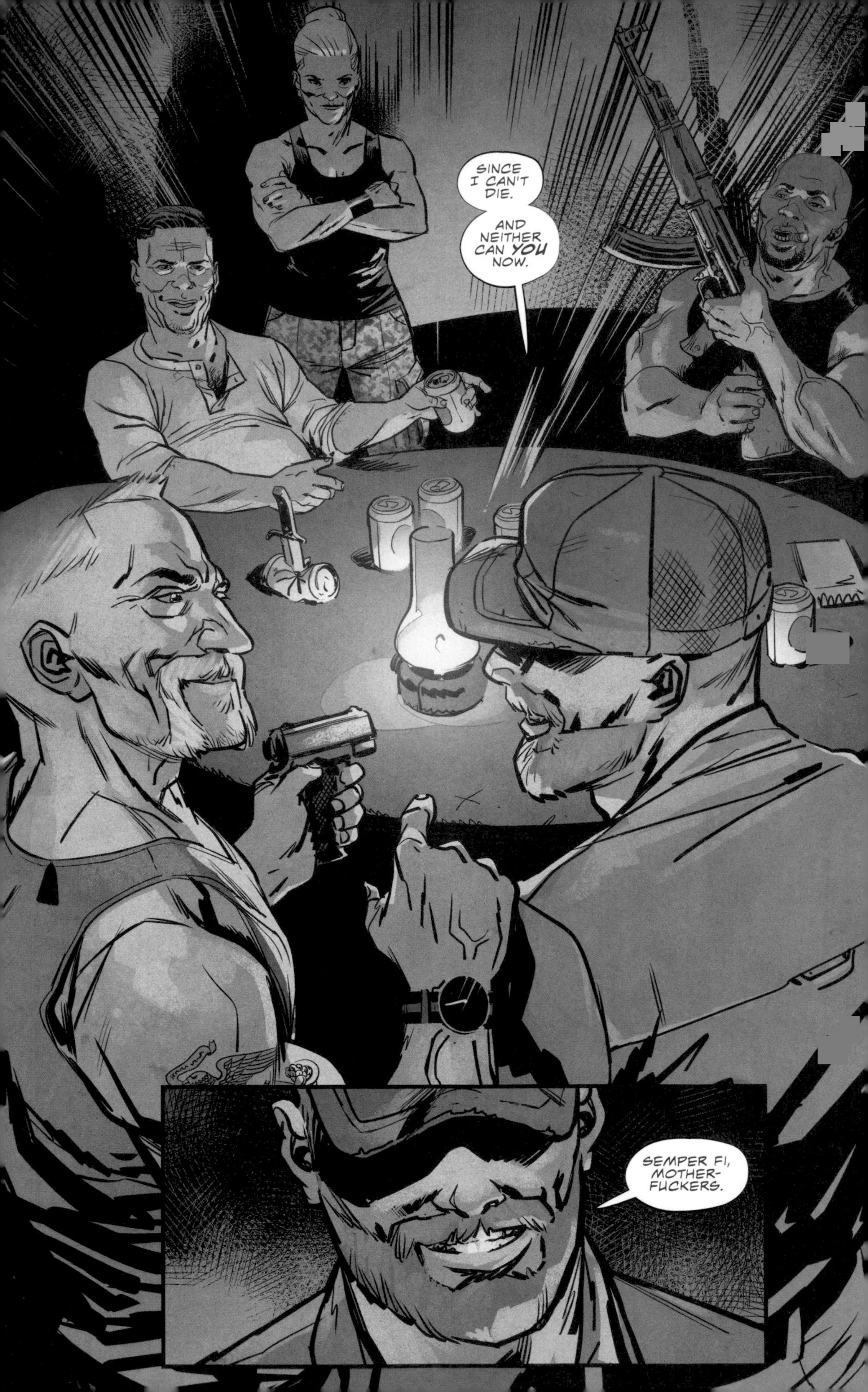
SINCE I CAN'T DIE.
AND NEITHER CAN YOU NOW.
SEMPER FI, MOTHER-FUCKERS.

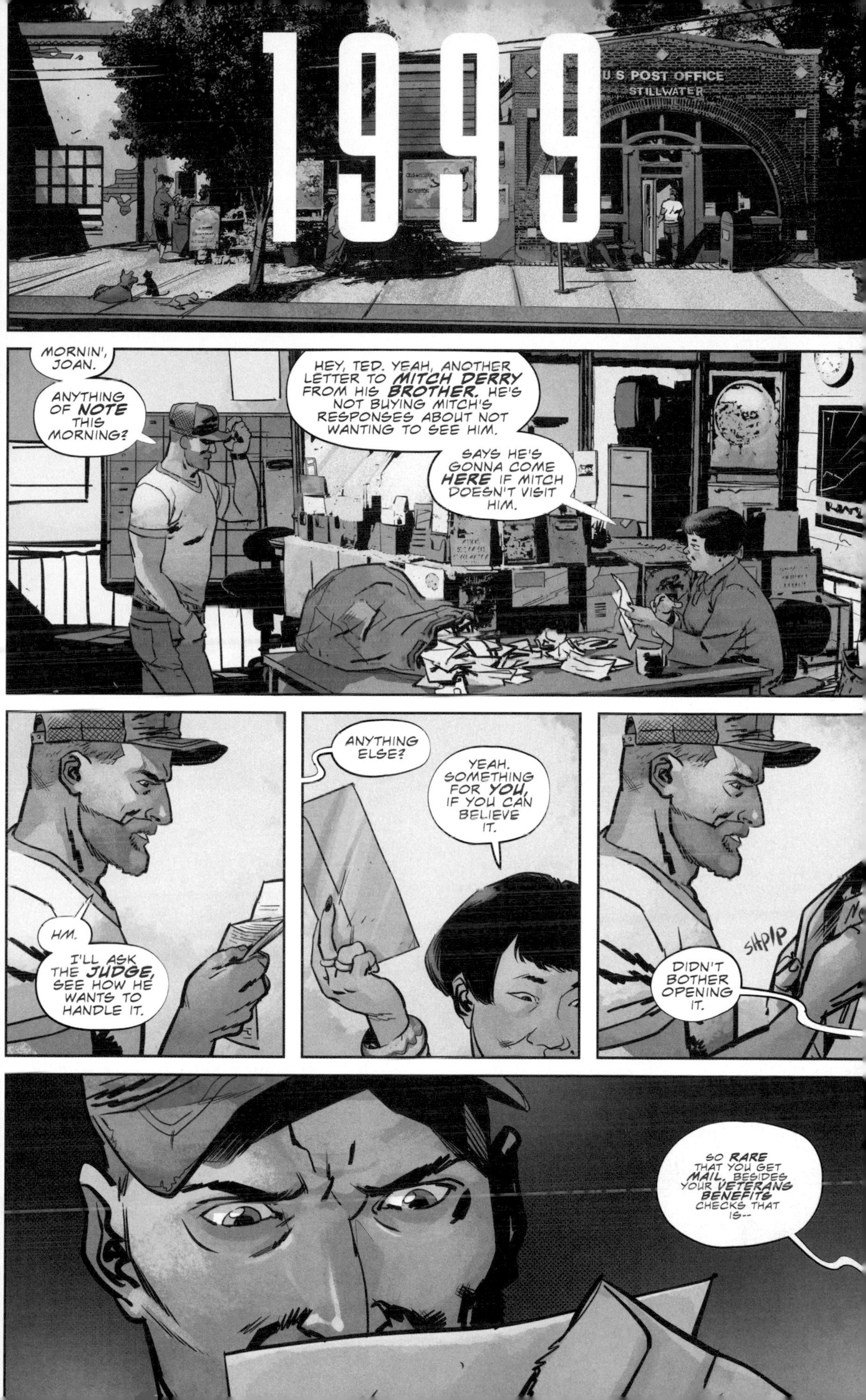
1999
U S POST OFFICE
STILLWATER
MORNIN', JOAN.
ANYTHING OF NOTE THIS MORNING?
HEY, TED. YEAH, ANOTHER LETTER TO MITCH DERRY FROM HIS BROTHER. HE'S NOT BUYING MITCH'S RESPONSES ABOUT NOT WANTING TO SEE HIM.
SAYS HE'S GONNA COME HERE IF MITCH DOESN'T VISIT HIM.
HM.
I'LL ASK THE JUDGE, SEE HOW HE WANTS TO HANDLE IT.
ANYTHING ELSE?
YEAH. SOMETHING FOR YOU, IF YOU CAN BELIEVE IT.
SHPIP
DIDN'T BOTHER OPENING IT.
SO RARE THAT YOU GET MAIL, BESIDES YOUR VETERANS BENEFITS CHECKS THAT IS--

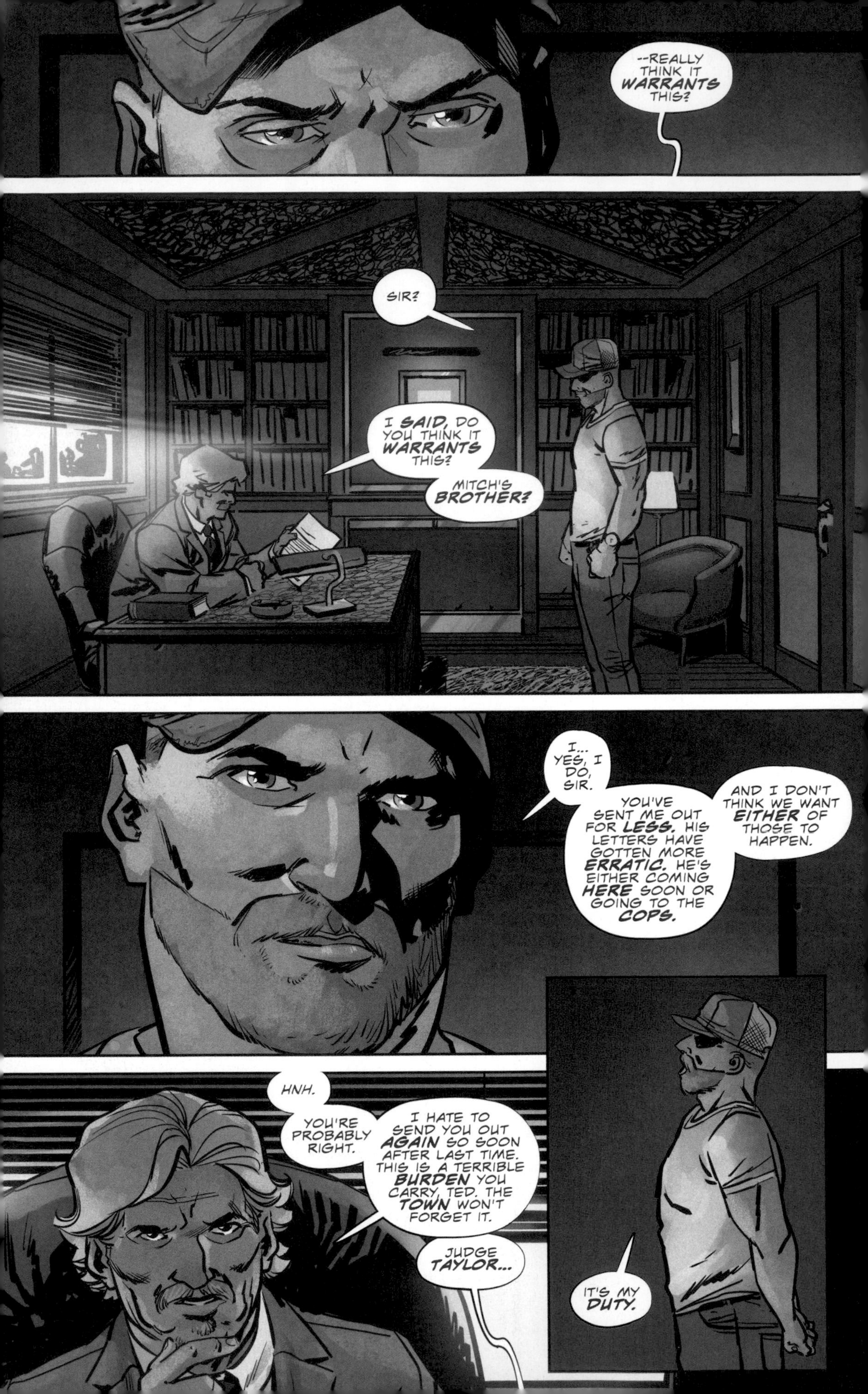
--REALLY THINK IT WARRANTS THIS?
SIR?
I SAID, DO YOU THINK IT WARRANTS THIS?
MITCH'S BROTHER?
I... YES, I DO, SIR.
YOU'VE SENT ME OUT FOR LESS. HIS LETTERS HAVE GOTTEN MORE ERRATIC. HE'S EITHER COMING HERE SOON OR GOING TO THE COPS.
AND I DON'T THINK WE WANT EITHER OF THOSE TO HAPPEN.
HNH.
YOU'RE PROBABLY RIGHT.
I HATE TO SEND YOU OUT AGAIN SO SOON AFTER LAST TIME. THIS IS A TERRIBLE BURDEN YOU CARRY, TED. THE TOWN WON'T FORGET IT.
JUDGE TAYLOR...
IT'S MY DUTY.

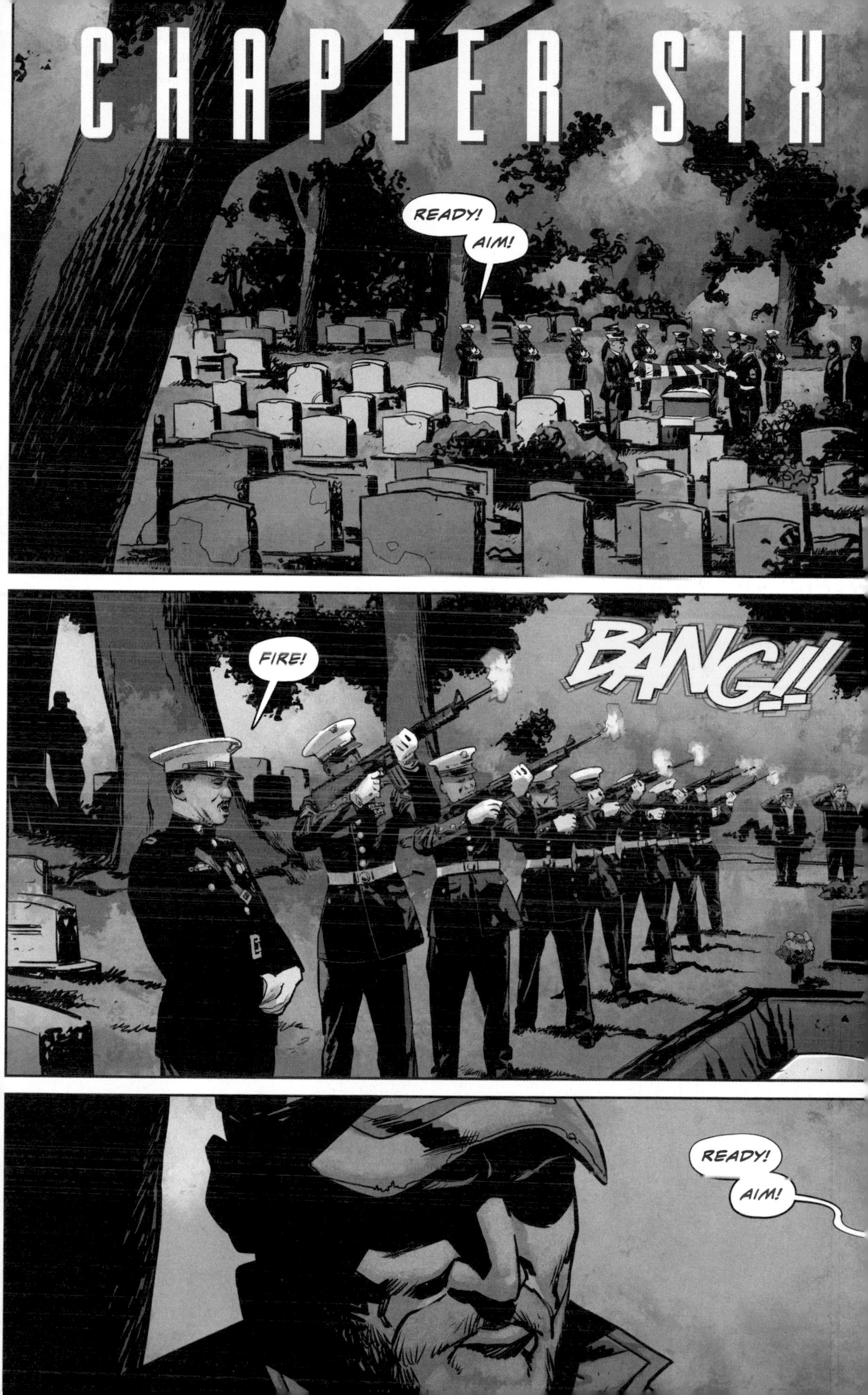
CHAPTER SIX
READY! AIM!
FIRE!
BANG!!
READY! AIM!

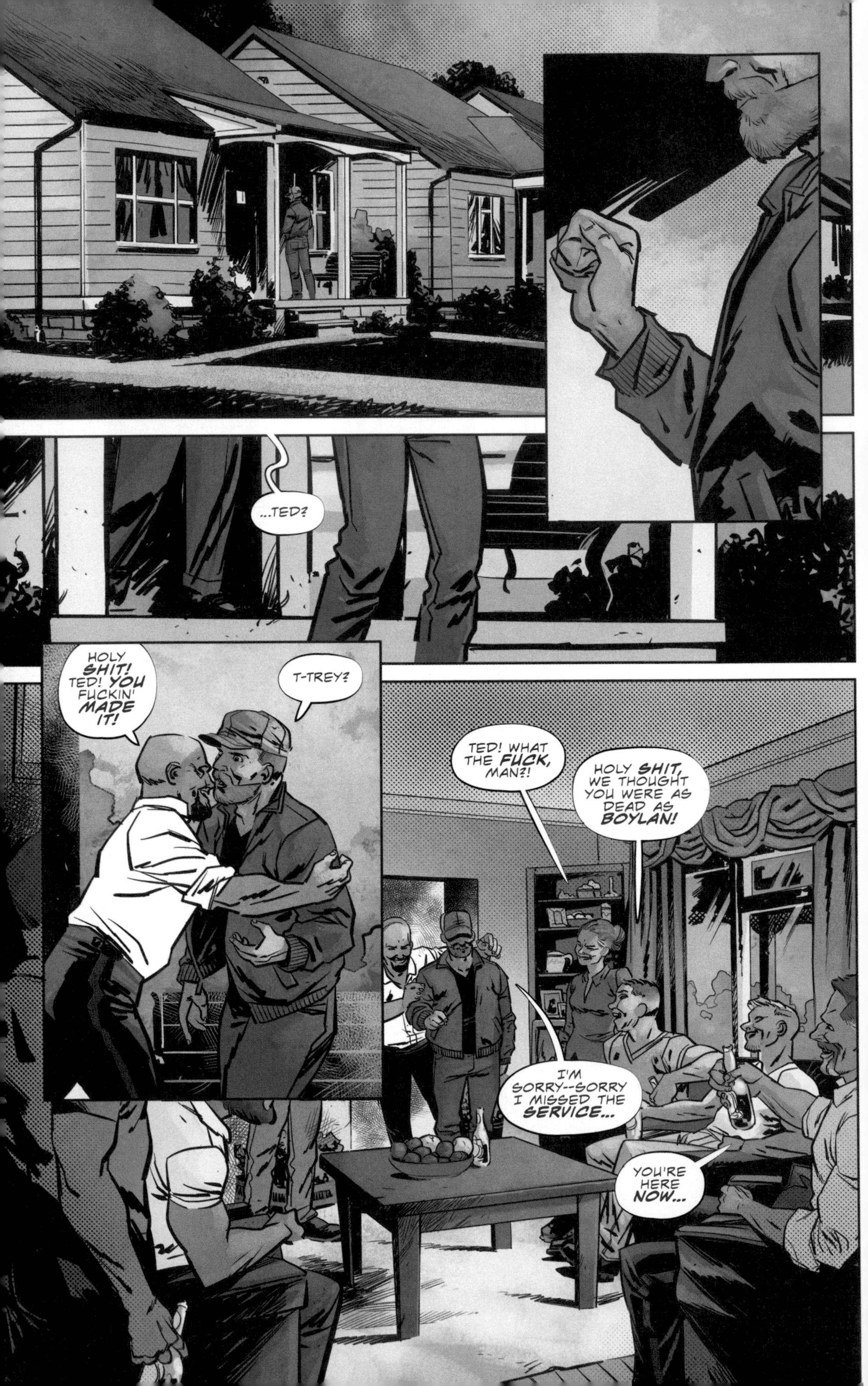
...TED?
HOLY SHIT! TED! YOU FUCKIN' MADE IT!
T-TREY?
TED! WHAT THE FUCK, MAN?!
HOLY SHIT, WE THOUGHT YOU WERE AS DEAD AS BOYLAN!
I'M SORRY--SORRY I MISSED THE SERVICE...
YOU'RE HERE NOW...

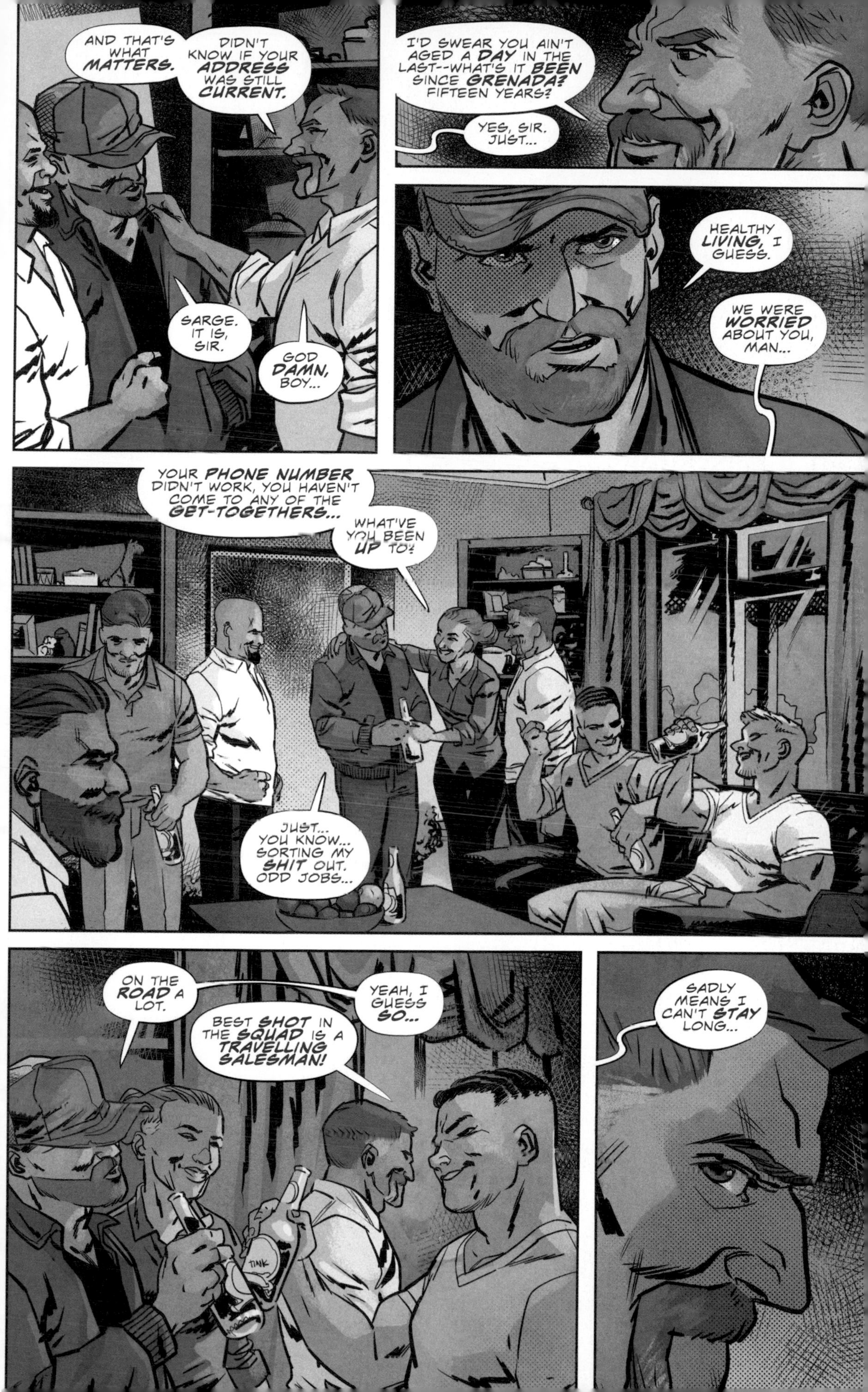

DIDN'T KNOW IF YOUR ADDRESS WAS STILL CURRENT.
AND THAT'S WHAT MATTERS.
SARGE. IT IS, SIR.
GOD DAMN, BOY...
I'D SWEAR YOU AIN'T AGED A DAY IN THE LAST--WHAT'S IT BEEN SINCE GRENADA? FIFTEEN YEARS?
YES, SIR. JUST...
HEALTHY LIVING, I GUESS.
WE WERE WORRIED ABOUT YOU, MAN...
YOUR PHONE NUMBER DIDN'T WORK, YOU HAVEN'T COME TO ANY OF THE GET-TOGETHERS...
WHAT'VE YOU BEEN UP TO?
JUST... YOU KNOW... SORTING MY SHIT OUT. ODD JOBS...
ON THE ROAD A LOT.
YEAH, I GUESS SO...
BEST SHOT IN THE SQUAD IS A TRAVELLING SALESMAN!
TINK
SADLY MEANS I CAN'T STAY LONG...

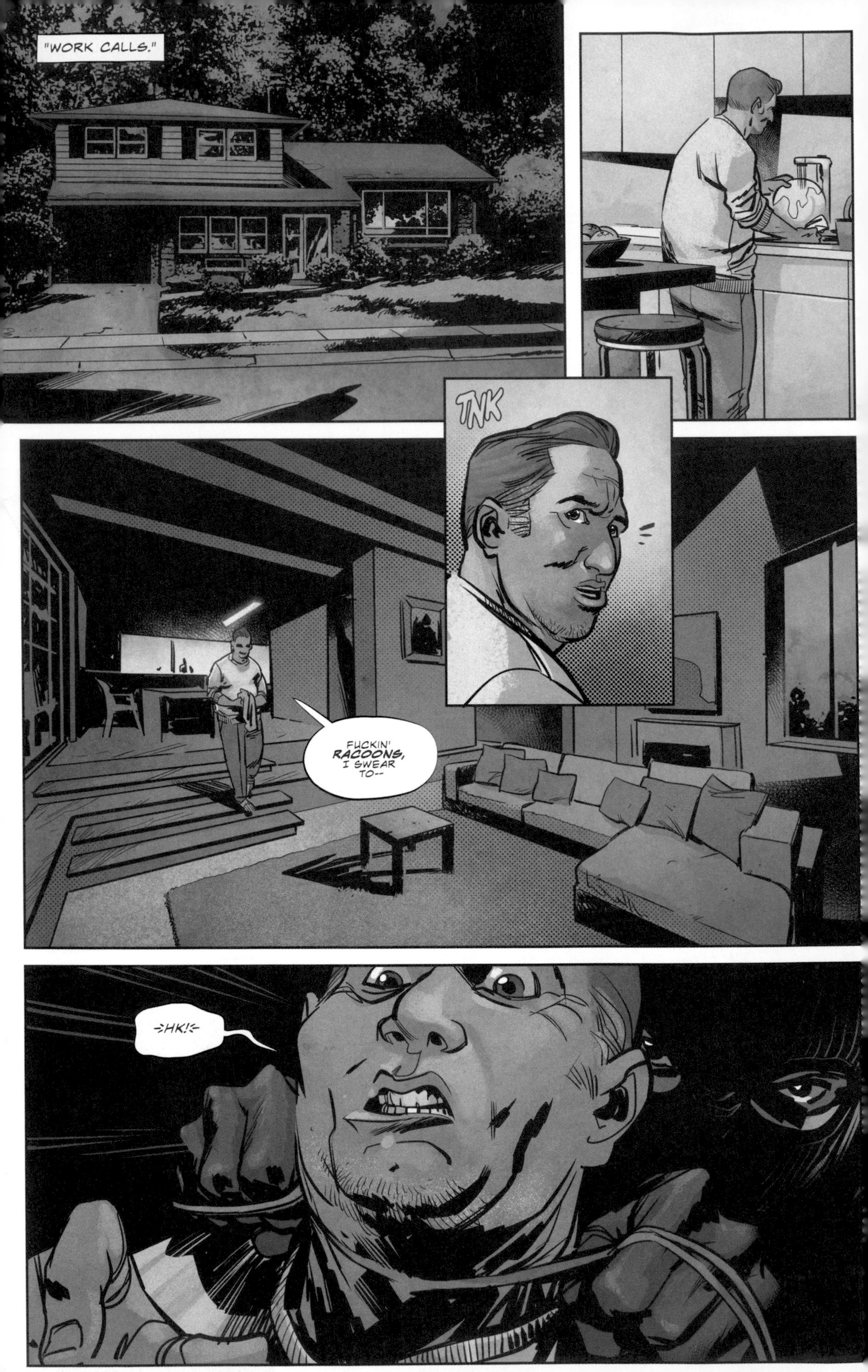
"WORK CALLS."
TNK
FUCKIN' RACOONS, I SWEAR TO--
HK!

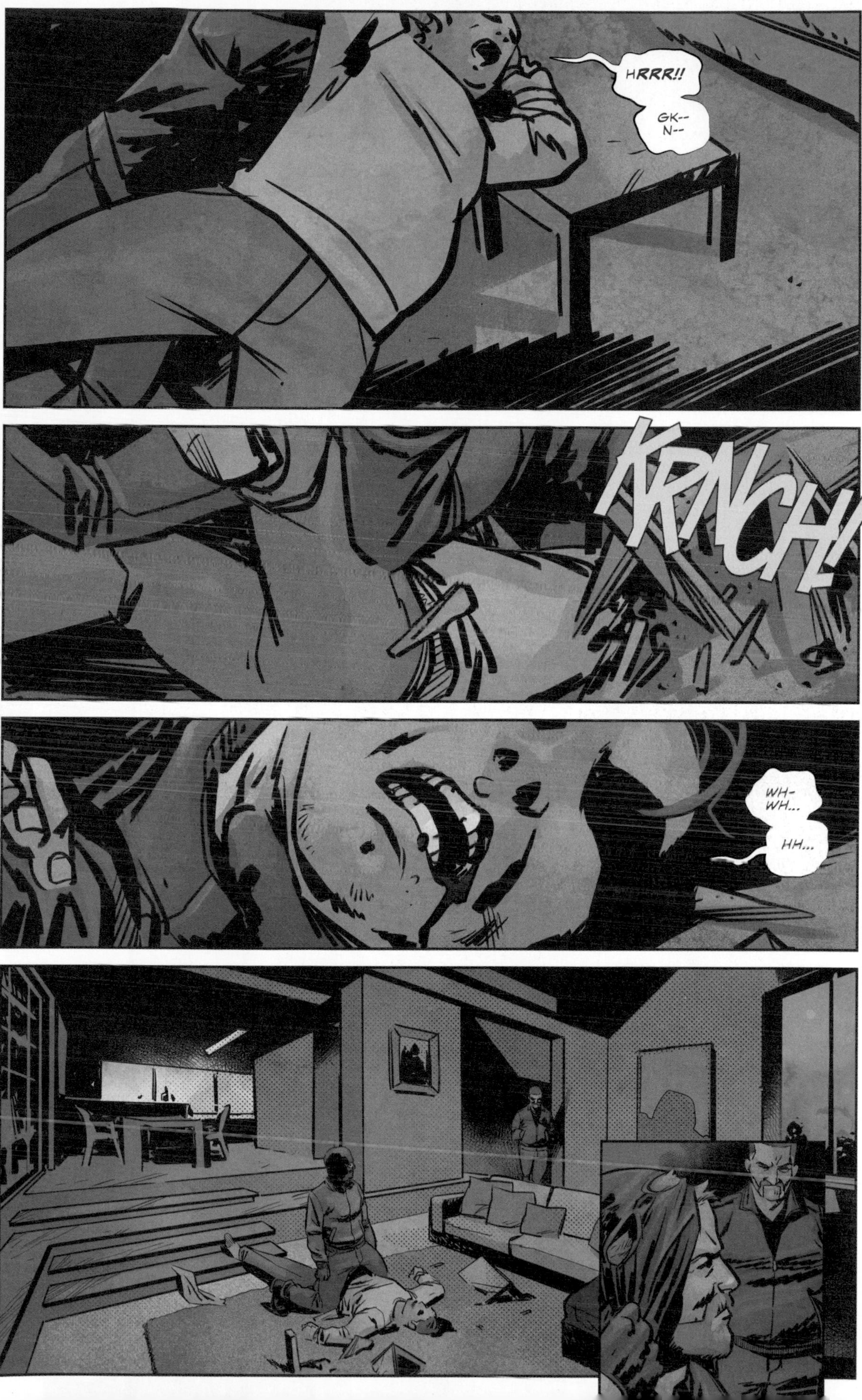
HRRR!!
GK--
N--
KRNCH!
WH-
WH...
HH...

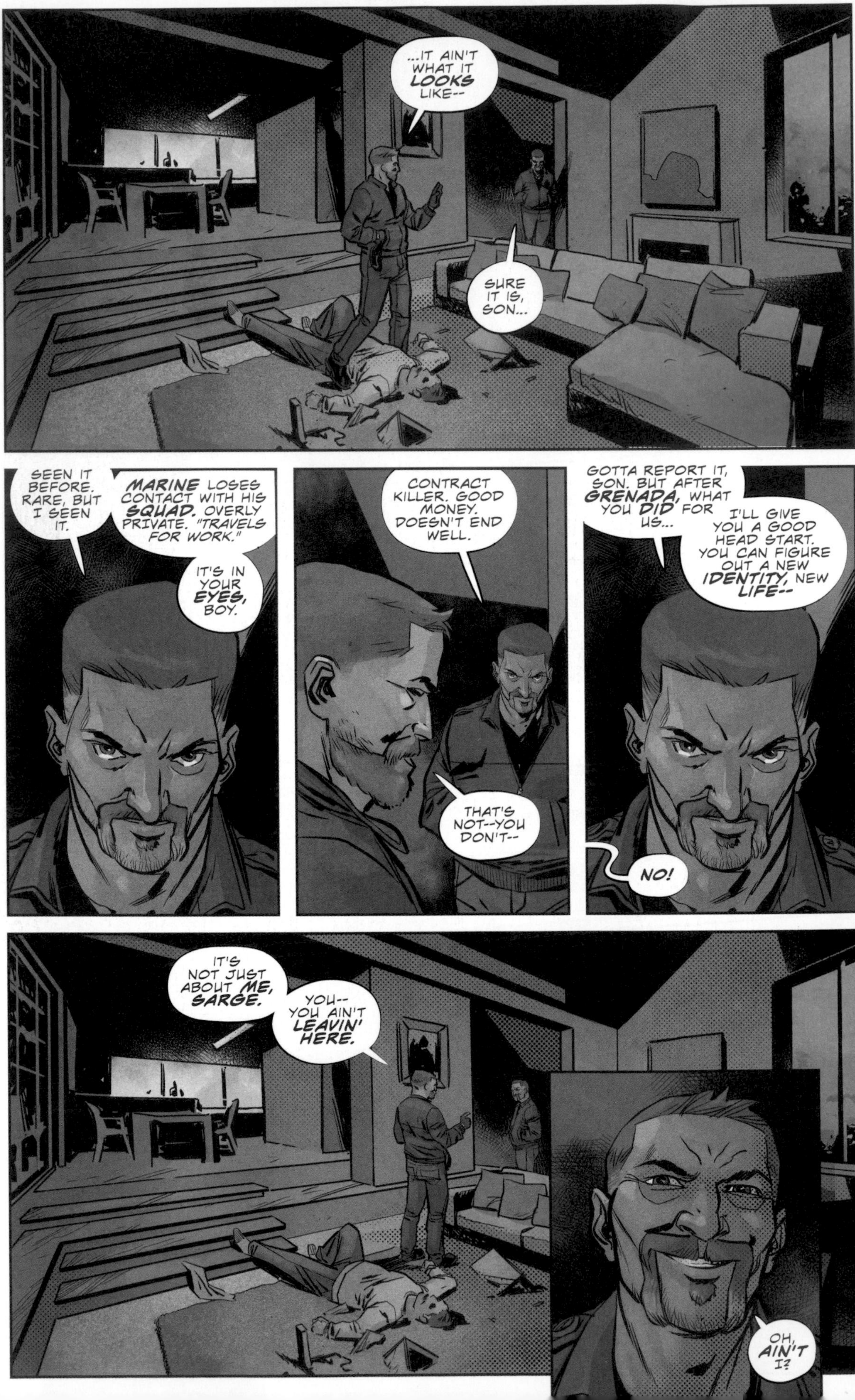
...IT AIN'T WHAT IT LOOKS LIKE--
SURE IT IS, SON...
SEEN IT BEFORE. RARE, BUT I SEEN IT.
MARINE LOSES CONTACT WITH HIS SQUAD. OVERLY PRIVATE. "TRAVELS FOR WORK."
IT'S IN YOUR EYES, BOY.
CONTRACT KILLER. GOOD MONEY. DOESN'T END WELL.
THAT'S NOT--YOU DON'T--
GOTTA REPORT IT, SON. BUT AFTER GRENADA, WHAT YOU DID FOR US...
I'LL GIVE YOU A GOOD HEAD START. YOU CAN FIGURE OUT A NEW IDENTITY, NEW LIFE--
NO!
IT'S NOT JUST ABOUT ME, SARGE.
YOU-- YOU AIN'T LEAVIN' HERE.
OH, AIN'T I?

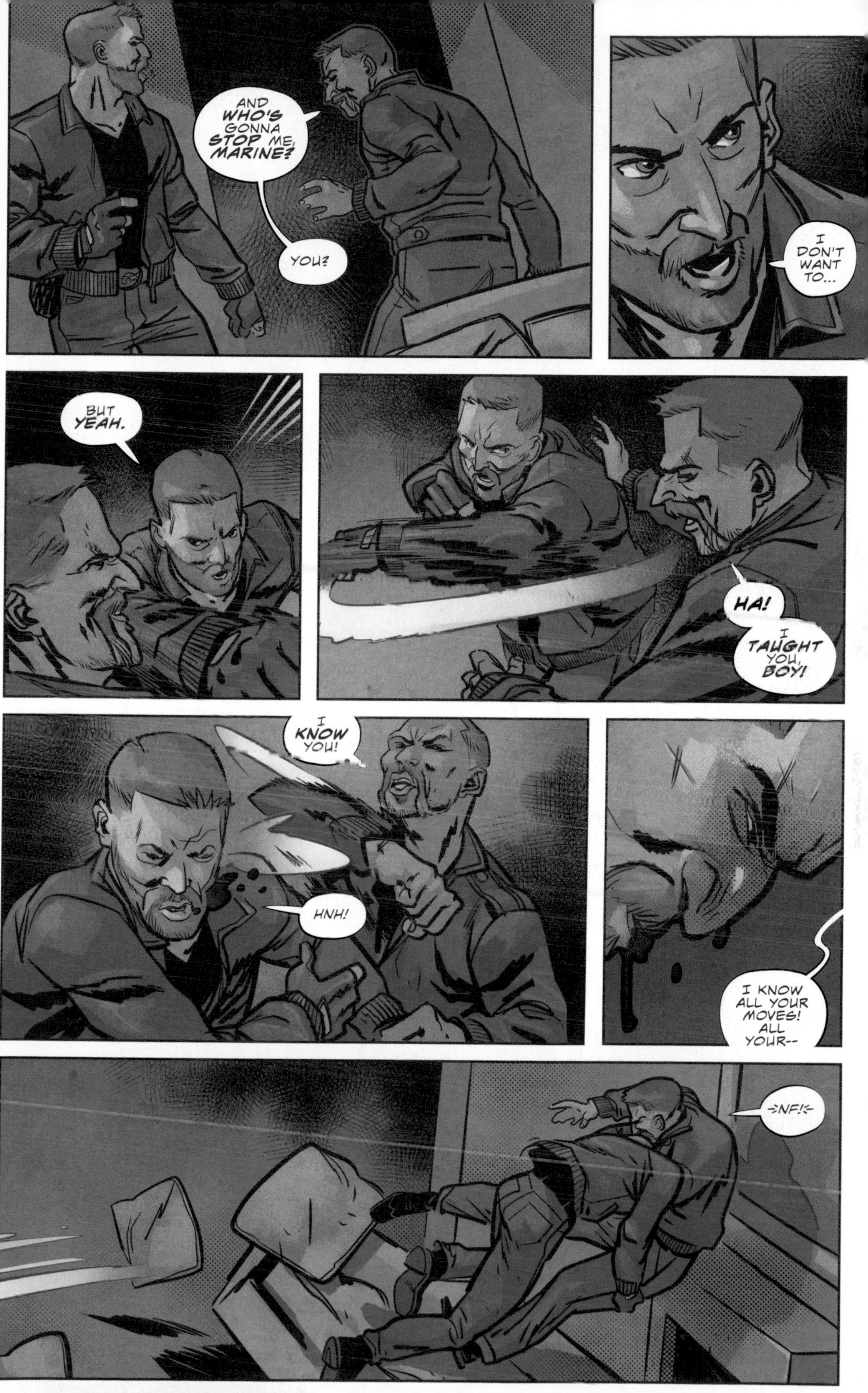
AND WHO'S GONNA STOP ME, MARINE?
YOU?
I DON'T WANT TO...
BUT YEAH.
HA! I TAUGHT YOU, BOY!
I KNOW YOU!
HNH!
I KNOW ALL YOUR MOVES! ALL YOUR--
NF!

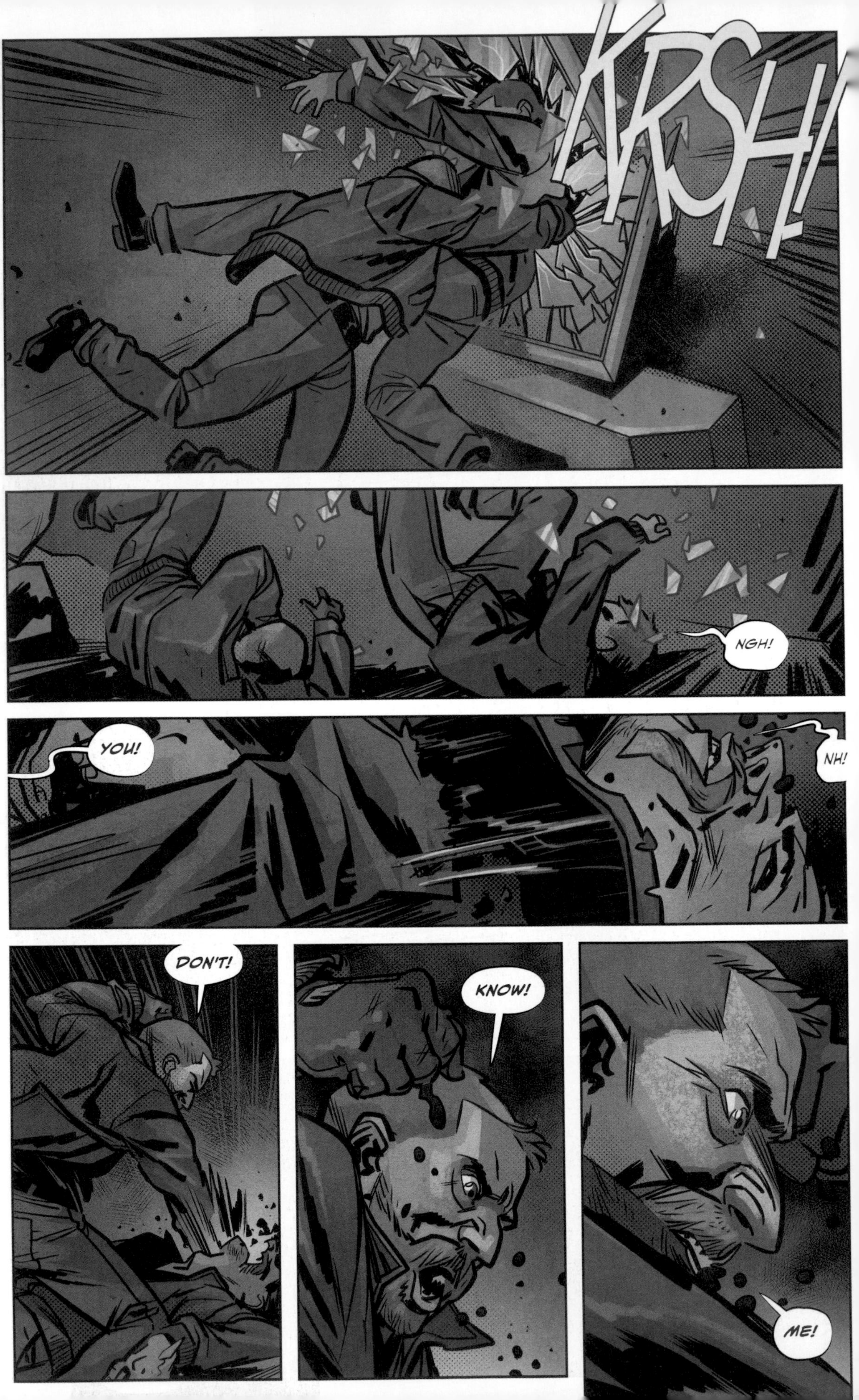
KRSH!
NGH!
YOU!
NH!
DON'T!
KNOW!
ME!

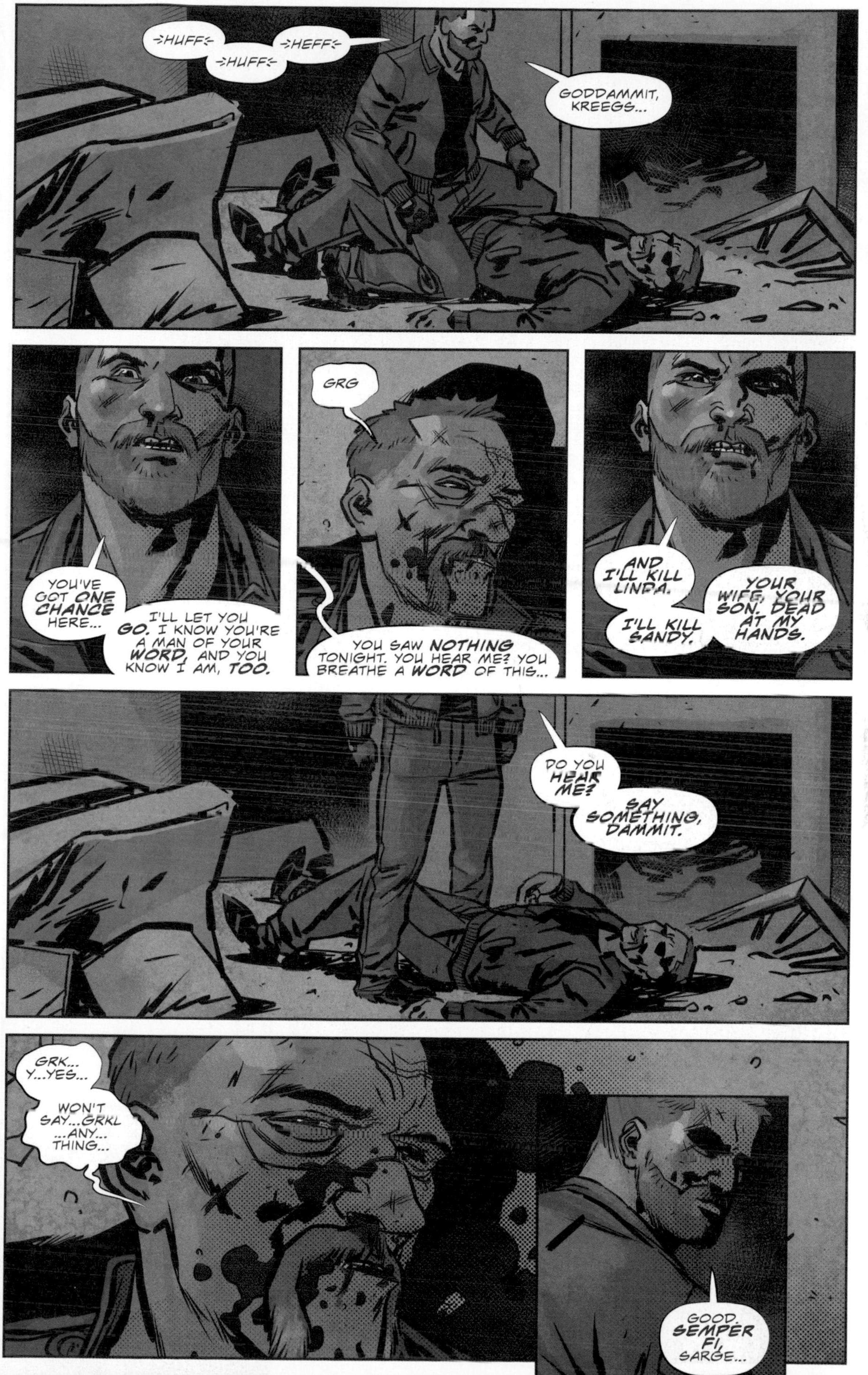

-HUFF-
-HUFF-
-HEFF-
GODDAMMIT, KREEGS...
YOU'VE GOT ONE CHANCE HERE...
I'LL LET YOU GO. I KNOW YOU'RE A MAN OF YOUR WORD, AND YOU KNOW I AM, TOO.
GRG
YOU SAW NOTHING TONIGHT. YOU HEAR ME? YOU BREATHE A WORD OF THIS...
AND I'LL KILL LINDA.
I'LL KILL SANDY.
YOUR WIFE, YOUR SON. DEAD AT MY HANDS.
DO YOU HEAR ME?
SAY SOMETHING, DAMMIT.
GRK... Y...YES...
WON'T SAY...GRKL ...ANY... THING...
GOOD. SEMPER FI, SARGE...

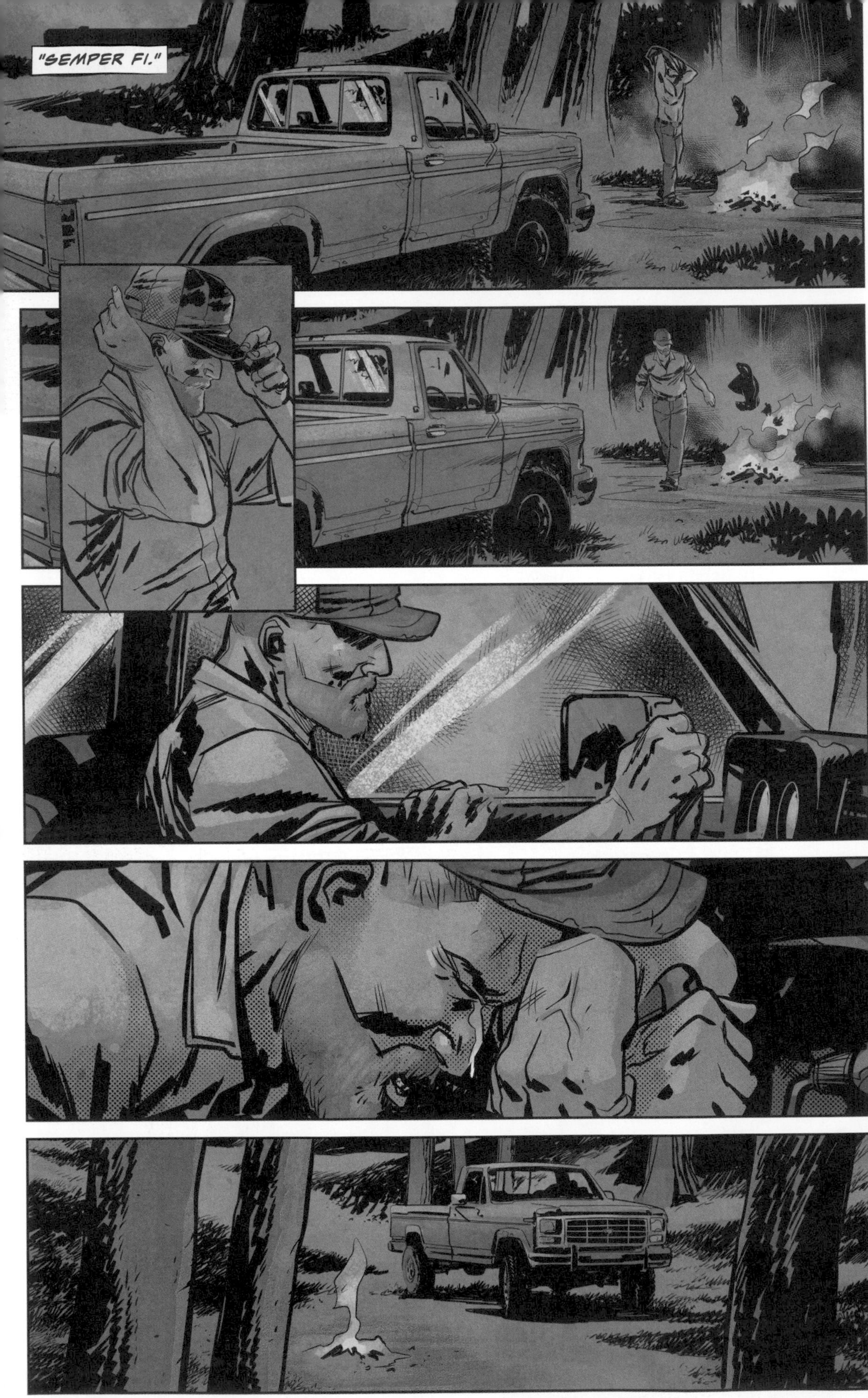
"SEMPER FI."

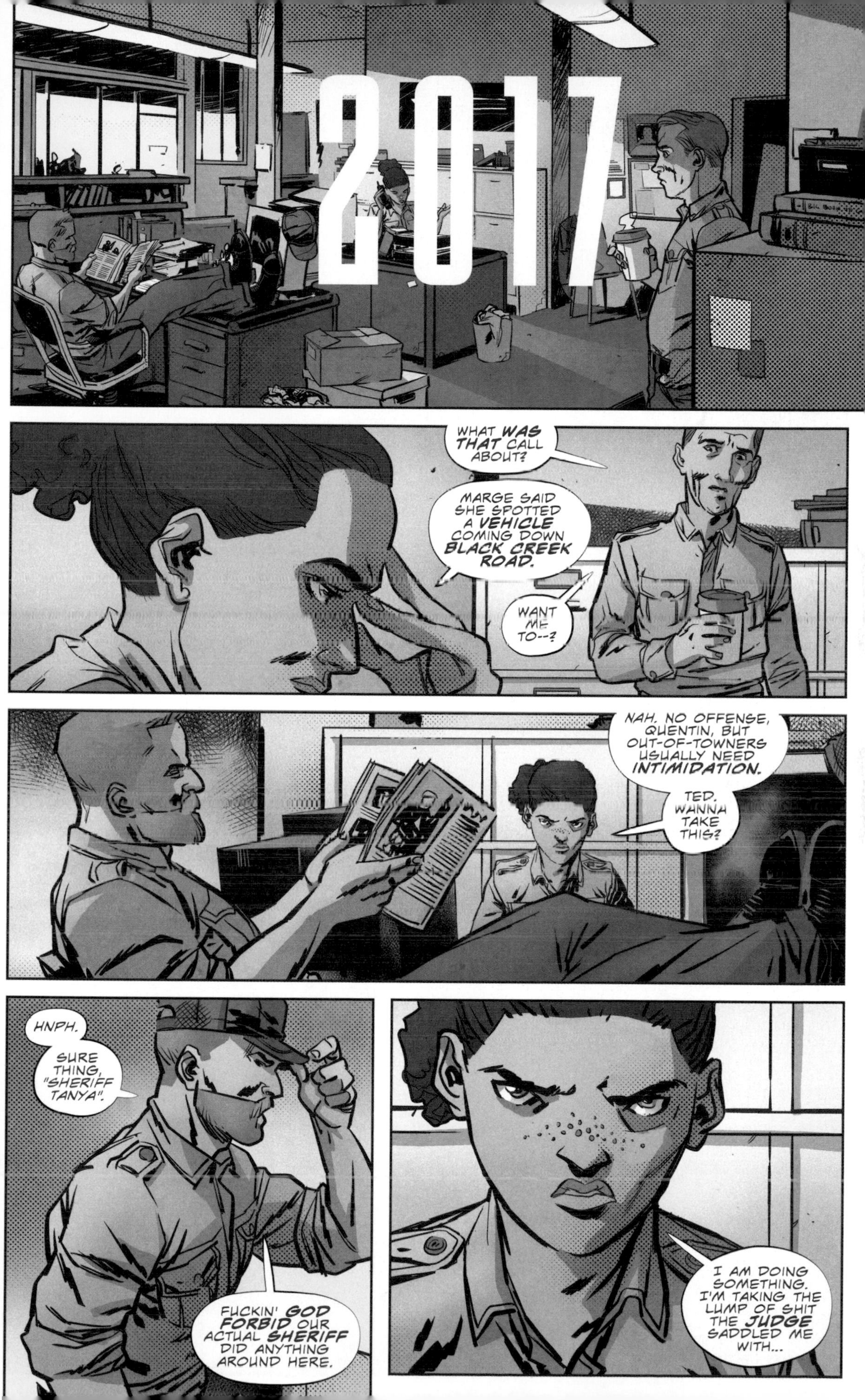
2017
WHAT WAS THAT CALL ABOUT?
MARGE SAID SHE SPOTTED A VEHICLE COMING DOWN BLACK CREEK ROAD.
WANT ME TO--?
NAH. NO OFFENSE, QUENTIN, BUT OUT-OF-TOWNERS USUALLY NEED INTIMIDATION.
TED. WANNA TAKE THIS?
HNPH.
SURE THING, "SHERIFF TANYA".
FUCKIN' GOD FORBID OUR ACTUAL SHERIFF DID ANYTHING AROUND HERE.
I AM DOING SOMETHING. I'M TAKING THE LUMP OF SHIT THE JUDGE SADDLED ME WITH...

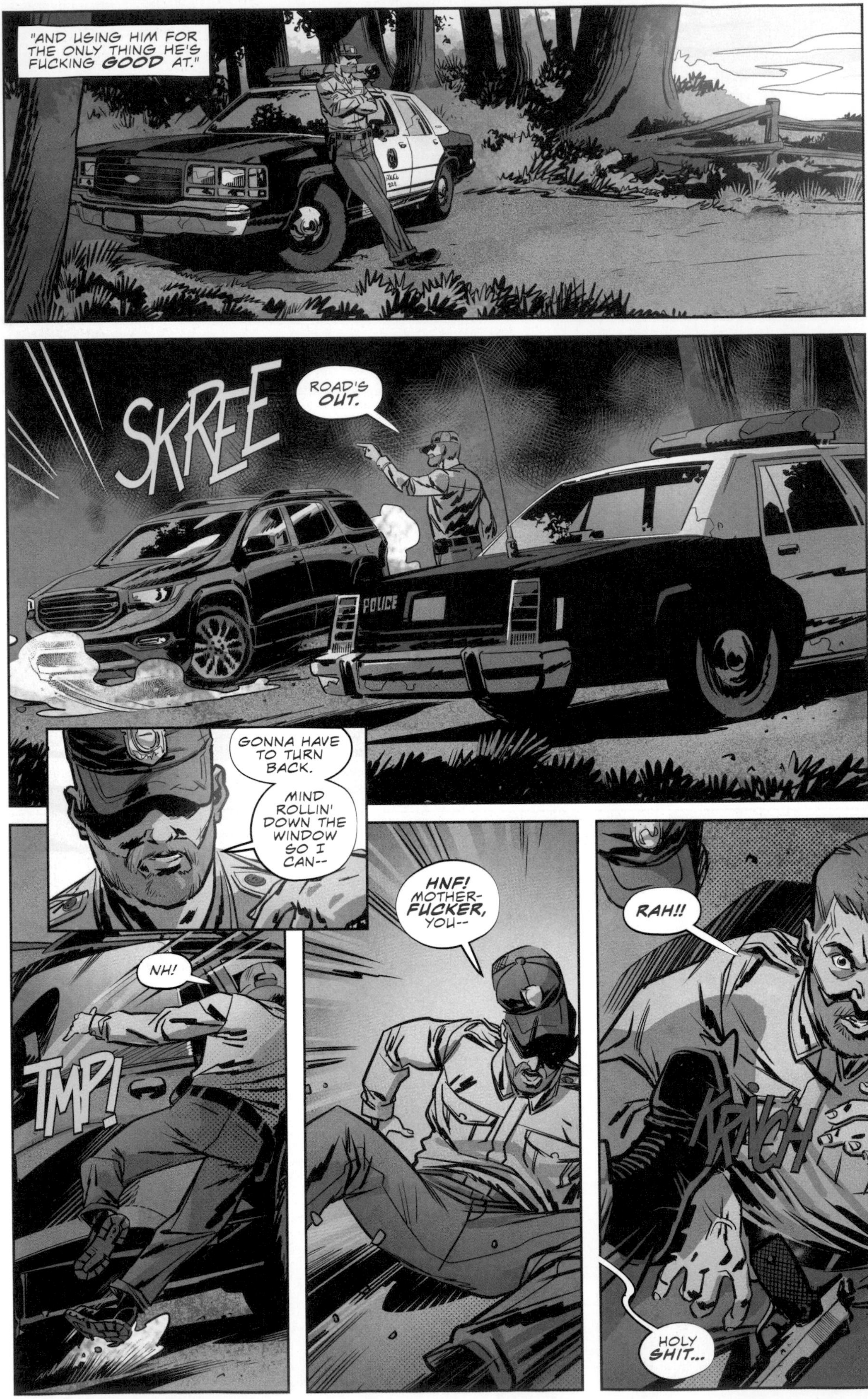
"AND USING HIM FOR THE ONLY THING HE'S FUCKING GOOD AT."
SKREE
ROAD'S OUT.
POLICE
GONNA HAVE TO TURN BACK.
MIND ROLLIN' DOWN THE WINDOW SO I CAN--
NH!
TMP!
HNF! MOTHER-FUCKER, YOU--
RAH!!
KRNCH
HOLY SHIT...

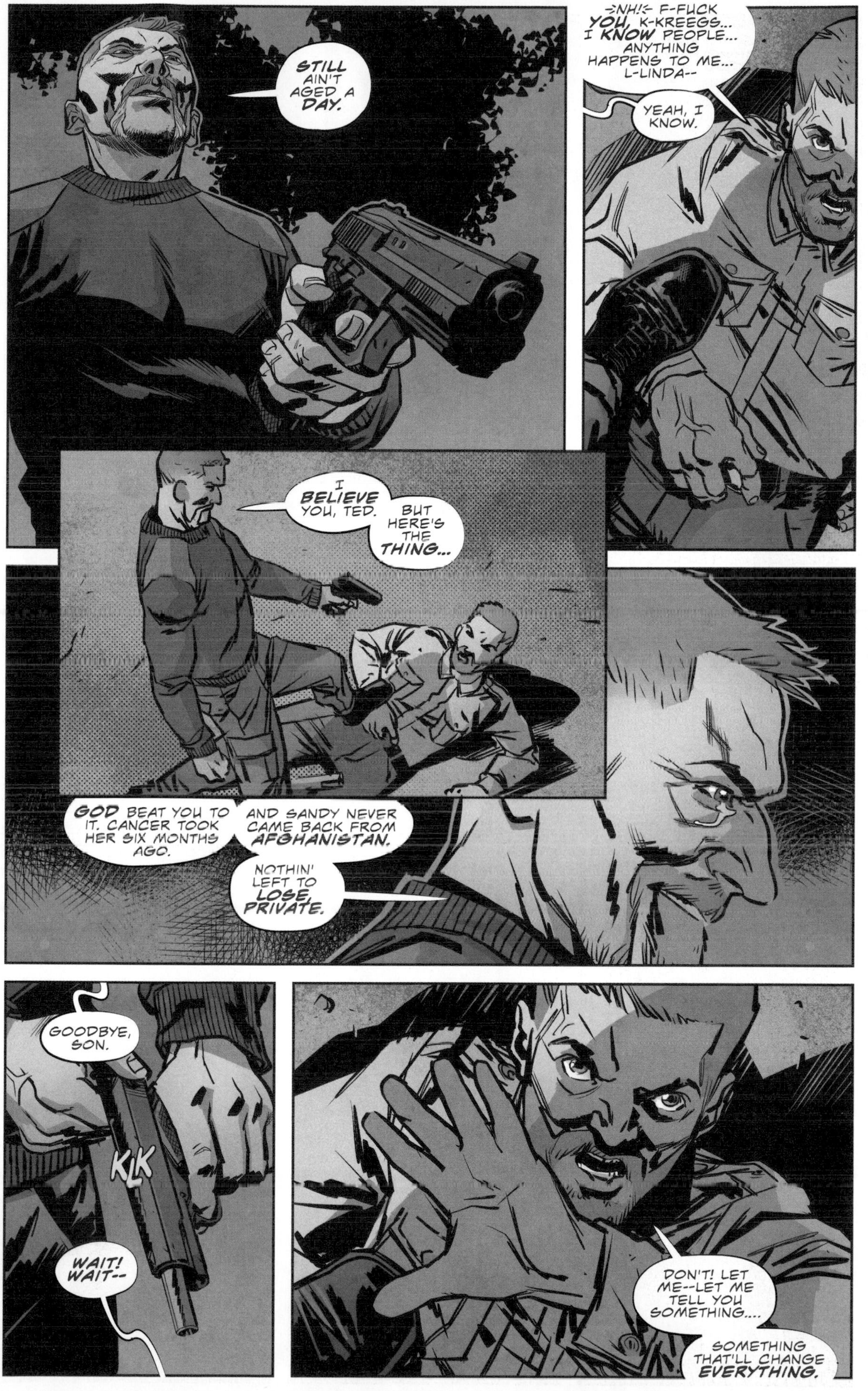
STILL AIN'T AGED A DAY.
-NH!- F-FUCK YOU, K-KREEGS... I KNOW PEOPLE... ANYTHING HAPPENS TO ME... L-LINDA--
YEAH, I KNOW.
I BELIEVE YOU, TED.
BUT HERE'S THE THING...
GOD BEAT YOU TO IT. CANCER TOOK HER SIX MONTHS AGO.
AND SANDY NEVER CAME BACK FROM AFGHANISTAN.
NOTHIN' LEFT TO LOSE, PRIVATE.
GOODBYE, SON.
KLK
WAIT! WAIT--
DON'T! LET ME--LET ME TELL YOU SOMETHING....
SOMETHING THAT'LL CHANGE EVERYTHING.

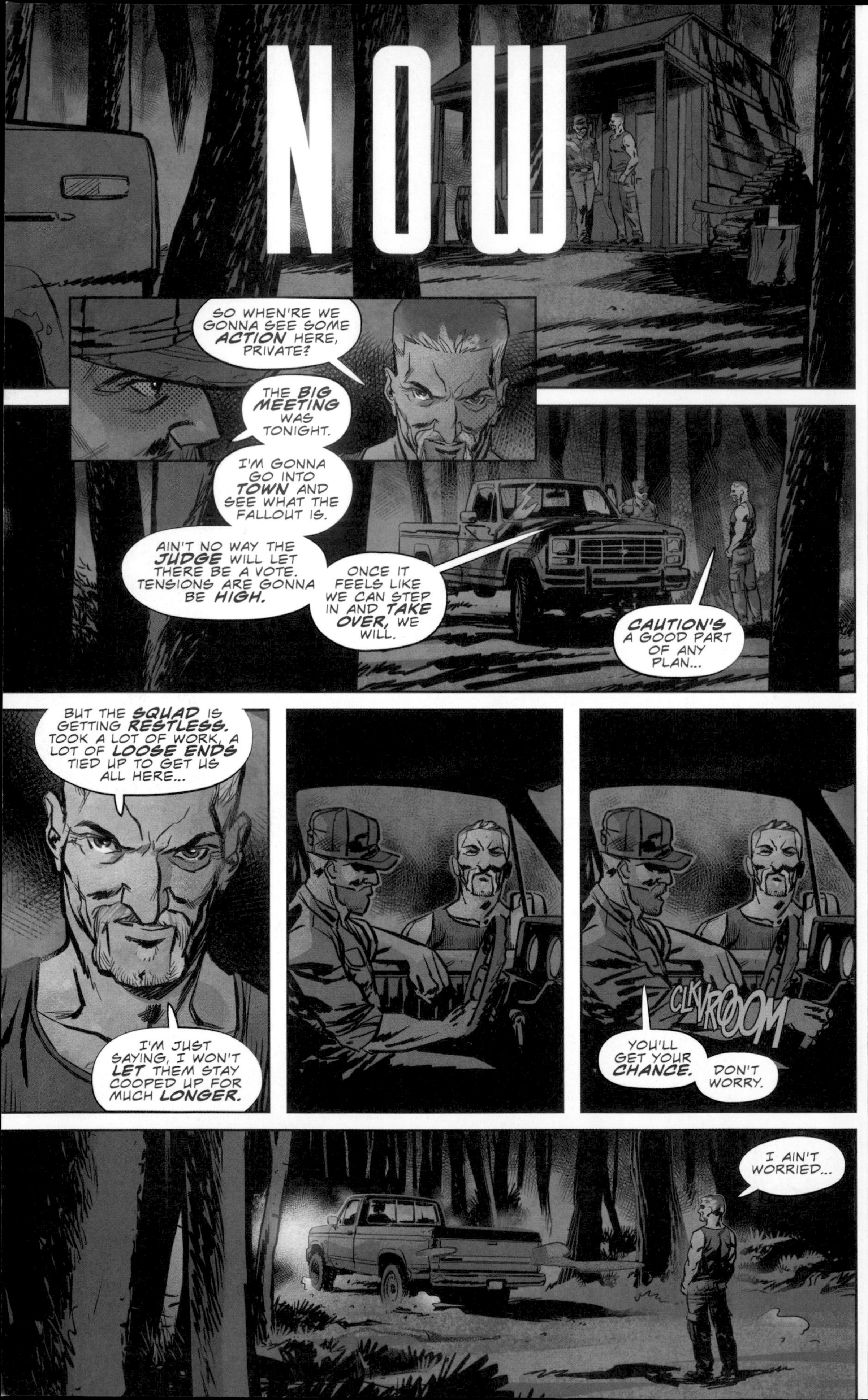
NOW
SO WHEN'RE WE GONNA SEE SOME ACTION HERE, PRIVATE?
THE BIG MEETING WAS TONIGHT.
I'M GONNA GO INTO TOWN AND SEE WHAT THE FALLOUT IS.
AIN'T NO WAY THE JUDGE WILL LET THERE BE A VOTE. TENSIONS ARE GONNA BE HIGH.
ONCE IT FEELS LIKE WE CAN STEP IN AND TAKE OVER, WE WILL.
CAUTION'S A GOOD PART OF ANY PLAN...
BUT THE SQUAD IS GETTING RESTLESS. TOOK A LOT OF WORK, A LOT OF LOOSE ENDS TIED UP TO GET US ALL HERE...
I'M JUST SAYING, I WON'T LET THEM STAY COOPED UP FOR MUCH LONGER.
CLKVROOOM
YOU'LL GET YOUR CHANCE.
DON'T WORRY.
I AIN'T WORRIED...

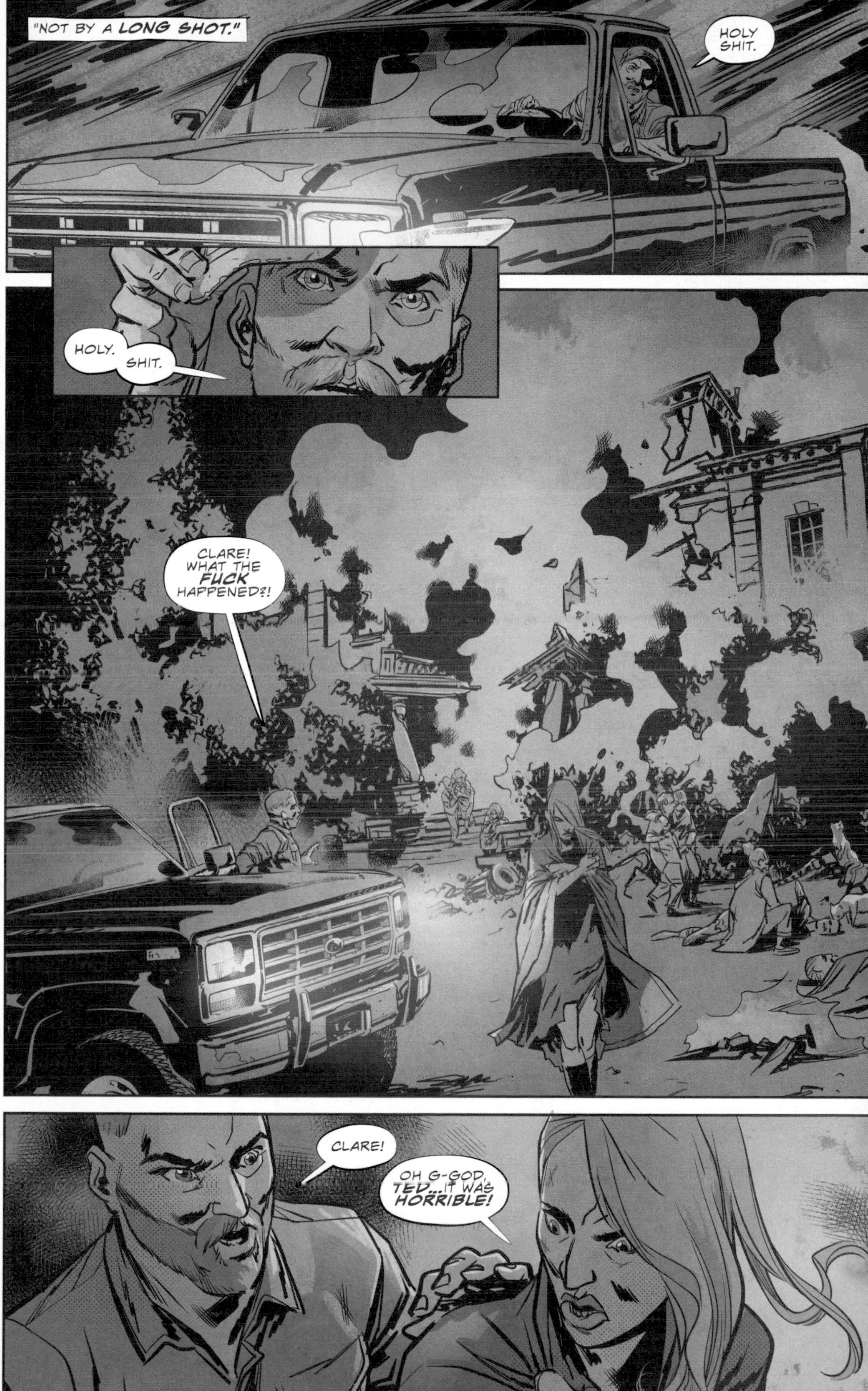
"NOT BY A LONG SHOT."
HOLY SHIT.
HOLY.
SHIT.
CLARE! WHAT THE FUCK HAPPENED?!
CLARE!
OH G-GOD, TED... IT WAS HORRIBLE!

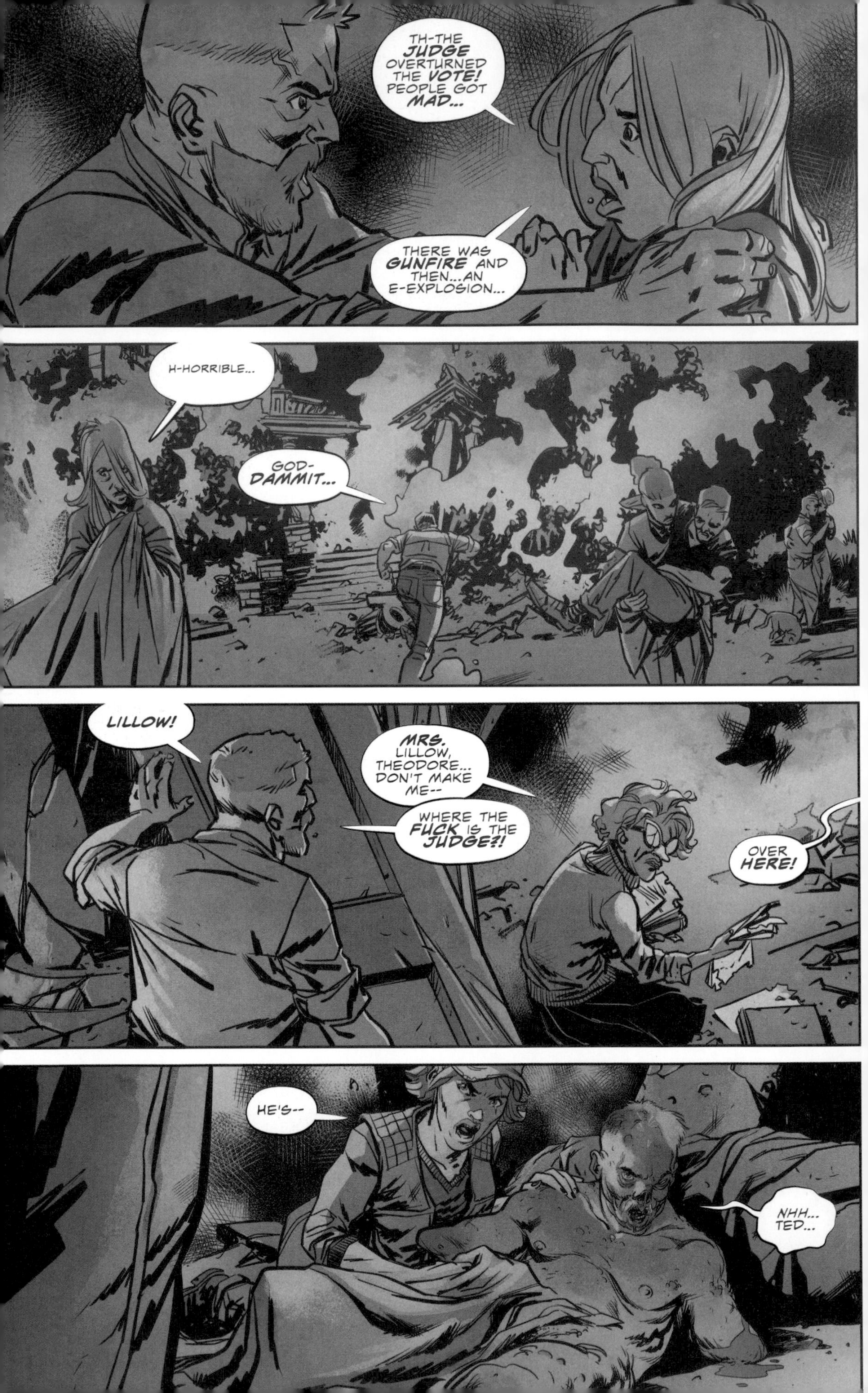
TH-THE JUDGE OVERTURNED THE VOTE! PEOPLE GOT MAD...
THERE WAS GUNFIRE AND THEN...AN E-EXPLOSION...
H-HORRIBLE...
GOD-DAMMIT...
LILLOW!
MRS. LILLOW, THEODORE... DON'T MAKE ME--
WHERE THE FUCK IS THE JUDGE?!
OVER HERE!
HE'S--
NHH... TED...

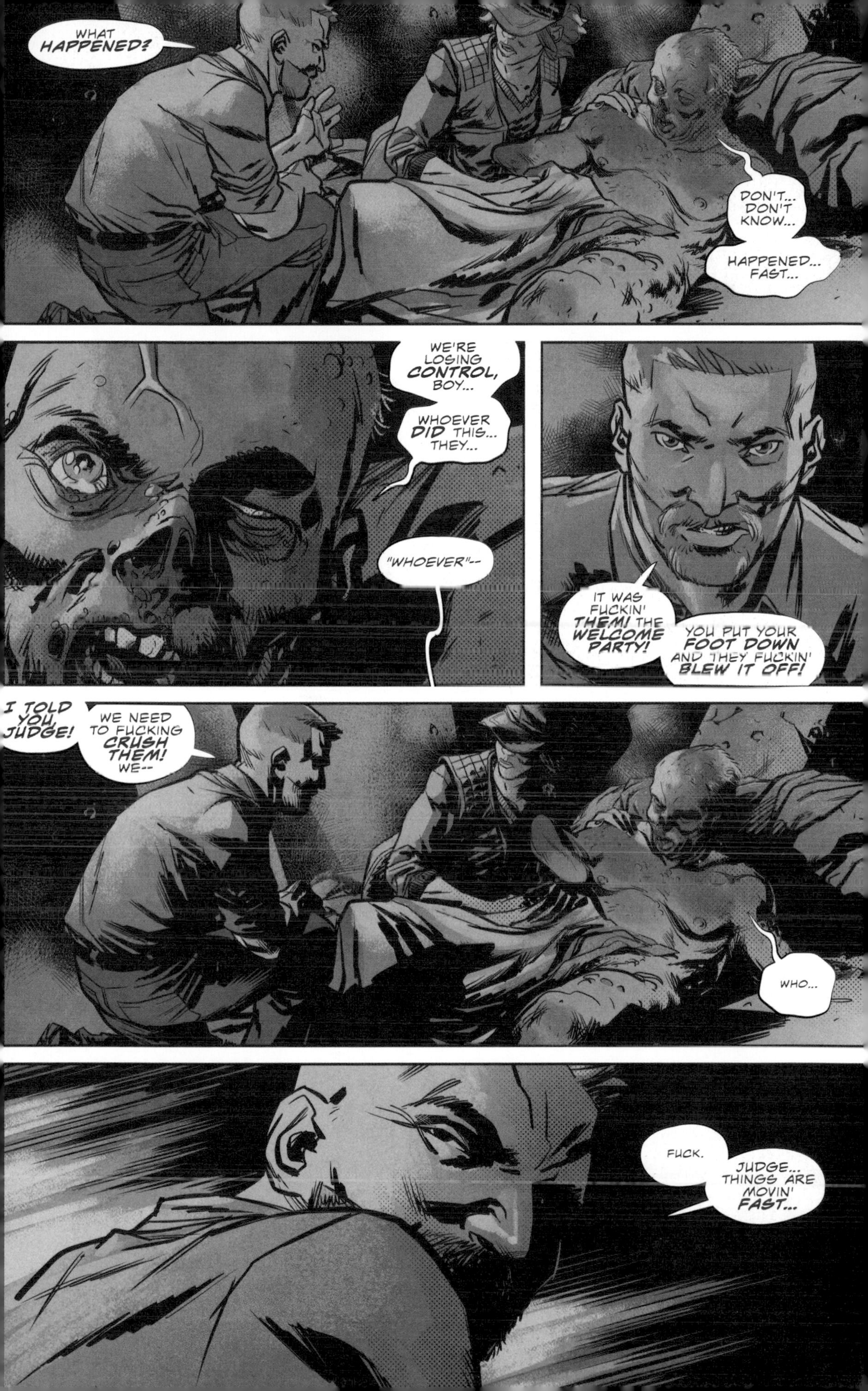
WHAT HAPPENED?
DON'T... DON'T KNOW...
HAPPENED... FAST...
WE'RE LOSING CONTROL, BOY...
WHOEVER DID THIS... THEY...
"WHOEVER"--
IT WAS FUCKIN' THEM! THE WELCOME PARTY!
YOU PUT YOUR FOOT DOWN AND THEY FUCKIN' BLEW IT OFF!
I TOLD YOU, JUDGE!
WE NEED TO FUCKING CRUSH THEM! WE--
WHO...
FUCK.
JUDGE... THINGS ARE MOVIN' FAST...

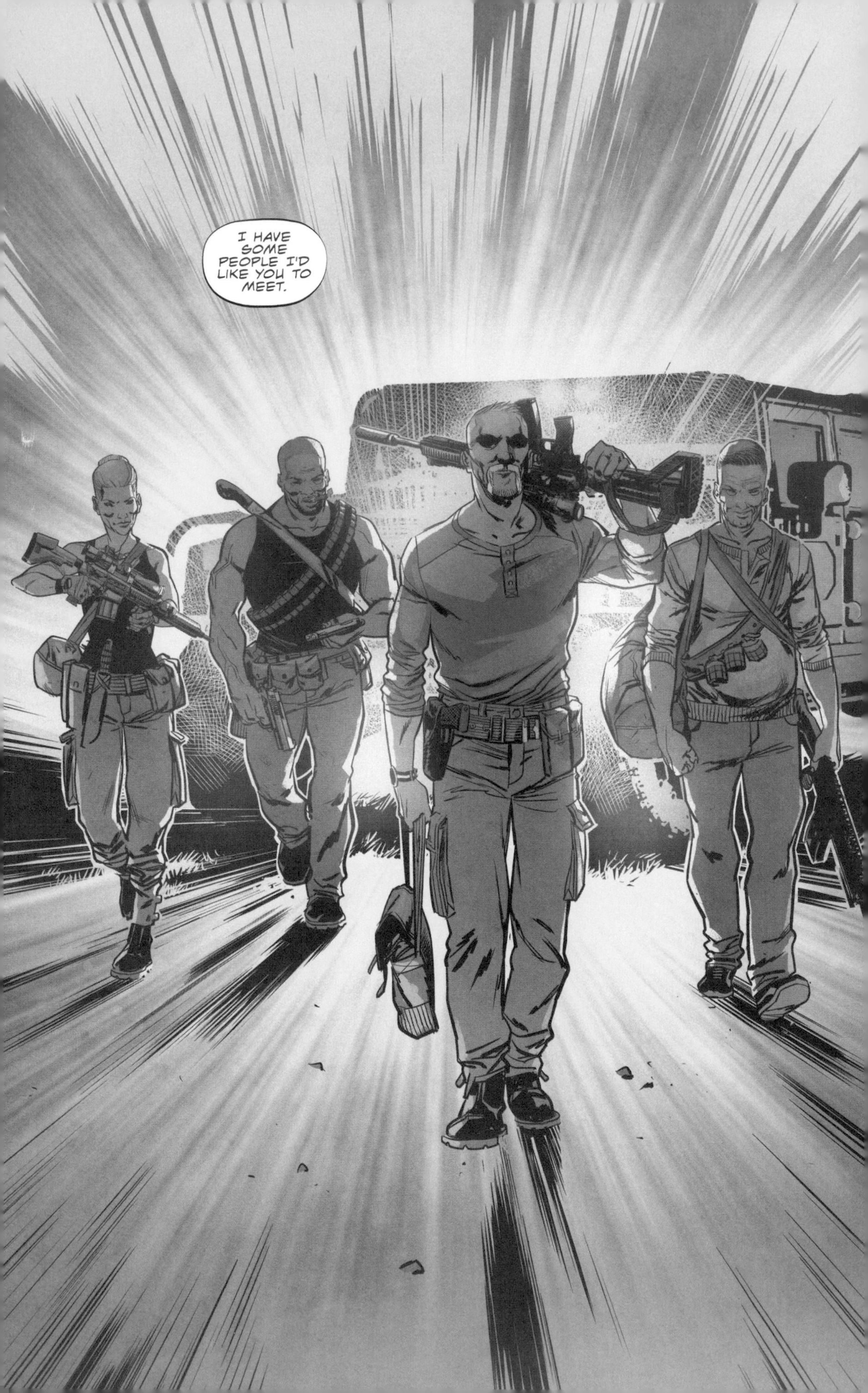
I HAVE SOME PEOPLE I'D LIKE YOU TO MEET.

TO BE
CONTINUED...

For more tales from ROBERT KIRKMAN and SKYBOUND

BRANDON THOMAS • KHARY RANDOLPH • EMILIO LOPEZ
EXCELLENCE
VOLUME ONE
KILL THE PAST

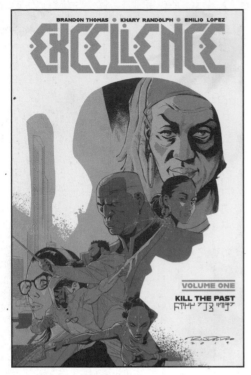

VOL. 1: KILL THE PAST
ISBN: 978-1-5343-11362-0
$16.99

ROBERT KIRKMAN
CHRIS SAMNEE
FIRE POWER
WITH MATT WILSON AND RUS WOOTON
VOLUME 2 HOME FIRE

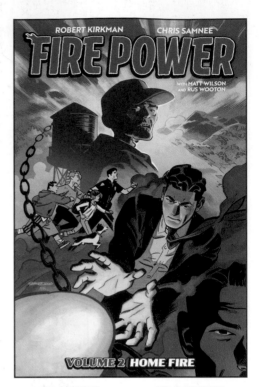

VOL. 1: PRELUDE
ISBN: 978-1-5343-1655-3
$9.99

VOL. 2: HOME FIRE
ISBN: 978-1-5343-1718-5
$16.99

WILLIAMSON
BRESSAN
VOLUME NINE
WAR OF THE WORLDS

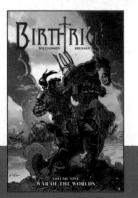

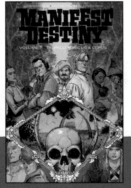

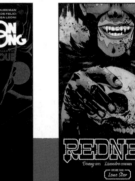

VOL. 1: HOMECOMING TP
ISBN: 978-1-63215-231-2
$9.99

VOL. 2: CALL TO ADVENTURE TP
ISBN: 978-1-63215-446-0
$12.99

VOL. 3: ALLIES AND ENEMIES TP
ISBN: 978-1-63215-683-9
$12.99

VOL. 4: FAMILY HISTORY TP
ISBN: 978-1-63215-871-0
$12.99

VOL. 5: BELLY OF THE BEAST TP
ISBN: 978-1-5343-0218-1
$12.99

VOL. 6: FATHERHOOD TP
ISBN: 978-1-53430-498-7
$14.99

VOL. 7: BLOOD BROTHERS TP
ISBN: 978-1-5343-1053-7
$14.99

VOL. 8: LIVE BY THE SWORD TP
ISBN: 978-1-5343-1368-2
$14.99

VOL. 9: WAR OF THE WORLDS TP
ISBN: 978-1-5343-1601-0
$14.99

MANIFEST DESTINY

VOL. 1: FLORA & FAUNA TP
ISBN: 978-1-60706-982-9
$9.99

VOL. 2: AMPHIBIA & INSECTA TP
ISBN: 978-1-63215-052-3
$14.99

VOL. 3: CHIROPTERA & CARNIFORMAVES TP
ISBN: 978-1-63215-397-5
$14.99

VOL. 4: SASQUATCH TP
ISBN: 978-1-63215-890-1
$14.99

VOL. 5: MNEMOPHOBIA & CHRONOPHOBIA TP
ISBN: 978-1-5343-0230-3
$16.99

VOL. 6: FORTIS & INVISIBILIA TP
ISBN: 978-1-5343-0513-7
$16.99

VOL. 7: TALPA LUMBRICUS & LEPUS TP
ISBN: 978-1-5343-1589-1
$16.99

ROBERT KIRKMAN
LORENZO DE FELICI
ANNALISA LEONI
OBLIVION SONG

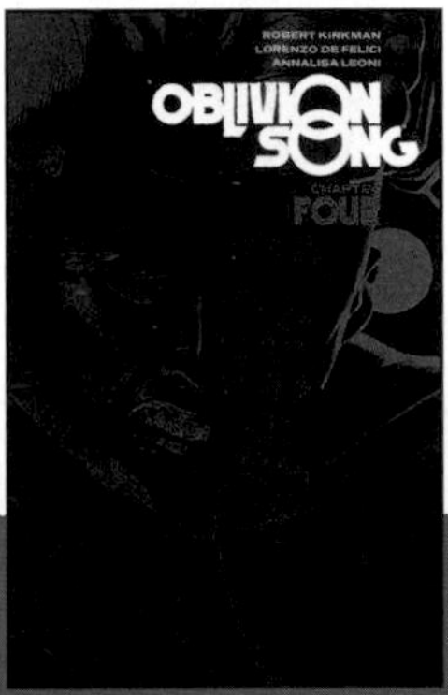

CHAPTER 1
ISBN: 978-1-5343-0642-4
$9.99

CHAPTER 2
ISBN: 978-1-5343-1057-5
$16.99

CHAPTER 3
ISBN: 978-1-5343-1326-2
$16.99

CHAPTER 4
ISBN: 978-1-5343-1517-4
$14.99

REDNECK
Lone Star

VOL. 1: DEEP IN THE HEART
ISBN: 978-1-5343-0331-7
$16.99

VOL. 2: EYES UPON YOU
ISBN: 978-1-5343-0665-3
$16.99

VOL. 3: LONGHORNS
ISBN: 978-1-5343-1050-6
$16.99

VOL. 4: LONE STAR
ISBN: 978-1-5343-1367-5
$16.99